MERGING ACROSS BORDERS

ANNE-MARIE SØDERBERG

EERO VAARA

Editors

MERGING ACROSS BORDERS

PEOPLE, CULTURES AND POLITICS

Copenhagen Business School Press

Merging across borders
People, cultures and politics

© *Copenhagen Business School Press*
Printed in Denmark
1. edition 2003

ISBN 87-630-0115-2

Distribution:

Scandinavia
Djoef/DBK, Siljangade 2-8, P.O. Box 1731
DK-2300 Copenhagen S, Denmark
Phone: +45 3269 7788, fax: +45 3269 7789

North America
Copenhagen Business School Press
Books International Inc.
P.O. Box 605
Herndon, VA 20172-0605, USA
Phone: +1 703 661 1500, fax: +1 703 661 1501

Rest of the World
Marston Book Services, P.O. Box 269
Abingdon, Oxfordshire, OX14 4YN, UK
Phone: +44 (0) 1235 465500, fax: +44 (0) 1235 465555
E-mail Direct Customers: direct.order@marston.co.uk
E-mail Booksellers: trade.order@marston.co.uk

CONTENTS

PREFACE

We are a pan-Nordic research team studying a pan-Nordic organization created through cross-border mergers and acquisitions. This was the starting point of our research project, which was initiated in 2001 by Ingmar Björkman (Swedish School of Economics, Helsinki), Tore Hundsnes (The Norwegian School of Economics and Business Administration, Bergen), Christine B. Meyer (The Norwegian School of Economics and Business Administration, Bergen), Annette Risberg, (Copenhagen Business School), Anne-Marie Søderberg (Copenhagen Business School), Janne Tienari (Lappeenranta University of Technology) and Eero Vaara (Helsinki School of Economics and Ecole de Management de Lyon). What could be more appropriate for an understanding of perceived cultural differences, occasional banal nationalism, practical difficulties in arranging meetings in different places, knowledge transfer, coordination of cross-border work processes, gender issues or strong pressure to achieve visible results?

Nordea and its representatives have given us, as researchers within the field of international mergers and acquisitions, unique access and have allowed us to dig into the problems and challenges of post-merger integration and organizational change. In our view, Nordea with its quadruple cross-border merger is a pioneering case. It is, however, not difficult to foresee that we will soon see other significant and complex cross-border mergers and acquisitions in a

European context. In many ways, Nordea is also a very promising case. Creating an effective pan-Nordic organization out of four previously separate national players is in itself an achievement that calls for recognition. The speed of this restructuring adds to the accomplishment.

As researchers, however, we have chosen to focus on the problematic issues in cross-border mergers and acquisitions. Consequently, we analyze and elaborate on the problems that merged organizations have experienced, as well as on the challenges encountered. The main lesson is that even the most well-planned organizational change projects and the most sincere decisions might have unintended cultural or socio-political consequences. And the difficult thing about this is that these consequences are often very difficult for top management to control.

By digging into difficulties and highlighting problematic issues, we are not claiming that Nordea has handled the post-merger integration unprofessionally. We can point out a number of successful change processes, exemplary efforts by key managers and others, and the development and use of effective integration practices. In fact, companies going through major structural and organizational changes have a lot to learn from examples set by Nordea and its management.

There are many people who deserve special thanks for their important input to our research process. On Nordea's side, we are especially grateful that Peter Forsblad, Karl-Olof Hammarkvist and Flemming Dalby Jensen as 'liaison officers' between the research group and top management have made this research project possible. They have cleared our path of bureaucracy and have provided insightful comments at various stages of the research project. Many other people have also served as key informants. We are particularly thankful to all those managers and employees at Nordea who have taken the time to be our interviewees.

Research also requires funding, and we are especially grateful that Nordea, the Copenhagen Business School and the Finnish OKO Bank Group Research Foundation have supported our research efforts by covering the costs. For crucial help in the final stages of the editing process we wish to thank The Language Center, Copenhagen Business School, and Virva Haltsonen, Helsinki School of Economics.

12.5.2003

Anne-Marie Søderberg   Eero Vaara

CONTRIBUTORS

INGMAR BJÖRKMAN is professor of international management and organization at Department of Organization and Management, Swedish School of Economics and Business Administration. Contact address: ibjorkma@shh.fi

KARL-OLOF HAMMARKVIST is adjunct professor of Stockholm School of Economics and former EVP of Nordea. Contact address: dhoh@hhs.se

CHARLOTTE HOLGERSSON is doctoral candidate, member of Fosfor (Feminist organization studies) at the Center for Management and Organization, Stockholm School of Economics. Contact address: charlotte.holgersson@hhs.se

TORE HUNDSNES is doctorate student of strategic management and organization at Department of Strategy and Management, Norwegian School of Economics and Business Administration. Contact address: tore.hundnes@nhh.no

ANNETTE RISBERG is assistant professor of intercultural management at Department of Intercultural Communication and Management, Copenhagen Business School. Contact address: ari.ikl@cbs.dk

ANNE-MARIE SØDERBERG is professor of organizational communication at Department of Intercultural Communication and Management, Copenhagen Business School. Contact address: ams.ikl@cbs.dk.

JANNE TIENARI is professor of management and organization at the Department of Business Administration, Lappeenranta University of Technology, Finland. Contact address: janne.tienari@lut.fi

EERO VAARA is professor of strategy at Ecole de Management de Lyon. Contact address: Vaara@em-lyon.com

Chapter 1

INTRODUCTION

Anne-Marie Søderberg & Eero Vaara

Mergers[1] and acquisitions in general and cross-border mergers and acquisitions in particular are more popular than ever. This is the case even though they frequently fail to deliver the synergistic or other benefits strived for, lead to human resource and cultural problems, result in power plays, and often produce problematic consequences for various internal and external stakeholders. Why is this the case? Apparently there are pressures to keep up with the pace of industrial restructuring, a need to respond to competitor moves, and benefits that cannot be achieved without sufficient size. Restructuring provides specific opportunities for rationalization, and joining forces usually creates all kinds of lucrative possibilities for synergistic cooperation, transfer of knowledge or capabilities, and learning. There are also

---

[1] The term 'merger' has two meanings in the context of combining organizations. 'Merger' can refer to any form of combination of organizations, initiated by different types of contractual arrangements. The more specific meaning that separates mergers from acquisitions is that a merger is a combination of organizations which are rather similar in size and which create an organization where neither party can clearly be seen as the acquirer.

special reasons for cross-border deals such as the lack of domestic growth opportunities or the fact that many synergies appear even more attractive when moving across the borders. But there are also other motives at play – financial rewards, fame, prestige and power.

Whatever the motives for specific mergers and acquisitions, people in merging organizations face specific problems and challenges after the merger or acquisition has taken place. It is this post-merger or post-acquisition phase that arguably determines whether the synergistic or other benefits are realized and which kinds of social problems are created by the changes.

It is not, however, easy to cope with – not to speak of managing – post-merger integration. This is due to several reasons. First, it is usually not clear for all people as to what the organizational changes will actually be. Even though the people in charge may have clear visions as to what is needed to bring about the synergies strived for, the details of these plans and their implementation usually have to be worked out along the process. Other organizational members expect to be informed by the management, but at the same time they are often sceptical as to whether they are told the whole truth about the coming changes. Second, related to the previous point, it usually happens that not all changes are embraced by all people. In fact, mergers and acquisitions due to rationalization often imply drastic changes, such as layoffs, for particular people. Neither do all managers succeed in getting the positions that they covet for. This means that post-merger integration is often characterized by resistance to change and politics – overt or covert.

Third, post-merger changes tend to take time. During this time, the environment, the people and the ideas about integration also usually change. For example, new mergers and acquisitions may take place while the previous integration tasks seem far from accomplished. In fact, complexity and unpredictability usually characterize post-merger integration. Fourth, in cross-border settings in particular, cultural differences – 'real' or imaginary – tend to create confusion in the post-merger organization. This is specifically the case when making difficult decisions concerning organizational integration.

Post-merger integration is thus a process that is difficult to conceptualize and even more difficult to manage. Against this background, it is unfortunate that most of the organizational and management literature on post-merger integration has not dealt with the socio-political dynamics of these processes. In fact, while looking for clear-cut advice and quick fixes, especially the more practitioner-oriented literature on post-merger integration tends to oversimplify the actual organizational and managerial problems and challenges. This is arguably one of the key reasons why so many post-merger integration processes fail to deliver the synergies planned for and tend to generate surprisingly complicated human resource, cultural and political problems.

In this research project we concentrate on the socio-political dynamics of post-merger processes. For that purpose, we focus on a particularly revealing case. This is the construction of the Nordic financial services group Nordea through a series of cross-border mergers and acquisitions. In particular, this case allows us to examine the social, cultural and political dynamics of post-merger integration, to point to the specific features of cross-border integration, and to develop an understanding of consequent managerial dilemmas and challenges.

In the following chapter 2, we will provide an overview of the existing literature on post-merger integration. In this overview, we distinguish different approaches to post-merger or post-acquisition integration. On this basis, we argue that there is a need to move from managerialistically-oriented analyses towards more 'in-depth' studies of the socio-cultural, political and discursive dynamics. We then outline our sensemaking approach that serves as an overall theoretical framework for the different analyses included in this book. We also present and discuss our methodological choices and focus in particular on our narrative interviews.

We have written this book for both reflective practitioners and people studying post-merger integration. We have therefore tried to make explicit our theoretical and methodological choices but avoided overly academic jargon. Nevertheless, more practically oriented readers might want to skip chapter 2 where we position our research project both in a theoretical and a methodological context and proceed directly to the empirically oriented chapters. More theoretically-oriented students in international mergers and acquisitions can, in turn, at times need more in-depth theoretical or methodological discussion. For that purpose, we have tried to pay special attention to the references to other studies, not only here but throughout the book.

In chapter 3, we provide background information for our Nordea case. In a historical outline the tremendous pace of restructuring in the Nordic financial services sector in general and in our case in particular are summarized. As this chapter summarizes the key events, it thus serves as an historical introduction for the chapters to follow. We also look at some specifics of the Nordic context, similarities as well as differences between the four Nordic societies. We expect this introduction to be useful especially for non-Nordic readers who might expect the Nordic region to be a homogenous entity. But it can also be helpful for Nordic readers as it points to historical relationships between the Nordic countries that according to our experiences seem to play an important role in the cultural dynamics we are analyzing.

The core of the book are eight chapters focusing on specific issues in post-merger or post-acquisition integration. These analyses conducted by different members of our research team raise a number of important points concerning the social, cultural and political dynamics of cross-border mergers and acquisitions.

In chapter 4, we point out that banal nationalism is an unavoidable part of cross-border mergers and acquisitions. In particular, we concentrate on national stereotyping that seems to be an inherent part of post-merger or post-acquisition sensemaking processes in international contexts. We focus on the stereotypes reconstructed in the interviews both by the representatives of that particular nation and the other Nordic communities. According to these categorizations, Swedes were often presented as consensus-driven, Finns as action-oriented, Danes as negotiating merchants and Norwegians as people who go straight to the point in decision-making. The analysis thus highlights the paradox that even though the Nordic region is often perceived by outsiders to be a relatively homogenous area, people in the four Nordic nations themselves perceive significant differences between their respective national cultures. The analysis demonstrates that, at least in the initial phase of the integration process, Swedish, Finnish, Danish and Norwegian senior executives made frequent use of an available cultural repertoire of national stereotypes when describing themselves and the other national groups involved in the cross-border merger. This was especially the case when they tried to make sense of critical events in relation to decision-making processes involving managers from all the merging companies.

Introduction

In chapter 5, we highlight the political processes that often characterize international mergers and acquisitions. We focus on the internal politics concerning top managerial positions and illustrate how international mergers often involve a principle of 'balance of power' manifested and symbolized by an even distribution of important positions. This principle is effective, for example, in selling the merger idea to internal and external stakeholders unwilling to surrender control. It also seems to serve as a means to prevent 'unnecessary' politicking by committing and disciplining top decision-makers. The 'balance of power' principle, however, triggers and appropriates national confrontation. Over time, the 'balance of power' principle also seems to produce another kinds of inequality as it conflicts with other principles such as competence-based career development.

A strategy of locating and transferring knowledge around 'best practices' can, at best, be an effective integration mechanism in merging multinational organizations. It focuses attention on concrete questions. Reflection around processes and practices can thereby become a key source of learning for the actors involved. This can also lead to the invention of new 'best' ways of doing things. The concept of 'best practices' has also been actively used in Nordea at the different stages of building the organization. But knowledge transfer does not necessarily work out as planned by the merger strategists; some people do not become committed in the process, and all kinds of socio-cultural obstacles complicate the transfer of 'best practices' from one location to another. In chapter 6, we illustrate and reflect on these complex socio-political aspects related to knowledge transfer in a multinational organization.

The frequent use of national stereotyping illustrated in chapter 4 demonstrates the need for initiatives to integrate people in the merging companies. The creation of Nordea as a multinational corporation and as an integrated group of companies offering a wide range of financial services is thus an important managerial challenge. Initiating a socio-cultural integration process means building bridges over perceived differences between national cultures, corporate cultures as well as professional cultures involved in a multinational corporation encompassing diverse business units. In chapter 7, we introduce and analyze some initiatives taken in Nordea to manage socio-cultural integration of the multinational workforce.

The human resource (HR) function is often encouraged by academics, consultants and practitioners to play more 'strategic' roles in their organization. This is the case especially with dramatic organizational changes such as cross-border mergers and acquisitions. Given the apparent significance of people management in post-merger processes, it is, however, unfortunate that we know little about how the HR function develops and implements interventions, policies and procedures that contribute to the integration of workforces and cultures. In chapter 8, we explore the roles played by the HR function in the large-scale post-merger change processes in Nordea. It helps us to uncover the inherent problems in managing HR issues in the post-merger organization, and specifically highlights the difficulties in giving HR issues a 'strategic' status.

In chapter 9, we focus on organizational learning. We examine how key managers make sense and use of their previous merger experiences. We focus on four central issues in the integration process: development and communication of a corporate vision, choice of corporate language, location of headquarters, and cultural training. In our analysis, we point out that such learning is inherently context-specific, that it often involves ambiguity, and that the significance attributed to specific learning experiences depends on the dominant coalition. Based on this reflection, we offer some suggestions as to how to avoid most simplistic ideas about learning but foster effective exploitation of past experiences in cross-border mergers.

On a general level, the Nordic societies carry a gender egalitarian image and women's participation rate is higher than in most other European countries. Against this background, it is highly conspicuous that there are very few women in the top management of private companies, and in mergers and acquisitions it seems as if the competition between key individuals for top positions makes it even more difficult for women to make a career. In chapter 10, we take up the making of Nordea as an example to illustrate some of the gendered problematics in contemporary 'globalizing' business. Our findings from interviews with senior executives suggest that organizational legacies, persistent perceptions of family obligations, and specific notions of managing change and transformation play a crucial role in the ways in which top management is constructed and reconstructed as a pure male terrain.

Mergers and acquisitions are also dramatic events. They can be a source of anxiety, fatigue, frustration and stress for members of the focal organizations. In chapter 11, we examine the pressures and demands that managers as individuals face in the midst of post-merger and post-acquisition change processes. We in particular point to the extra work created by the merger process, special problems caused by travelling, an ever-changing social environment, and constant uncertainty as sources of stress. We also discuss measures taken to alleviate these problems in the Nordea group.

Chapter 2

THEORETICAL AND METHODOLOGICAL CONSIDERATIONS

Anne-Marie Søderberg & Eero Vaara

The purpose of this chapter is to outline the theoretical and methodological foundations of this research project. In the following we provide a brief overview of previous research on post-merger and post-acquisition integration, outline a 'sensemaking' approach that serves as an overall theoretical framework for this project, and describe our methodological choices that are to a large extent based on narrative interviews.

AN OVERVIEW OF LITERATURE ON POST-MERGER INTEGRATION

What is 'post-merger' or 'post-acquisition' integration might appear self-evident for many researchers and practitioners. Yet this area of organizations and management research, like most others, is characterized by a diversity of perspectives drawing on different traditions. In the following, we outline strategic, human resource, cultural and discursive perspectives on post-merger and post-acquisition integration. This serves as a basis for arguing that there is a need for processual studies that look deeper into the sensemaking around these phenomena.

In brief, one can distinguish strategic, human resource and cultural perspectives in research on post-merger or post-acquisition integration. Some earlier studies pointed to the significance of the period following the initial merger or acquisition (e.g. Kitching, 1967), but the discussion concerning organizational change processes following mergers and acquisitions did not really start until the mid-1980s. Most of this research has since concentrated on strategic questions such as which acquisition choices are likely to lead to success (Salter and Weinhold, 1979; Kusewitt, 1985; Fowler and Schmidt, 1989), what types of mergers and acquisitions (related or unrelated) lead to better results in terms of synergy or financial performance (Lubatkin, 1987; Chatterjee, 1986; Porter, 1987; Singh and Montgomery, 1987; Shelton, 1988; Chatterjee and Lubatkin, 1990; Seth, 1990) and how performance is linked with resource deployment (Capron, Dussauge and Mitchell, 1998; Capron, Mitchell and Swaminathan, 2001).

Gradually, however, more and more scholars have become interested in the processes following merger or acquisition decisions and thereby 'integration' questions. Researchers have concentrated on issues such as how management can bring about the potential synergistic benefits (Lindgren, 1982; Shrivastava, 1986; Larsson, 1990; Ingham et al., 1992; Larsson and Finkelstein, 1999, Birkinshaw, Bresman and Håkansson, 2000), create value (Haspeslagh and Jemison, 1991), transfer knowledge or capabilities from one organization to another (Bresman, Birkinshaw and Nobel, 1999; Ranft and Lord, 2002) or enhance learning (Leroy and Ramanantsoa, 1997).

These studies have also listed obstacles to integration from a managerial perspective (Hunt, 1990; Haspeslagh and Jemison, 1991; Pablo, 1994; Birkinshaw, Bresman and Håkansson, 2000). For instance, Haspeslagh and Jemison (1991) mention determinism (inability to modify one's plans when integration processes unfold), value destruction (changes that destroy existing competences and capabilities in the target organization), and a leadership vacuum (lack of managers taking up the overall responsibility for the new post-merger organization) as impediments to integration. Researchers in this camp (Hunt, 1990; Larsson, 1990; Olie, 1990; Haspeslagh and Jemison, 1991) have also concluded that there are several types of integration approach that can be adopted. Haspeslagh and Jemison (1991), for example, distinguish between 'holding', 'preservation', 'symbiosis' and 'absorption' types.

Most of the studies mentioned above have actually also considered socio-cultural and political factors and thereby provided us with insightful models of decision-making in post-merger or post-acquisition integration processes. However, many other, especially more 'practitioner'-oriented studies on post-merger or post-acquisition integration, tend to be overly one-sided in their 'managerialist'[1]

---

[1] 'Managerialism' is here seen as an ideology according to which enhancing organizational performance – usually defined by relatively short-term financial measures – is the primary objective of management. This is achieved by exercising managerial control through different types of processes and practices. Deviant views and behavior not aligned with objectives defined and set by management are often seen as 'organizational resistance'. Success and failure are thus attributed to managers' actions, while other explanations are less central in this kind of thinking.

orientation. Apart from the dominant managerial perspective, there has been little appreciation, not to speak of legitimization, of other kinds of view. For example, the concerns and reactions of the personnel have most often been seen as 'resistance', the overcoming of which has been portrayed as a key post-merger or post-acquisition implementation challenge. What is 'management' has also more often than not been portrayed in an overly simplistic way. There has been a lack of understanding of how the decision-makers and managers themselves are often divided, how their actions form an inherent part of the power games and internal politics of mergers and acquisitions, and how they experience the same kinds of cultural and identity-related problem as the employees.

Motivated by general interest in the 'soft aspects' of mergers and acquisitions, other scholars have adopted a perspective focusing on people issues (Levinson, 1970; Marks and Mirvis, 1986; Schweiger et al., 1987; Buono and Bowditch, 1989; Napier et al., 1989; Schweiger and DeNisi, 1991; Cartwright and Cooper, 1990, 1992, 1993; Greenwood et al., 1994; Fried et al., 1996). Particular attention has in such analyses been focused on the uncertainty, anxiety and stress that people involved in post-merger or post-acquisition change processes experience and the consequent motivational or resistance problems at the organizational level (Marks and Mirvis, 1986; Buono and Bowditch, 1989). The organizational – employee or managerial – reactions to merger or acquisition news as well as anticipated or concrete changes have been central objects of study (Cartwright and Cooper, 1993; Greenwood et al., 1994; Fried et al., 1996; Lohrum, 1996; Bouwen and Overlaet, 2001; Risberg, 2001), as have communication issues (Bastien, 1987; Schweiger and DeNisi, 1991).

Although not always linked with 'human aspects', there are also studies that have examined mergers and acquisitions from a 'justice' perspective, thereby highlighting the complex cognitive processes that underlie people's reactions (Very et al., 1997; Meyer, 2001). Likewise, there are also some studies that look at the political perspectives of post-merger or post-acquisition integration (e.g. Hambrick and Cannella, 1993; Vaara, 2001). These studies have emphasized the importance of power struggles and internal politicking in mergers and acquisitions. It should be noted that researchers have taken various kinds of 'human' perspective on processes that are often only considered from a 'managerialist' perspective. For example, Empson has analyzed the human side of knowledge transfer (2001).

Although many of these studies have been motivated by a willingness to understand the causes and consequences of 'organizational resistance' to better 'manage' these processes, they have also reflected genuine 'humanistic' concerns. In fact, in most studies representing the 'human side' of mergers and acquisitions has been a priority *per se* (e.g. Buono and Bowditch, 1989). There are, however, few analyses that draw on more critical traditions in sociological and organizational research influenced by humanistic understandings and approaches. Studies on topics such as gender inequality have, nevertheless, showed how merger processes also have consequences such as increased gender segregation (Tienari, 2000).

When organizational scholars discovered 'culture' as a convenient metaphor for various types of organizational phenomena, researchers started to analyze organizational change processes following mergers and acquisitions from a cultural perspective. This literature has concentrated on the organizational cultural integration processes and sought explanations for post-merger problems in terms of 'cultural clashes' between merger parties (Davis, 1968; Sales and Mirvis, 1984; Marks and Mirvis, 1986; Buono, Bowditch and Lewis, 1985; Walter, 1985; Altendorf, 1986; Datta, 1991; Chatterjee et al., 1992; Weber and Schweiger, 1992; Larsson, 1993; Elsass and Veiga, 1994; Weber, 1996). In international settings, researchers have focused not only on organizational, but also on national cultural differences (Olie, 1994; Calori, Lubatkin and Very, 1994; Morosini and Singh, 1994; Villinger, 1996; Weber, Shenkar and Raveh, 1996; Very et al., 1997; Gertsen, Søderberg and Torp, 1998; Lubatkin et al., 1998; Larsson and Lubatkin, 2001).

Most cultural research on mergers tends to see integration problems as being caused by objective cultural differences. For example, Datta (1991) and Chatterjee et al. (1992) have analyzed the impact on organizational cultural differences on post-merger performance and suggested that such a positive relationship exists. In international settings, drawing on Hofstede's (1991) and Trompenaars' (1993) work, this has resulted in research arguing that mergers between culturally closer nations lead to better outcomes than those between more distant national cultures (see Morosini and Singh, 1994). The contrary argument that cultural differences may also be a source of value has received little attention until recent studies. Krishnan, Miller and Judge (1997) and Morosini, Shane and Singh (1998) have, however, illustrated how cultural diversity can benefit top management decision-making.

Most researchers in this field share an ambition to find out which organizational cultures can co-exist and how. According to the 'cultural fit' or 'cultural compatibility' perspective (Cartwright and Cooper, 1992; Larsson, 1993), the most problematic situations are those where the beliefs and values of the organizational members are contradictory. According to this view, beliefs and values that do not conflict are not likely to create particular problems. Others, like Nahavandi and Malekzadeh (1988), Morosini and Singh (1994) and Calori, Lubatkin and Very (1994), have also developed the argument that the adopted integration strategies should be 'culturally compatible'.

Researchers in this field also mostly share a normative goal - to advance general instructions as to how to 'manage' cultural differences. Though different models are proposed, and somewhat different conclusions reached, researchers with this approach have generally assumed that cultural analyses of the companies involved carried out before the merger will make it possible to predict problems of integration and adjust the management's integration strategy accordingly.

This kind of approach is something that has lately been strongly criticized (Gertsen, Søderberg and Torp, 1998; Vaara, 1999; Søderberg and Holden 2002). This is because such approach reflects a 'naïve realist' or 'essentialist' view on cultural phenomena at odds with most contemporary sociological and anthropological research where the emphasis is on the 'social construction' of cultures through negotiation and sensemaking. From a practical stance, essentialist cultural analyses also tend to oversimplify the phenomena at hand, ignoring the comparative perspective from which a specific culture is described, and the culture-bound categorizations used in the descriptions.

Some organization and management scholars have also studied 'integration' from discursive perspectives. Although only representing a 'marginal' stream of research, it is important to acknowledge these research efforts as attempts to 'dig deeper' in the social and discursive construction of change. Researchers have, for example, analyzed the narratives of post-merger or post-acquisition integration (Gertsen and Søderberg 2000; Søderberg, 2003; Vaara, 2002) and shown that the actors' sensemaking of post-merger or post-acquisition organizational changes is indeed more complex and fluid than usually expected. Studies have also examined cultural confrontation by use of metaphors (Vaara, Tienari and Säntti, 2003), thereby adding to our knowledge, for example, of the mythical underpinnings of cultural conceptions and the power involved in cultural stereotypes.

Researchers have also analyzed media coverage around mergers and acquisitions. These studies have shown how the media constructs certain kinds of images of specific mergers and acquisitions and of mergers and acquisitions in general. Hirsch and Andrews (1983) and Hirsch (1986) have, for example, examined the vocabularies of hostile takeovers. Schneider and Dunbar (1992) have provided a psychoanalytic reading of texts in hostile takeover events. Vaara and Tienari (2002) have studied the discourses used in the media coverage of merger and acquisition cases. They found that 'rationalistic' discourse tended to dominate the discussions and that within this discursive framework particular decisions and actions were more easily justified and legitimated than within alternative discursive frameworks.

Subsequent analyses by Hellgren et al. (2002) and Risberg, Tienari and Vaara (2003) have further highlighted the role of different kinds of discourse type and discursive practice in the social construction of mergers and acquisitions. Such discourse analyses can 'deconstruct' commonly held conceptions concerning the inevitability of mergers and acquisitions and highlight how specific ideas are justified, legitimized and naturalized. Such analyses also show how specific ideas and ideologies around mergers and acquisitions in general and integration in particular are not only (re)constructed within the organizational boundaries but also, for example, in the media.

TOWARDS A SENSEMAKING PERSPECTIVE

This brief and selective review of literature can be read as a description of how critical organization and management scholars in this area – like others – have started to view the necessity of providing a counter-weight to the managerially-oriented analyzes in order to create more 'in-depth' understanding of the complex social phenomena around post-merger or post-acquisition integration. This has been achieved by adopting ideas from human resource and cultural theories in organization and management studies as well as drawing on discourse analysis.

The emerging interest in what can be called a 'sensemaking' approach in the recent cultural and discursive analyses is particularly noteworthy as it represents a conscious focus on the socially-negotiated and constructed meaning around post-merger or post-acquisition changes. It is this kind of analysis that our research project is built on – precisely to be able to 'dig deeper' into the social, cultural and political aspects of post-merger and post-acquisition integration.

What sensemaking is has intrigued scholars in organization and management studies for about two decades (see Weick, 1995). The concept of 'sensemaking' has been given different definitions, to the extent that there is significant ambiguity concerning what sensemaking does or does not mean (see e.g. Dutton and Jackson, 1987; Porac, Thomas and Baden-Fuller, 1989; Dutton and Dukerich, 1991; Gioia and Chittipeddi, 1991; Czarniawska-Joerges, 1992; Weick, 1995; Gioia and Thomas, 1996; Vaara, 2000; Søderberg 2003).

Theory and methodology

In this research project, we understand 'sensemaking' as an overall perspective that focuses attention on the interpretative processes through which organizational actors enact their organizational reality. A key assumption is that sensemaking is grounded in identity construction. This means that when people make sense of different events, issues, questions, problems, opportunities, threats, challenges, processes, or practices, they do it by constructing meanings for themselves. Another key assumption is that sensemaking is closely associated with organizational action. This means that it is the meaning given to specific actions, at the time of the action or retrospectively, that is important in terms of organizational consequences.

From a cognitive perspective, sensemaking processes can be seen as processes through which collective discussions lead to the formation of specific cognitive maps. In the merger setting, the organizational learning processes are especially interesting. In these processes, the actors make sense of the characteristics – for example strengths and weaknesses – of the previously separate organizations and their representatives. In cross-border cases, especially perceived national cultural differences pose specific cognitive challenges. Sensemaking may help people in the merging organizations to develop a better understanding of the institutional and cultural differences at play, but also frequently involve stereotyping.

Mergers also trigger emotional processes among the actors. The organizational changes may appear positive or negative from the perspective of the organizational members. Positive changes are likely to lead to sensemaking processes that portray the merger as favorable. If the organizational changes are seen as negative, for example, if 'good old' procedures and routines are changed leaving the actors with a feeling of being threatened and made insecure about their future tasks, they will tend to emphasize problematic features of the merger. What is important is not only whether the total gains are positive or negative when added up, but also whether the effects, positive or negative, are perceived by the organizational actors as distributed in an equal and fair manner. Thus, a merger that, all in all, benefits both sides, may still be interpreted in a negative manner by those who feel that they have suffered injustice. Such an emotional experience of injustice may be turned into a general conception of 'lack of synergy' and conviction of 'cooperation problems'.

Sensemaking processes also involve politics, that is, purposeful use of meanings for the promotion of organizational or personal interests. In the merger context, organizational actors often deliberately influence the collective sensemaking processes by 'management of meaning'. The clearest manifestation of this sensegiving is probably management's work to justify the merger decision, to seek social acceptance for their plans, and to motivate people to work for the new joint organization. In fact, a crucial part of their leadership role is precisely this management of the organizational change processes at the symbolic level. Other organizational actors, however, are also likely to promote different or conflicting agendas to further their own careers or other interests by attaching alternative meanings to the issues discussed.

OUR METHODOLOGICAL APPROACH

Our empirical research efforts have been guided by a methodology where narratives of post-merger and post-acquisition change have played a key role. In the following, we will first outline the methodological premises of our approach to organizational and managerial discourses and then describe 'how we did it' with a focus on the specific problems and challenges encountered.

Our understanding of the social and organizational relations and identities produced in the interviews is informed by a social constructionist approach (Gergen 1999). We rest on the premise that people in their discursive practices constitute their social relations, identities, and their social reality whereby they maintain or change social structures. This view implies that language is not just a transparent medium for reflecting the way things are, and not merely a kind of conduit through which information and ideas are transmitted from a sender to a receiver, as many managerial conceptions of communication still assume. On the contrary, a specific use of language and certain discursive practices constitute social relations, social identities and the social world according to position and perspective (Fairclough and Wodak, 1997).

In this book, we examine the implications of these premises for the understanding of social relations and identities in a specific organizational setting. Our approach regards organizations as social entities that emerge in complex interactive processes:

[...] when we speak of organizational discourse, we do not simply mean discourse that occurs in organizations. Rather we suggest that organizations exist only in so far as their members create them through discourse. This is not to claim that organizations are 'nothing but' discourse, but rather that discourse is the principal means by which organization members create a coherent social reality that frames their sense of who they are. (Mumby and Clair, 1997: 181)

We claim that discursive practices not only shape organizational structures, but are also simultaneously shaped by them. In the same way, discursive practices form social relations, social identities, and views of the organizational world, but they are also formed by them. Hence, organizational identities are neither stable nor well-defined entities. On the contrary they must be viewed as products of ongoing construction and negotiation of meaning:

> *[...] identities are never unified and, in late modern times, increasingly fragmented and fractured; never singular but multiply constructed across different, often intersecting and antagonistic, discourses, practices and positions. They are subject to a radical historicization, and are constantly in the process of change and transformation.* (Hall 1996: 4)

According to this view organizational actors' interpretation and sensemaking processes must be seen as firmly linked with their identity construction processes. When people (more or less consciously) make sense of themselves and others, as well as the activities taking place in the organization, they ask questions such as: Who am I? Who are we? Who are the others?

Social constructionism thus emphasizes that constructions of individual as well as organizational identities are relational; any identity construction takes place in relation to 'the other' that is marginalized or excluded. It is obvious that neither managers' nor employees' commitment to the new company and its goals can be expected to be realized without problems. A commitment to live and work according to a company's corporate values occurs through a struggle over meaning in which the company and its members compete over definitions of organizational reality (Mumby, 2000). Therefore, we also focus on relations of and struggles over power, delving into different Nordea top managers' positions and perspectives on the corporation, and we try to display how different meanings and sensemaking practices are constructed as part of the socio-cultural integration processes, legitimizing certain interests over others.

We acknowledge that interviewing organizational actors can never be a method for tapping abundant, objective 'facts' and 'information' about any organizational 'reality' (Czarniawska, 2001), as it is sometimes assumed in management and organization studies. One of the primary reasons for focusing on narrative interviews is to be able to examine the ongoing and shifting construction and reproduction of organizational actors' identifications, with a national community, a corporate culture, a business unit, a professional role, or whatever it may be. In the collected interviews, storytelling about 'us' and 'them' is very prominent in situations where dramatic organizational changes may threaten the organizational actors' 'normal' ways of making sense of the world.

Our narrative perspective underpins the importance of the managers' and employees' dynamic and shifting understandings and representations. Furthermore, the narrative approach enables us as researchers to grasp the interviewed managers' and employees' different sensegiving and sensemaking efforts, and to analyze and reflect upon different linguistic representations of the organizational reality in their becoming, for example emerging stereotyped descriptions of the nationalities involved in the merger (see chapter 4).

A narrative approach also encourages a *polyphonic* understanding of the world. By giving voice to a great number of key organizational actors within the four merging companies, to managers operating within the different business units and to people in different positions in the organizational hierarchy, our overall research approach and agenda are rather different from the mainstream approach in studies of international mergers and acquisitions. We have listened to a multitude of voices and thus encouraged different understandings and interpretations of the complex organizational world rather than looked for 'one truth out there'.

Apart from the interview situation, another key element in our research framework is our own understanding of the social context of the interview situations where the accounts are produced. The interview statements quoted in the different chapters in this book are not coincidental or arbitrary. It is not 'acceptable' to utter just anything in an organized encounter between a senior executive and a management scholar. There are inherent 'rules' for such accounts, because the interviews take place within normal working hours and in a specific organizational context, and in most cases in the manager's own office.

In our analysis, we also try to place the interviews in a wider political, economic and historic context. It is our understanding of this context that enables us to come up with more in-depth readings of the interview transcripts and to construct links between different interviewees' statements and accounts, but also links to other kinds of texts, for example company documents and media texts about the company.

There are no ultimate 'truths' in analyzing and theorizing talk and discourse. As authors of this book, we put forth our interpretations of the accounts and meanings produced by the senior executives and other interviewees. We are positioned by the available discourses as much as our interviewees (cf. Hardy et al., 2000). In effect, then, what we present in the following chapters is our reconstruction of the

Nordic senior managers' storytelling in interview situations of critical events and actions as they have experienced them in the post-merger integration processes. Such interview statements do not lend themselves to simple and direct interpretation. So even though we as researchers try to make the empirical material inspire our theoretical ideas and conceptualizations, we must also use different theoretical frames of reference in the different chapters of this book as our interpretive repertoire (see Alvesson and Deetz, 2000: 183).

THE EMPIRICAL MATERIAL

We decided to start our empirical investigations of Nordea by conducting interviews with top managers in the four merging Nordic companies. We outlined the main objectives for these interviews as follows:

- *To reconstruct the decision-making processes leading to the creation of Nordea with a focus on 'integration decision-making' and 'cultural politics'*

- *To collect stories told by the key decision-makers about critical events and actions during the negotiations and the following post-merger integration processes*

- *To provide a basis for future research efforts focusing e.g. on post-merger issues in specific business units or on specific tasks and projects*

The initial round of 53 in-depth interviews took place during the fall of 2001 and early 2002. We also carried out other kinds of fieldwork in different parts of the multinational organization.

Supplementary interviews with both managers and employees were conducted during 2002 to cover certain themes and issues such as corporate identity and branding, corporate communications and the development of a new multinational HR organization. Hence, we had opportunities to follow ongoing developments in the merger companies and shifting interpretations of the socio-cultural integration processes over a longer period of time, even though, of course, we only obtained 'snapshots' of a long course of events when we visited the company for shorter periods. The primary method for collection of our empirical material was semi-structured narrative interviews, but in addition, we collected company documents, surveys, and consultancy reports. Press releases from Nordea as well the media coverage of Nordea in different Nordic newspapers and magazines were also gathered to shed light on certain issues.

In this context, it is also important to note that several members of our research team have previously conducted research on this company and its predecessors. The empirical material gathered in these previous research projects as well as the informal contacts developed over time with people working in Nordea have also been of great value in this research project.

THE INTERVIEW SITUATIONS

A key part of our interview strategy was to let each interviewee tell his/her story, but at the same time cover the topics in our interview guide (see appendix). Focus was therefore to be on personal experience and reflections – not on the 'official versions' of why and how the company was created through mergers and acquisitions.

Theory and methodology

Our interview guide was gradually modified in the specific interview context to take advantage of emerging themes, and we tried hard not to impose our definitions of what was important or especially interesting. A common set of themes and issues for all interviews allowed us to analyze significant differences in the top managers' retrospective interpretations and sensemaking of certain events and actions, and to observe changes in their presentation, if they were interviewed several times.

Most interviews were carried out by one researcher, a few by two researchers of the same nationality as the interviewee, using a shared idiom. All interviews were performed *in situ*, in the senior executive's office during regular business hours, and on average they lasted from one and a half hours to two hours. We recorded the interviews, took field notes and wrote diaries about our participant observations. Afterwards, all interviews were transcribed *verbatim* and distributed within the research team.

As interviewers, we have been co-authors of the narratives told. We have taken the initiative to interview the senior executives; we have asked certain questions, commented on answers and otherwise contributed to the senior executives' accounts. Most of the interviews conducted were narrative in nature, that is, the interviewees were deliberately encouraged to describe their work situation and their perception of critical events in relation to the cross-border mergers and the following integration processes, and to do it in their own words with as few interruptions as possible from the interviewer. We tried to elicit stories by asking relatively few, yet very open questions after having explained the objective of our research.

The interviewees may have retold stories, which already circulated in the organization and gave sense to events and actions attracting attention and calling for interpretation. But the interview situations themselves should also be seen as a site for narrative production (Czarniawska 2001). Therefore, the *co-authorship* of the collected stories must be taken into consideration. As Gabriel puts it:

> *(...) they are part of the dyadic research relationship rather than of organizational discourse proper. Nevertheless, in as much as certain stories become embedded in an organization's culture or subcultures, they may be re-created for the benefit of the researcher in a very telling manner, as though they were significant artefacts or heritage figures, unchanged by the circumstances of their presentation* (Gabriel 2000: 137).

The researcher may ask clarifying questions to further elucidate particular aspects of the stories told. However, it is crucial that the organizational storyteller feels that these questions are asked in the interest of a 'deeper' understanding of his or her world and are driven by the interviewer's empathy. Gabriel (2000) recommends that the researcher takes on the role of a 'fellow-traveller' during the narrative, showing interest and pleasure in the storytelling process; this understanding of the interviewer's role has been guiding our efforts. We found it very interesting to get such privileged insights into the key decision-makers' considerations and interpretations of critical actions and events. But many of our interviewees also spontaneously commented on the interviews as a welcome opportunity to reflect on the integration process and their experiences of it and to do it from a wide perspective that cut across the way they traditionally reported on success and failure in their positions within the company.

In spite of a negotiated interview strategy and a certain degree of standardization concerning the issues to be touched upon and the questions to be raised, the interviews did not all take the same form. As researchers, we are not only Danish, Norwegian, Swedish and Finnish; some are more experienced scholars and field-workers than others, and finally we are also a team of women and men. Some of the executives talked to a man, some to a woman, some to an interview team of a man and a woman or to a team of two men. This may have played a specific role in the section of the interviews concerning gender issues, on which we base our analysis in chapter 10.

Finally, it should also be mentioned that interviewing the corporate elite also produces specific methodological challenges (Welch et al., 2002). Many of our interviewees possess much more societal and economical power than we do as researchers. They are professional communicators who have a long working experience in giving sense to their decisions and actions in a way that is legitimate within the company. Some of them have even been trained in media performance by professional journalists and communication consultants. We wanted to conduct narrative interviews where they told us their story with as few interruptions as possible. It was not difficult to make our interviewees talk, but our concern was how we could avoid getting the 'official story' which we could read in press releases and annual reports. Our challenge was to create a trustful relation that paved a way to their individual sensemaking and reflections on the merger experiences.

THE NORDIC RESEARCH TEAM

We have already reflected on the co-authorship of the stories told by the managers, and especially on the fact that the research team consists of both men and women studying a male-dominated organization. But the examples mentioned above should lead us to a more thorough reflection on the advantages and disadvantages of conducting empirical organization studies of a Nordic merger in a team consisting of researchers from the four Nordic countries involved.

The fact that we were employed at business schools located in the four different Nordic countries meant that we did not have the opportunity of face-to-face contact on a daily basis with more than one or two researchers from the team. We met in our own workshops 2-4 times a year; sometimes we also participated in the same international conferences and research seminars. But the rest of the time we communicated intensively by e-mail.

The different nationalities represented in the research group enabled us to conduct nearly all interviews in the mother tongue. The Danish scholar visited Unibank and Tryg-Baltica, a Swedish scholar the former Nordbanken, etc. This provided both the interviewees and the interviewers the best linguistic opportunities to give concise and detailed accounts. Furthermore, it gave the research team the privilege always to discuss the specific meaning of certain interview statements and accounts with the scholars mastering the specific language as their mother tongue. The interviewers had also the benefit of an extensive knowledge of the specific national setting and the specific organizational context. They knew the history of the company studied and had insights, for example, into how the case had been presented and commented on in the national media.

At the same time, collaborating with scholars working in other countries created opportunities to compare our material and interpretations. The Nordic research team thus provided a basis for reducing ethnocentricity and national idiosyncracies as well as good opportunities for defamiliarizing cultural understandings and meanings.

It has been specifically interesting to study how the managers in the initial phase of the post-merger integration made sense of critical events and actions using stereotypes about different nationalities (see chapter 4). We have also seen it as a challenge to reflect on how we as a Nordic research team coped with the managers' statements about different nationalities, and how we handled perceptions of national differences within the research group in discussions about certain issues where consensus was difficult to obtain. Even though we are all internationally oriented scholars, we have also grown up in different Nordic societies and been socialized into slightly different academic traditions at the universities where we have studied and worked.

Finally, it could be seen as an asset that we have slightly different academic backgrounds and research profiles ranging from organizational communication to human resource management and international business studies. In our experience, this interdisciplinarity has enabled us to draw on different theories and methodologies in our joint research efforts.

REFERENCES

ALTENDORF, D. M. (1986). *When Cultures Clash: A Case Study of the Texaco Takeover of Getty Oil and the Impact of Acculturation on the Acquired Firm.* Los Angeles: University of Southern California.

ALVESSON, M. and KÄRREMAN, D. (2000). 'Varieties of Discourse: On the Study of Organizations Through Discourse Analysis'. *Human Relations*, 53, 1124-1149.

BASTIEN, D. T. (1987). 'Common patterns of behaviour and communication in corporate mergers and acquisitions'. *Human Resource Management*, 26, 17-33.

BIRKINSHAW, J., BRESMAN, H. and HÅKANSON, L. (2000). 'Managing the post-acquisition integration process: How the human integration and the task integration processes interact to foster value creation'. *Journal of Management Studies,* 37, 395-425.

BOUWEN, J. E. and OVERLAET, B. (2001). 'Managing continuity in a period of takeover: The local management dealing with the experience of being a target'. *Journal of Management Inquiry,* 10, 27-38.

BRESMAN, H., BIRKINSHAW, J. and NOBEL, R. (1999). 'Knowledge transfer in international acquisitions'. *Journal of International Business Studies,* 30, 439-462.

BUONO, A.F., BOWDITCH, J.L. and LEWIS, J.W. (1985). 'When cultures collide: The anatomy of a merger'. *Human Relations,* 38, 477-500.

BUONO, A. F. and BOWDITCH, J. L. (1989). *The Human Side of Mergers and Acquisitions. Managing Collisions between People, Cultures, and Organizations.* San Francisco: Jossey-Bass.

CALORI, R., LUBATKIN, M. and VERY, P. (1994). 'Control mechanisms in cross-border acquisitions: An international comparison'. *Organization Studies,* 15, 361-79.

CAPRON, L., MITCHELL, W. and SWAMINATHAN, A. (2001). 'Asset divestiture following horizontal acquisitions: A dynamic view'. *Strategic Management Journal,* 22, 817-844.

CAPRON, L., DUSSAUGE, P. and MITCHELL, W. (1998). 'Resource deployment following horizontal acquisitions in Europea and North America, 1988-1992'. *Strategic Management Journal,* 19, 631-661.

CARTWRIGHT, S. and COOPER, C. L. (1990). 'The impact of mergers and acquisitions on people at work: Existing research and issues'. *British Journal of Management,* 1, 65-76.

CARTWRIGHT, S. and COOPER, C.L. (1992). *Mergers and Acquisitions: The Human Factor.* Oxford: Butterworth-Heinemann Ltd.

CARTWRIGHT, S. and COOPER, C. L. (1993). 'The psychological impact of merger and acquisition on the individual: A study of building society managers'. *Human Relations,* 46, 327-347.

CHATTERJEE, S. (1986). 'Types of synergy and economic value: The impact of acquisitions on merging and rival firms'. *Strategic Management Journal,* 7, 119-139.

CHATTERJEE, S. and LUBATKIN, M. (1990). 'Corporate mergers, stockholder diversification, and changes in systematic risk'. *Strategic Management Journal,* 11, 255-268.

CHATTERJEE, S., LUBATKIN, M. H., SCHWEIGER, D. M. and WEBER, Y. (1992). 'Cultural differences and shareholder value in related mergers: Linking equity and human capital'. *Strategic Management Journal*, 13, 319-34.

CZARNIAWSKA-JOERGES, B. (1992). *Exploring complex organizations: A cultural perspective*. Newbury Park: Sage.

CZARNIAWSKA, B. (2001). 'Narrative, interviews, and organizations'. In Gubrium, J.F. and Holstein, J.A. (eds.) *Handbook of interview research: Context & method*. Thousand Oaks, CA: Sage, 733-750.

DATTA, D. K. (1991). 'Organizational fit and acquisition performance: Effects of post-acquisition integration'. *Strategic Management Journal*, 12, 281-97.

DAVIS, R.E. (1968). 'Compatibility in corporate marriages'. *Harvard Business Review*, 46 (July-August), 86-93.

DUTTON, J.E. and JACKSON, S.E. (1987). 'Categorizing Strategic Issues: Links to Organizational Action'. *Academy of Management Review*, 12, 76-90.

DUTTON, J.E. and DUKERICH, J.M. (1991). ‚Keeping an Eye on the Mirror: Image and Identity in Organizational Adaptation'. *Academy of Management Journal*, 34, 517-554.

ELSASS, P.M. and VEIGA, J.F. (1994). 'Acculturation in acquired organizations: A force-field perspective'. *Human Relations*, 47, 431-453.

EMPSON, L. (2001). 'Fear of exploitation and fear of contamination: Impediments to knowledge transfer in mergers between professional service firms'. *Human Relations*, 54, 839-862.

FAIRCLOUGH, N. and WODAK, R. (1997). 'Critical Discourse Analysis'. In van DIJK, T.A. (ed.): *Discourse as social interaction*. London: Sage Publications, 258-284.

FOWLER, K.L. and SCHMIDT, D.R. (1989). 'Determinants of tender offer post-acquisition financial performance'. *Strategic Management Journal*, 10, 339-350.

FRIED, Y., TIEGS, R.B., NAUGHTON, T.J. and ASHFORD, B.E. (1996). 'Managers' reactions to a corporate acquisition: A test of an integrative model'. *Journal of Organizational Behavior*, 17, 401-427.

GABRIEL, Y. (2000). *Storytelling in organizations: Facts, fictions, and fantasies*. Oxford: Oxford University Press.

GERGEN, K. (1999). *An Invitation to Social Construction*, London: Sage Publications.

GERTSEN, M. C. and SØDERBERG, A.-M. (2000). 'Tales of Trial and Triumph. A narratological perspective on international acquisition'. In Cooper, C. and Gregory, A. (Eds.): *Advances in International Mergers and Acquisitions*. Vol. 1, JAI Press. London: Elsevier Science.

GERTSEN, M. C., SØDERBERG, A.-M. and TORP, J. E. (1998). *Cultural Dimensions of International Mergers and Acquisitions*. Berlin: Walter de Gruyter.

GREENWOOD, R., HININGS, C. R. and BROWN, J. (1994). Merging professional service firms'. *Organization Science*, 5, 239-57.

GIOIA, D. A. and CHITTIPEDDI, K. (1991). 'Sensemaking and sensegiving in strategic change initiation'. *Strategic Management Journal*, 12, 433-448.

GIOIA, D. A. and THOMAS, J. B. (1996). 'Identity, image, and issue interpretation: Sensemaking during strategic change in academia'. *Administrative Science Quarterly*, 41, 370-403.

HALL, S. (1996). 'Introduction: Who needs 'Identity'?'. In Hall, S. and du Gay, P. (Eds.). *Questions of Cultural Identity*. London: Sage Publications.

HARDY, C., PALMER, I. and PHILLIPS, N. (2000). 'Discourse as a strategic resource'. *Human Relations*, 53, 1227-1248.

HAMBRICK, D. and CANNELLA, A. (1993). 'Relative standing: A framework for understanding departures of acquired executives'. *Academy of Management Journal*, 36, 733-62.

HASPESLAGH, P. C. and JEMISON, D. B. (1991). *Managing Acquisitions: Creating Value through Corporate Renewal*. New York: The Free Press.

HELLGREN, B., LÖWSTEDT, J., PUTTONEN, L., TIENARI, J., VAARA, E. and WERR, A. (2002). How issues become constructed in the media: 'Winners' and 'Losers' in the AstraZeneca merger. *British Journal of Management*, 13(2), 123-140.

HIRSCH, P. M., and ANDREWS, J. A. (1983). Ambushes, shootouts, and the knights of the round table: The language of corporate takeovers. In Pondy, L., Frost, P., Morgan, G., and Dandrige, T. (eds.) *Organizational symbolism*. Greenwhich, CT: JAI Press.

HIRSCH, P. M. (1986). From ambushes to golden parachutes: Corporate takeovers as an instance of cultural framing and institutional integration. *American Journal of Sociology*, 91, 800-837.

Theory and methodology

HOFSTEDE, G. (1991). *Cultures and organizations: Software of the mind.* New York: McGraw-Hill.

HUNT, J. W. (1990). 'Changing pattern of acquisition behaviour in takeovers and the consequences for acquisition processes'. *Strategic Management Journal*, 11, 69-77.

INGHAM, H., KRAN, I. and LOVESTAM, A. (1992). 'Mergers and profitability: A managerial success story?'. *Journal of Management Studies*, 29, 195-208.

KITCHING, J. (1967). 'Why do mergers miscarry?' *Harvard Business Review*, 46 (November-December), 84-101.

KRISHNAN, H. A., MILLER, A. and JUDGE, W. Q. (1997). 'Diversification and top management team complimentarity: Is performance improved by merging similar or dissimilar teams?'. *Strategic Management Journal*, 18, 361-374.

KUSEWITT, J.B. (1985). An exploratory study of acquisition factors relating to performance. *Strategic Management Journal*, 6, 151-169.

LARSSON, R. (1990). *Coordination of Action in Mergers and Acquisitions. Interpretive and Systems Approaches towards Synergy.* Lund: Lund University Press.

LARSSON, R. (1993). 'Barriers to acculturation in mergers and acquisitions: Strategic human resource implications'. *Journal of European Business Education*, 2, 1-18.

LARSSON, R. and FINKELSTEIN, S. (1999). 'Integrating strategic, organizational and human resource perspectives on mergers and acquisitions: A case survey of synergy realization'. *Organization Science*, 10, 1-26.

LARSSON, R. and LUBATKIN, M. (2001). 'Achieving acculturation in mergers and acquisitions: An international case study'. *Human Relations*, 54, 1573-1607.

LEROY, F. and RAMANANTSOA, B. (1997). 'Cognitive and behavioural dimensions of organizational learning in a merger: An empirical study'. *Journal of Management Studies*, 34, 871-894.

LOHRUM, C. (1996). *Post-Acquisition Integration: Towards an Understanding of Employee Reactions.* Helsinki: Swedish School of Economics and Business Administration.

LEVINSON, H. (1970). 'A Psychologist diagnoses merger failures'. *Harvard Business Review*, 48, 139-147.

LINDGREN, U. (1982). *Foreign acquisitions: Management of the integration process*. Stockholm: IIB/EFI.

LUBATKIN, M.H. (1987). 'Merger strategies and stockholder value'. *Strategic Management Journal*, 8, 39-53.

LUBATKIN, M., CALORI, R., VERY, P. and VEIGA, J. F. (1998). 'Managing mergers across borders: A two-nation exploration of a nationally bound administrative heritage'. *Organization Science*, 9, 670-684.

MARKS, M.L. and MIRVIS, P.M. (1986). 'The merger syndrome'. *Psychology Today*, 20, 36-42.

MEYER, C.B. (2001). 'Allocation processes in mergers and acquisitions: An organizational justice perspective', *British Journal of Management*, 12 (1), 47–66.

MOROSINI, P., SHANE, S. and SINGH, H. (1998). 'National cultural difference and cross-border acquisition performance'. *Journal of International Business Studies*, 29, 137-158.

MOROSINI, P. and SINGH, H. (1994). 'Post-cross-border acquisitions: Implementing national-culture-compatible strategies to improve performance'. *European Management Journal*, 12, 390-400.

MUMBY, D. K. (2000). 'Power and Politics'. In Jablin, F.M. and Putnam, L. L. (Eds.): *The New Handbook of Organizational Communication*. Thousand Oaks, CA: Sage Publications.

MUMBY, D. K. and CLAIR, R. P. (1997). 'Organizational Discourse'. In van Dijk, T. A., (Ed.): *Discourse as social interaction*. London: Sage Publications, 181-205.

NAHAVANDI, A. and MALEKZADEH, A. R. (1988). 'Acculturation in mergers and acquisitions'. *Academy of Management Review*, 13, 79-90.

OLIE, R. (1990). 'Culture and integration problems in international mergers and acquisitions'. *European Management Journal*, 8, 206-15.

OLIE, R. (1994). 'Shades of culture and institutions in international mergers'. *Organization Studies*, 15, 381-405.

PABLO, A. (1994). 'Determinants of acquisition integration level: A decision-making perspective'. *Academy of Management Journal*, 37, 803-36.

PORAC, J.F., THOMAS, H. and BADEN-FULLER, C. (1989). 'Competitive Groups as Cognitive Communities: The Case of Scottish Knitwear Manufacturers'. *Journal of Management Studies*, 26, 397-416.

Theory and methodology

PORTER, M. E. (1987). 'From competitive advantage to corporate strategy'. *Harvard Business Review*, 65 (May-June), 43-59.

RANFT, A. L. and LORD, M. D. (2002). 'Acquiring new technologies and capabilities: A grounded model of acquisition implementation'. *Organization Science*, 13, 420-441.

RISBERG, A. (2001) 'Employee experiences of acquisitions.' *Journal of World Business*, 6(1), 58-84.

RISBERG, A., TIENARI, J. and VAARA, E. (2003). 'Making sense of a transnational merger: Media texts and the (re)construction of power relations'. *Culture and Organization*, 9(2).

SALES, A. L. and MIRVIS, P. H. (1984). 'When cultures collide: Issues in acquisitions'. In Kimberley, J. and Quinn, R. (Eds), *New futures: The challenge of managing corporate transitions.* Homewood, Illinois: Dow Jones-Irwin.

SALTER, M.S. and WEINHOLD, W.S. (1979). *Diversification through acquisition.* New York: Free Press.

SCHNEIDER, S. C. and DUNBAR, R. L. M. (1992). A psychoanalytic reading of hostile takeover events'. *Academy of Management Review*, 17, 337-567.

SCHWEIGER, D. M. and DENISI, A. S. (1991). 'Communication with employees following a merger: A longitudinal field experiment'. *Academy of Management Journal*, 34, 100-35.

SETH, A. (1990). 'Value creation in acquisitions: A re-examination of performance issues'. *Strategic Management Journal* 11, 99-115.

SHELTON, L. (1988). 'Strategic business fits and corporate acquisition: Empirical evidence'. *Strategic Management Journal*, 9, 279-288.

SHRIVASTAVA, P. (1986). 'Post-merger integration'. *Journal of Business Strategy*, 7, 65-76.

SINGH, H. AND MONTGOMERY, C. (1987). 'Corporate acquisition strategies and economic performance'. *Strategic Management Journal*, 8, 377-386.

SØDERBERG, A.-M. and HOLDEN, N. (2002). 'Rethinking cross-cultural management in a globalizing business world'. *International Journal of Cross Cultural Management*, 2(1), 103-121.

SØDERBERG, A.-M. (2003). 'Sensegiving and sensemaking in an integration process. A narrative approach to the study of an international acquisition'. In Czarniawska, B. and Gagliardi, P. (Eds.). *Narratives we organize by.*

Narrative approaches in organization studies. Amsterdam/Philadelphia: John Benjamins.

TIENARI, J. (2000) 'Gender segregation in the making of a merger', *Scandinavian Journal of Management*, 16(2), 111–144.

TROMPENAARS, F. (1993). *Riding the waves of culture: Understanding cultural diversity in business*. London: Brealey.

VAARA, E. (1999). 'Cultural differences and postmerger problems: Misconceptions and cognitive simplifications'. *Nordic Organization Studies/Nordiske Organisasjonsstudier*, 1(2), 59-88.

VAARA, E. (2000). 'Constructions of cultural differences in postmerger change processes: A sensemaking perspective on Finnish-swedish cases'. *M@n@gement*, 3, 81-110.

VAARA, E (2001). 'Role-bound actors in corporate combinations: A sociopolitical perspective on post-merger change processes'. *Scandinavian Journal of Management*, 17, 481-509.

VAARA, E. AND TIENARI, J. (2002). 'Justification, legitimization and naturalization of mergers and acquisitions: A critical discourse analysis of media texts'. *Organization,* 9(2), 275-303.

VAARA, E., TIENARI, J. and SÄNTTI, R. (2003). 'The international match: Metaphors as vehicles of social identity building in cross-border mergers'. *Human Relations*, 56, 419-451.

VERY, P., LUBATKIN, M., CALORI, R. and VEIGA, J. (1997). 'Relative standing and the performance of recently acquired European firms'. *Strategic Management Journal*, 18, 593-614.

VILLINGER, R. (1996). 'Postacquisition managerial learning in Central East Europe'. *Organization Studies*, 17, 181-206.

WALTER, G. A. (1985). 'Culture collisions in mergers and acquisitions'. In Frost, P. J., Moore, L. F., Louis, M. R., Lundberg, C. C. and Martin, J. (Eds.). *Organizational culture*. Beverly Hills: Sage.

WEBER Y. (1996). 'Corporate cultural fit and performance in mergers and acquisitions'. *Human Relations*, 49, 1181-1202.

WEBER, Y. and SCHWEIGER, D.M. (1992). 'Top management culture conflict in mergers and acquisitions'. *The International Journal of Conflict Management*, 3, 1-17.

WEBER, Y., SHENKAR, O. and RAVEH, A. (1996). 'National and corporate cultural fit in mergers/acquisitions: An exploratory study'. *Management Science*, 42, 1215-27.

Theory and methodology

WEICK, K. (1995). *Sensemaking in Organizations*. Thousand Oaks: Sage.

WELCH, C., MARSCHAN-PIEKKARI, R., PENTTINEN, H. and TAHVANAINEN, M. (2002). 'Corporate Elites as informants in qualitative international business research'. *International Business Review*, 11, 611-628.

Chapter 3

THE NORDEA CASE AND THE NORDIC SETTING

Ingmar Björkman, Tore Hundsnes,
Karl-Olof Hammarkvist, Anne-Marie Søderberg,
Janne Tienari and Eero Vaara

The purpose of this chapter is to provide background information concerning our case. We will first describe the construction of this pan-Nordic financial services group through a series of cross-border mergers and acquisitions. At the end of this section, we will also provide a summary of what Nordea is today. We will then offer an overview of the Nordic setting and highlight key similarities and differences between the Nordic countries. This is important as national differences have played a key role in the organizational change processes that we are analyzing. Furthermore, being Nordic is a part of the organizational identity of the group.

THE CONSTRUCTION OF NORDEA THROUGH A SERIES OF CROSS-BORDER MERGERS AND ACQUISITIONS

The finance sector has traditionally been closely linked with the national institutional systems. This has meant that banks, insurance companies and other actors have been operating within national institutional frameworks characterized by relatively clearly specified legal and normative rules. However, following the deregulation measures of the 1980s and 1990s, these institutional conditions have changed radically, opening up new areas of operation and competition. Specifically, the development of the European Union-wide directives and regulations and the EMU institutions have created a new emerging pan-European market.

Technological development has been another important driving force behind industrial and organizational restructuring in the European financial services sector. It has provided a great deal of possibilities for improved efficiency. It has also created new services such as e-banking. This development has meant that organizations have been able to – and forced to – rationalize their existing operations, implying most notably cutbacks in workforce. New entrants basing their operations on low costs have put in this respect extra pressure on the traditional banks. At the same time, the costs of renewing the IT systems of large banks – the backbone of the operations – have increased tremendously, making it difficult for medium-sized banks to carry out radical changes on their own.

A third force driving changes in the European financial services sector has been the blurring of boundaries between banking, insurance and other financial services. Especially banks and insurance companies have been increasingly offering similar kinds of products and services and joining forces in specific areas. Also, for example, retail chains and telecom companies have started to plan expansion to areas traditionally governed by banks.

All these developments have especially in markets such as the Nordic countries meant that the leading banks have been increasingly looking for possibilities to join forces. Due to the fact that these Nordic markets have been characterized by more consolidation and fewer players than in many other European markets, it is no wonder that the Nordic banks have been pioneers in the restructuring of the European banking sector. In fact, for example the EU regulations concerning competition have made it increasingly difficult for the leading Nordic banks to grow through domestic expansion.

The history of Nordea can be traced to the middle of the 1990s, although many of its parts were established already in the 19th century. The banks in the Nordic countries had gradually recovered from the financial crises in the late 1980s and early 1990s. The governments in Norway and Sweden had started to decrease their ownership in the banks that were state-controlled, and competition had increased in most product areas. In these circumstances, it was natural for the Nordic banks to reconsider their future strategies. For example, as first movers, Svenska Handelsbanken (SHB) and Danske Bank started to expand to other Nordic countries by establishing branch offices while Skandinaviska Enskilda Banken (SEB) and Föreningssparbanken (FSB) were looking at the Baltic states.

In Finland, the merger in 1995 between Union Bank of Finland (UBF) and Kansallis had created Merita, a banking group with market shares well above 40 per cent in the private market and from 60 per cent and upwards in the corporate market. Merita was by far the dominant bank in the Finnish market at that time, and due to its corporate customers it was internationally-oriented. In this situation, future growth and development had to be found outside the domestic markets. It was therefore natural that top management in Merita, in the fall of 1996, cast a glance at Sweden.

Nordea and the Nordic setting

Nordbanken, a middle-sized player in the Swedish market, had acquired Gota Bank in 1993. A couple of years later, the corporate management felt that the company was running the risk of being left behind as a domestic retail oriented bank group. As mentioned above, the other three leading Swedish banks had in different ways started a Nordic expansion while Nordbanken was still trying to come into terms with the domestic acquisition of Gota Bank. In the fall of 1996 Nordbanken and SEB started discussing a possible merger, but in June 1997 it came to an unsuccessful end. Nordbanken had then already concluded that organic growth into the other Nordic countries would be a long and cumbersome road to profitable expansion. Mergers and acquisitions were regarded as a better alternative, and Merita came up as an interesting partner. It then became clear that the Merita's top management had already in April 1997 approached the Swedish government, the majority owner of Nordbanken.

The discussions between the top management groups of Nordbanken and Merita concerning strategic fit, synergies, valuation and structural issues proceeded well, and in October 1997 the merger was announced. In the press release, one could read that this was the first step towards the creation of a pan-Nordic bank of significant size. It was genuinely felt that a Finnish-Swedish bank was simply not enough. In order to build a competitive platform, a presence in Denmark and Norway was regarded as necessary. Therefore, the owners and senior managers indicated that further geographical expansion in the Nordic and Baltic regions was part of the bank's future strategy and invited others to join forces.

The first bank to answer MeritaNordbanken's call was the Danish Unibank. Discussions were held between the representatives of the two parties, but the top management of Unibank wanted to first go ahead with domestic restructuring. In 1999, Unibank merged with Tryg-Baltica, one of the leading Danish insurance companies. As a result, Unidanmark, a strong Danish financial services group, was created. For the eventual negotiations with MeritaNordbanken, the increased market capitalization of the Danish group removed one of the major obstacles for a 'merger between equals'.

In the meanwhile, the corporate management of MeritaNordbanken turned its attention towards Norway, and in October 1999 made a bid for Christiania Bank og Kredittkasse (CBK), the second largest banking group in Norway. This led to a heated debate, various counter bids, attempts to block the bid, and finally a change in legislation to allow foreign ownership in Norwegian banks. The complex process ended with the Norwegian government, as the majority owner, accepting the bid in October 2000.

However, already in March 2000, the representatives of MeritaNordbanken and Unidanmark had announced their merger. This created the largest Nordic-based financial services group. After the acquisition of CBK, the pan-Nordic financial services group was complete. In 2001, the new group was named Nordea, referring to the Nordic ideas they claimed its identity to be based on.

As a result of these restructurings, Nordea is today (May 2003) the largest financial services group in the Nordic region with approximately EUR 250 billion in total assets. It has a world-leading Internet banking and e-commerce operation with 3.4 million customers. It has significant market shares in banking – 40 percent in Finland, 25 percent in Denmark, 20 percent in Sweden and 15 percent in Norway – as well as significant positions in Nordic life insurance markets. Nordea has the largest customer base of any financial services group in the Nordic region, including 9.7 million personal customers, one million corporate customers and 500 large corporate customers. It has the most comprehensive distribution network in the region including 1,240 bank branch offices. Finally, it is a leading asset manager in the Nordic financial market with EUR 96 billion under management. Nordea Group had about 37,600 employees corresponding to approximately 34,600 full time equivalents as of year-end 2002. (see www.nordea.com)

THE NORDIC SETTING

Sweden, Denmark, Finland, Norway and Iceland form the Nordic region in Europe together with the self-ruling regions the Aaland Islands, Greenland and the Faroe Islands.

With a population of almost 9 million, Sweden is by far the biggest of the Nordic countries. It is also the largest in geographical size (450,000 km2); roughly the size of California or Spain. In terms of population, Denmark, Norway and Finland are relatively similar in size: Denmark with 5.37 million, Norway with 5.19 million and Finland with 4.53 million inhabitants (2002). Denmark is markedly smaller in geographical size (43,094 km2) than Sweden, Finland and Norway.

In a number of ways, the Nordic countries share a web of common histories. But while Sweden and Denmark are old 'nations', Norway and Finland gained their independence only relatively recently, in 1905 and 1917 respectively.

Gustav I Vasa, King of Sweden 1520-1560, is generally considered as the creator of the centralized Swedish state. A strong military power during the 17th century, Sweden has not participated in any war in almost two centuries. Sweden also managed to preserve an armed neutrality in both World Wars, while Denmark and Norway were occupied by the Germans during the second World War. Finland, in turn, fought two wars against the Soviet Union and one against Germany. A Soviet attack on Finland set the stage for the Winter War in 1939-1940. In its continuation in 1942-1944, Finland joined Germany in a war against the Soviet Union. In the War of Lapland in 1944-1945, Finnish troops fought the Germans out of the country.

The Danish kingdom was once a major North European power reigning over areas which now belong to UK, Germany, Iceland, Norway and Sweden. In the late 17th century Sweden conquered rich agricultural areas from Denmark, constituing today the southern regions of Sweden (Skåne, Halland and Blekinge). As a result of the Napoleonic wars, Denmark lost the hegemony over Norway in 1814. The southern regions of the Danish kingdom, Schleswig and Holstein, were conquered by the Prussians in the late 19th century. These events altogether weakened Denmark as an economical and political power.

In 1397, Norway was absorbed into a union with Denmark that was to last for more than four centuries. In 1814, Norwegians resisted the cession of their country to Sweden and adopted a new constitution. As part of the Vienna peace treaty following the Napoleonic wars, Norway entered into a personal union with Sweden, which nevertheless agreed to let Norway keep its constitution in return for accepting the union under a Swedish king. Rising nationalism throughout the 19th century led to a 1905 referendum granting Norway independence as a kingdom. The new Norwegian king was called from the Danish royal family.

When Finland is introduced to the setting, the web of historical relations becomes even more complex. Already in 1150, King Erik of Sweden led a crusade to what is today the southwestern part of

Finland. From the peace treaty of 1323 until 1809, Finland was a Dukedom in the Kingdom of Sweden. In 1809, Finland was incorporated as a Grand Duchy within Imperial Russia. In 1917, Finland for the first time gained its independence. A republic was formed after heated discussions, but a kingdom had, in fact, been a serious option. A Prussian prince, notably not a Swedish one, had already been selected to the throne.

The people who in the Viking-age lived in Denmark, Norway and Sweden as well as in Iceland spoke a common language, Norse, with less significant differences than those we experience today between the Scandinavian languages. It does not mean that the Vikings also felt attachment to a common Nordic identity, which the many mutual wars within the region witness. But the linguistic community nevertheless created a kind of common ground for orientation towards foreign powers. This linguistic and cultural community was revitalized in the mid-19th century where 'Scandinavism' emerged as a movement against German culture, and again in Norway and Denmark during the Second World War as a cultural-political movement against the German occupational force. According to recent data from the European Values System Study Group, there is still a feeling of mutual affiliation between Norway, Denmark and Sweden and more shared values than with countries outside the Nordic region.

The Swedish, Danish and Norwegian languages all belong to the Germanic language group. Today, they are similar to such an extent that the respective nationalities can relatively easily understand each other in an everyday communication where each part speaks his or her mother tongue. But while the written Scandinavian languages with a large group of common words constitute a stabilizing factor, the pronunciation of Danish has moved it far away from Norwegian and

Swedish, so often a mixture of the Scandinavian languages is preferred to facilitate mutual understanding.

In contrast to the three Scandinavian languages, the Finnish language is of completely different origin. It belongs to the rare Fenno-Ugrian language group, which is not an indo-European language, and thus has no relations with the other Nordic languages. As a consequence of centuries with Swedish colonization, however, there is still today a Swedish-speaking minority in Finland, now amounting to approximately six percent of the population. This Swedish-speaking minority has been extremely influential in, for example, the domains of culture and business, and the Finnish-speaking majority has generally regarded it as an elite. Alongside Finnish, Swedish remains an official language in Finland. Consequently, it is obligatory for all Finnish-speaking school children to study a certain amount of Swedish at school. Obligatory Swedish remains a contested topic.

The three Scandinavian countries cultivate a linguistic community. But all four Nordic states form a community when it comes to the form of government and the social conditions offered to its citizens. In cross-national comparisons of political systems, Denmark, Finland, Norway and Sweden are often grouped under the label 'the Nordic model'. Despite of differences, all four Nordic societies are deeply rooted democracies and highly developed welfare states. The states are relatively small, and the composition of inhabitants has been relatively homogeneous until the 1970s when larger groups of workers migrated and political refugees fled to the Nordic countries from distant regions of the world.

More specifically, the 'Nordic model' refers to a particular version of the state with a large public sector where all welfare services are financed by taxes and offered to everybody regardless of their social status. The Nordic societies are moreover characterized by a high degree of egalitarianism. A very high proportion of women are working full time. The development of the welfare states in the Nordic region is often explained by the role played by strong social democratic movements. For example, the Swedish model society – *Folkhemmet* (The (Swedish) People's Home) – was constructed by the social democratic party, which governed in Sweden for decades. However, also other parties have traditionally supported the welfare state ideology in the Nordic countries.

On the one hand, geographical proximity and the web of common histories mean that the Nordic nations appear to be characterized by similar traits. Many of the institutions and traditions have the same origins. The legislation in the four countries is relatively harmonized. The Nordic countries have – especially after the Second World War – worked consciously to create institutions and procedures to foster Nordic cooperation and values. The Nordic Council was established in 1952 as a public institution for collaboration between the Nordic parliaments and governments. Since 1954 Nordic citizens have been able to move freely across the borders without a passport, and in the same year the Nordic countries decided to form a common labor market which means that citizens in the four Nordic countries can move to and work in other Nordic countries without applying for formal permission.

On the other hand, it is evident that the Nordic countries in other respects do not form a monolithic block. In particular, the economical structures of the countries are relatively different. Sweden's huge natural resources (timber, hydropower and iron) constitute the resource base of an economy heavily oriented towards foreign trade with many large-scale companies. Finland has traditionally relied on its vast forest resources. It is also noteworthy that Swedish corporations began to internationalize already in the latter part of the 19th century. The early pattern of Finnish industrialization was characterized by scattered mill communities in remote forest areas. Finland's key economic sector is manufacturing – principally the wood, metals, engineering, telecommunications, and electronics industries. Forestry, an important export earner, provides a secondary occupation for the rural population besides agriculture that is solely aimed at the domestic market.

Norway has been a pronounced fishing and shipping nation. The country is richly endowed with natural resources – petroleum, hydropower, fish, forests and minerals – and is highly dependent on its crude oil industry. In Denmark, small-scale farmers played an important role in the modernization process, which was characterized by co-operation between the state and the peasants; the peasants also formed co-operatives and modernized the Danish agricultural sector from the grassroots level to high-tech agriculture. Denmark has through centuries also relied on trade. It is still characterized by a relatively decentralized structure of small- and medium size enterprises.

The four countries also differ in significant respects in terms of current political and military alliances. Denmark has been part of the European Union since 1973. However, Denmark has opted out of the European Union's Maastricht Treaty, the European Monetary Union (EMU), and issues concerning certain internal affairs. Denmark and Norway were together with Iceland founding member states of the North Atlantic Treaty Organization (NATO). Norway has, however, in two referendums chosen to stay outside the EEC (1972) and EU (1994). After similar referendums, Sweden and Finland joined the EU in the beginning of 1995. Sweden has chosen to stay outside the EMU, while Finland joined it immediately upon establishment in the beginning of 2002. Neither Sweden nor Finland are NATO member states.

This complex web of historical relations between Swedes, Danes, Finns and Norwegians briefly described in this introduction continues to flavor social interaction between representatives of the four nations, as we will also show in the analysis of interview statements in different chapters of this book. For Danes, Finns and Norwegians, the history makes Sweden a natural reference point. For Norwegians, this is also the case with Denmark.

Chapter 4

NATION TALK

THE CONSTRUCTION OF NATIONAL STEREOTYPES IN A MERGING MULTINATIONAL

Eero Vaara, Anette Risberg[1],
Anne-Marie Søderberg and Janne Tienari

INTRODUCTION

Whether we like it or not, international interaction involves talk about cultural differences. And talk about cultural differences, as we know, involves stereotyping, that is, reconstruction of widely held images of oneself and the other. This is the case also with multinational corporations in general and merging multinationals in particular. In fact, in the merger setting, cultural stereotypes are likely to play a key role when the people involved make sense of the new situation, the role and identity of themselves and others, the organizational changes or the joint future.

What is interesting about these stereotypes is *not* whether they represent facts or refer to any particular kind of organizational reality,

---

[1] The last three authors are listed in alphabetical order.

but that they – at a certain time and in a specific context – represent shared meanings. Thereby, they also represent attitudes, preferences and prejudices of the people involved. It is therefore important from both theoretical and practical perspectives to try to uncover typical stereotyping patterns and unravel the meaning of particularly strong stereotypes.

Even though the Nordic region is often perceived by outsiders – both management researchers and practitioners – to be a relatively homogenous area, people in the four Nordic nations seem to perceive differences between their respective national cultures. This makes the Nordic countries a specifically interesting setting for an analysis of cultural stereotyping and Nordea a particularly fruitful case. In this chapter, based on our extensive interview material, we therefore focus on the question *'how do senior executives make use of stereotypical categorizations when presenting themselves and describing the other national collectives involved in the making of Nordea?'*.

In our interviews it was evident that Swedish, Finnish, Danish and Norwegian senior executives made frequent use of an available cultural repertoire of national stereotypes when describing themselves and the other national groups involved. This was especially the case in relation to decision-making processes. Some of the stereotypes uttered represented widely shared descriptions used by both the representatives of that particular nation and the other national groups. According to these 'strong' stereotypes, Swedes were frequently seen as consensus-driven, Finns as action-oriented, Danes as negotiating merchants and Norwegians as people who go straight to the point in decision-making.

Based on our analysis, we claim that these strong stereotypes are rooted in the specific histories and mutual relationships of the four nations. However, their widespread enactment also requires that they have some 'explanatory power' vis-à-vis current experiences in organizational decision-making. When unraveling these strong stereotypes, we argue that they are 'flexible' and ambiguous. They are used in the construction of national uniqueness in a way that promotes a positive self-image of the representatives of that particular nation. For others, the same stereotypes can, however, at the same time accommodate completely different conceptions, laden with more negative attributes. It is this flexibility that is apparently needed for their widespread use in multi-national organizations such as Nordea. We conclude this chapter by pointing out that while it is easy to dismiss these stereotypes as interesting but unimportant, it is dangerous not to take a critical view of these cultural representations and categorizations, full of prejudice and political implications.

STEREOTYPES AS A MEANS TO RECONSTRUCT NATIONAL DIFFERENCES

Previous organizational research has thrown light on how organizations as cultures are embedded in specific national contexts (see Sackmann, 1997). Research has also shown how social identity construction and negotiation are particularly complex in multinational settings. Especially the more managerially oriented studies have often produced and reproduced representations of the Western ideal and the 'problems' of other cultures. Many of these 'problems' are caused by a naïve realist understanding of identity and cultures. This has led some scholars to question the rationale of focusing on differences or distinctive national identities as something objective (e.g. Westwood, 2001, Søderberg and Holden, 2002). Theories of self-identity and self-categorization provide insights into the dynamics of cultural identity building processes involving inclusion and exclusion. According to social identity theory (Tajfel, 1981), groups construct a social reality through dividing the world into 'us' and 'them'. In-groups thus tend to give themselves more favorable judgments than they would out-groups. They create a positive self-image and thereby boost their self-esteem. At the same time, they define their boundaries to other groups, which are often considered inferior. However, identities are constructed not only through self-definition, such as claimed by Tajfel (1981). On the contrary, we see identities as constructed through discourse and mutual negotiation, that is, both through self-definition and ascription by others.

According to these theories, social identity constructions are always *relational*. This means that the national characteristics ascribed in a specific situation will differ, dependent on the comparisons made. For example, Finns and Swedes are usually characterized as being very much alike when compared with, for example, the French or Italians. If, however, we concentrate on Finnish-Swedish relationships, the perceived national differences will be emphasized when Finns and Swedes are asked to describe themselves and their next-door neighbors. Again, in comparison with Danes and Norwegians, Finns and Swedes in some contexts form a group whereas, for example, Finns and Norwegians in other contexts form a group distinct from the others.

In this chapter, we will adopt a discursive approach to national identity formation and negotiation. One starting point is that a nation with a common culture in the past, present and future is a mental construct, an 'imagined community' (Anderson, 1983). Every nation is thus a socially constructed pattern of interpretation according to which the country and its inhabitants are seen from a standpoint of difference between 'us' and 'them'. Another starting point is that national identities are produced and reproduced, transformed as well as deconstructed, discursively (Wodak et al, 1999). This means that identity-constructions are always communicated and negotiated, whether the interlocutors are aware of the construction process or not. Constructions of national differences must thereby be considered as context-dependent and fluid.

Even though nationalism finds less passionate forms than in the past in many countries, it is still present in the form of 'banal nationalism' (Billig, 1995). In accordance with Billig (1995), we define banal nationalism as taken-for-granted views about specific nations and their representatives constructed and reproduced in everyday life; in the media, in social interaction, in jokes, in public settings such as sport and other competitions where a national belonging is expressed with a variety of national symbols.

National stereotypes[2] are part of banal nationalism, both when people express their perception of their own nation and its citizens (in auto-stereotypes), and when they characterize other nationalities (in hetero-stereotypes). This banal nationalism is usually not based on explicitly articulated national romantic ideas. In contrast, it is a discourse that has become a 'natural' or 'normal' way of making sense of one's own and others' national background and being. This

---

[2] We define stereotypes as shared cultural categorizations of social groups that help to create order in an otherwise complex social universe, and distinguish between auto-stereotypes (self-judgments) and hetero-stereotypes (judgments of other groups).

nationalist discourse may be matter-of-fact in tone, but can also be articulated in jokes (e.g. Gundelach, 2000). In any case, the very banality of this nationalism means that it is rarely critical or openly confrontational. According to our constructionist perspective on nationalist discourses, the frequently articulated ideas of specific national characteristics and attributes must be treated as 'a mere stereotypical phantasmagoria' (Wodak et al, 1999).

Nevertheless, such apparently harmless discursive practices may still influence the formation of groups within the multinational organization and serve to establish or conceal relations of power and dominance between the interlocutors. This is the main reason why it is important to pay attention to stereotypes in a study of post-merger integration processes. To illustrate how stereotypical representations of shared meanings about different nationalities are (re)constructed in social interaction, we now turn to the Nordea case.

ON NORDIC RELATIONSHIPS: THE BASIS FOR CATEGORIZATIONS

In order to make sense of national identity-building in the Nordic context, one has to look back at the historical relations between the nations involved. It is important to note that Sweden is by far the largest of the Nordic countries. Combined with the historical colonial role of the Swedes vis-à-vis the Finns and Norwegians, and the Swedes as conquerors over parts of the Danish kingdom, this makes Sweden very much a natural reference point in national comparisons across these countries.

For relatively new nation states such as Norway and Finland who did not gain independence until 1905 and 1917, nationalism and national identifications still appear to be of explicit importance in many contexts, not least in relation to the nation that earlier had the colonial power, that is, Denmark and Sweden, respectively. Against this background, it is no wonder that at times the Swedish-Finnish or Swedish-Norwegian relationships can mirror a sibling relationship where Sweden is considered the big brother and Finland and Norway the little brothers. A similar superiority-inferiority relationship may also be reflected in Danish-Norwegian relations, due to Norway's former status as Danish colony for hundreds of years.

In old nations such as Sweden, nationalism may at times be relatively implicit or 'hidden'. It has been pointed out that it is often customary for Swedes to project themselves as the 'norm' in cultural comparisons – this, again, being first and foremost a common hetero-stereotype. To Danes, Swedes are a natural reference point – or a 'hereditary enemy' (Gundelach, 2000: 121), Germans another. For Swedes, it may be more difficult than for Finns and Norwegians to find another national reference outside their own social collective.

We may expect stereotypes (re)constructed in Nordea to reflect these relationships between the Nordic nations. However, we may also assume that the emergent stereotypes are influenced by the specific processes through which Nordea has been constructed. In brief, for the Swedes and Finns, the Merita-Nordbanken merger in 1997 was a culmination point that made many individuals reflect upon, try to cope with, and manage conceptions of national cultural difference. Specific cultural projects carried out in the first merger also made people think about national differences and their significance in the merger context (see Säntti, 2001; Vaara, Tienari and Säntti, 2003). For the Finns in particular, this 'merger of equals' was often perceived as dominated by the Swedes.

When MeritaNordbanken merged with Unidanmark in another 'merger of equals' in March 2000, many Swedes and Finns viewed themselves in relation to the Danes and vice versa. Here, our interview material indicates that especially Swedes and Danes started to compare themselves to each other, and their relative influence within the multinational company. In many respects, they also started to 'fight' for power positions. As a Finnish interviewee put it with gleefulness:

They have a real fight going on. It involves a kind of hegemony power battle between the Danes and Swedes. And we Finns and Norwegians, what could be nicer than to look at this from the side. One has to remember that for the Danes [the] East starts in Malmö (city in Southern Sweden).

After the acquisition of CBK was approved in October 2000, the Norwegians started to position themselves against the other three nationalities as one group and to compare themselves to the three other nationalities in Nordea. Since CBK was acquired – not a 'merger of equals' as such – no one expected the Norwegians to rise to a dominant position as a group. This acquisition by a foreign company was a preferred alternative for the top managers and employees at CBK instead of a merger with a Norwegian company. A Norwegian interviewee described his perception of the relationships between the four companies as follows:

It is a fight with Danes on the one side, and Swedes and Finns on the other. The Danes thought that it's good that we came on board to help them a little in this fight ... We do that consciously and unconsciously because in some areas we are more like the Danes than the Swedes and Finns are ... It is the Danes and us on the one side and Finns and Swedes on the other on many

occasions, both on matters related to organization and concepts.
On the other hand, it is a bit like us three against the Danes on
some occasions as well. Danes want to run things their way.

In sum, we expect that the national stereotypes constructed by the
Swedes, Finns, Danes and Norwegians most often reflect both the
historical inter-national relationships and the more context-specific
relationships under construction in the making of the Nordea Group.

CONSTRUCTION OF DISTINCTIVE NATIONAL GESTALTS: SWEDES, FINNS, DANES AND NORWEGIANS AS DECISION-MAKERS

We look upon our interviews with the top decision-makers in Nordea
as narratives. As these 'narrative interviews' were designed to let the
interviewees tell their own versions of the events in their own words,
they provide an interesting material for the analysis of national
stereotypes concerning Swedes, Finns, Danes and Norwegians as
decision-makers. The interviews swarm with various kinds of national
stereotyping. In the following, we will take up four specifically robust
stereotypes that frequently emerged in the interviewees' accounts.

EGALITARIANISM OR BUREAUCRACY? THE IMAGE OF CONSENSUS-ORIENTED SWEDES

The Swedish senior executives described themselves frequently as
'consensus-driven' decision-makers. This was described by a Swedish
manager as follows:

In Sweden the discussion continues until the decision suddenly is
made. It could start with people disagreeing and then the person

> *who has disagreed the most starts to indicate 'well one could do it your way' through his body language and formulation. This way the group knows that we are getting close to making a decision and then the Swedish manager says 'Well let's say so', and then it is done.*

This seems to reflect a widespread Swedish auto-stereotype on decision-making practices. For example, in a volume presenting management in different European countries, Zander (2000: 345) describes the Swedish style: "The very employee-oriented Swedish management style is firmly rooted in Swedish culture and has evolved during the twentieth century in symbiosis with the political and industrial arena. Some of the most distinctive characteristics of management in Sweden include egalitarianism and empowering, cooperation and teamwork, conflict avoidance and consensus seeking, as well as rationality, fairness and pragmatism."

Also for Finnish top managers in Nordea, 'consensus-orientation' was a dominant characteristic of the Swedes. While this could be appreciated, it was also often portrayed in a problematic light. For example, Swedes could be seen as overly prone to 'discuss' issues and be painstakingly 'slow' in reaching decisions. The following is a typical comment by a Finnish executive:

> *It feels that the Swedes have kind of a discussion culture. They discuss, discuss and discuss. They (the Swedes) use the term 'anchoring' ('förankring'). You cannot make a final decision before the issue has been anchored here and there. Especially in the beginning it was often unclear for us Finns when a decision then really had been made, and if it had, what was the decision.*

At times, they could also give credit to this tendency by pointing out that this kind of approach does usually lead to effective implementation after reaching the consensus.

Danes also frequently mentioned 'consensus-orientation' as a typically Swedish characteristic. They often criticized the Swedes for this, especially in contexts where there had been confrontations between the two national groups. The following quotes are typical examples of Danes criticizing the Swedish consensus-orientation in decision-making:

The way they make decisions, it is simply consensus, consensus, consensus. We keep talking about the issues, and these issues are on the agenda until all resistance comes to an end.

I think that it is very clearly the Swedish organization that is the exception. It is markedly different from the three others. The Swedish organization or culture is much more consensus seeking than the three others, and they spend more time on the decision-making process in Sweden than elsewhere, and the organization is also much more bureaucratic.

This ascription of 'bureaucracy' to the Swedes as something rather negative is totally absent in the Swedes' self-descriptions. In fact, Swedes stressed that they were not as 'hierarchical' as, for example, the Finns (see the following section).

In a similar vein as Finns and Danes, Norwegians also frequently described the Swedes as consensus-oriented in their decision-making and action. A Norwegian top manager pointed to both positive and negative aspects of Swedish decision-making patterns:

They are kind of communists all of them, they discuss and chat and inform and talk and that takes a long time. But even if it takes a long time, they will do exactly what they have decided, and that's good; Swedes are thorough, skillful, and it yields results. As you can see, they have done well in their way of working so I'm not putting that down in any way, but it's just that it fits so poorly into the Danish way.

The jocular reference to 'communists' above is particularly interesting as it portrays the Swedish collectiveness in a somewhat dubious light in today's business world. At the same time, this jocular reference is not strange due to the long-lasting Social Democratic rule in Sweden, which has promoted democratic participation in various areas of society. The consensus decision-making may also reflect specific practices, in particular Swedish co-determination legislation. According to this law, the employer is obliged to call negotiations with the trade union concerning all important measures or changes, before a decision has been made. The employees are thus involved in all important measures and changes in the companies and the negotiations should lead to an agreement; otherwise an employee - employer conflict may occur.

EFFECTIVENESS OR AUTHORITARIANISM? THE IMAGE OF ACTION-ORIENTED FINNS

For the Finnish senior executives in Nordea, the self-descriptions often involved 'action-orientation'. This was most often perceived as a positive attribute that especially the Swedes were lacking. This is evident in the example above where the Finnish manager was amazed by the Swedes' endless discussions. The Finns refer to many things, but they frequently associate 'action-orientation' with effectiveness and stamina. The following statement by a Finnish executive illustrates this:

I don't want to brag too much but the Finnish stamina is several times better than the others'. They are really an amazing bunch, real Duracell bunnies, and I think it is because the Finnish organization has gone through the toughest school (i.e. experienced most challenging changes).

Unlike the others, the Finnish executives could at times also link these characteristics explicitly to Finns' war experiences. The following is an example where the Finnish war mythology pops up when reflecting upon the national differences in the Nordic countries:

But then you have also these softer issues where you try with experts to analyze why the societies are different and why people behave differently in Finland, Sweden, Denmark and Norway, what is behind that, are there significant differences in (societal) values, what is the role of history, what is the significance of the fact that Finns have gone through a war and Swedes not, and all these things.

Here, the Finnish interviewee develops discursive linkages between the Finns' war experiences and their action-orientation. This seems to reflect a widespread Finnish auto-stereotype on decision-making. In the same volume where Zander emphasized the egalitarianism in Swedish management style, Laurila (2000: 213-214) describes the Finnish style, after a lengthy description of its historical context: "Finnish managerial hierarchies are relatively stable and democratic.

[…] Finnish management is characterized by its high technical and operational efficiency."

This kind of image is also portrayed in popular analyses of the 'Finnish management style'. Staffan Bruun and Mosse Wallén, two Finnish journalists (or more precisely, Swedish-speaking Finns), write in their popular book on Nokia:

> *It is management by perkele – direct communication between managers and employees, and quick, unemotional decisions. The organization is flexible. There is readiness to confront change. […] It consists of countless small guerrilla units that carefully plan an attack and strike although the risk for failure is high. It is easier to be forgiven in Nokia than to get a permission to do something. The important thing is that one does not make the same mistake twice.* (Bruun and Wallén, 1999)

The Swedish views on Finns in Nordea often corresponded with this characteristic of the Finns as more 'action-oriented' compared to the more Swedish 'discussion-oriented' approach. However, the Finns could also be described by Swedes as overly authoritarian, which may be interpreted as another side of the war-army-action association. This is missing almost completely in the Finnish self-descriptions. Consequently, the Finnish organization was often presented by other groups as 'hierarchical' and the Finns as more 'formal', 'less open' and 'not very keen to discuss issues'. The following example is by a Swedish senior manager:

> *And if you are a manager in Finland you have to be more visible in a different way than in Sweden. You have to participate in conferences and give opening and closing speeches. But you also have to be visible in the corridors. I got the advice to make*

sure I had a room reflecting my position. To manage through others is an art not too developed as a management technique among the Finns.

In the Danish interviews, stereotypes on Finns were less pronounced than on the Swedish (who usually provided a natural reference point for the Danes). Often the Danes, however, shared the Swedish view and described the Finnish management as hierarchical and authoritarian:

As some of the Finns have described it themselves to me, the Finnish bank acts similarly to the army. There is one at the top of the organization who decides what is going to happen, and then it is implemented all the way down in the hierarchical organization.

Further, it was emphasized in the Danish narratives that the Finns can be very pragmatic and effective decision-makers producing impressive results. In such contexts, the Finns were frequently seen as very similar to the Danes themselves when compared to the Swedes. Also the Norwegians tended to produce a picture of the 'action-oriented' Finns:

Finns are very much 'head on' ... they just do things, and they are very authoritarian-oriented ... In Finland, a boss is a boss. There, you can just decide, and that's the way it is.

The Finns were also seen as 'introverts' by Norwegians, in contrast to the Swedes, for example, as in the following joke told by a Norwegian top manager:

Do you know what's the difference between an introvert and an
extrovert Finn? The introvert Finn looks down at his own shoes
when he talks to you. The extrovert Finn looks at your shoes.

BUSINESS-ORIENTATION OR POLITICS? THE IMAGE OF NEGOTIATING DANES

Danish senior executives tended to (re)construct themselves as more business-driven than the other national groups in Nordea. This meant that negotiation and management skills were often constructed as specific Danish virtues in this context. In particular, the negotiation-orientation was frequently mentioned in the Danish interviews, not least because the Danes had sensed that their tough negotiating behavior had often provoked others. Consequently, an image of an 'orientation towards negotiation' was strongly present in the Danish self-descriptions. From a Danish perspective, such an orientation was, however, only natural as the following explanation by a Danish senior manager illustrates:

We ask questions all the time, and we want to understand the
answers others give us. We are used to delegating managerial
responsibility, and then it is necessary to be very precise and
focused. Therefore we must also understand the reason why a
certain decision is made. If not, we cannot ask other people to
act according to these decisions.

Again, this seems to reflect a widespread auto-stereotype on decision-making. In a volume on management in European countries, Schramm-Nielsen (2000: 203) provides a summary of the tradition and present context in Denmark:

Danish management is characterized by slow and gradual but continuous adaptation to external and internal changes. At the organizational level we find a high degree of pragmatism, and Danish managers are action- and outcome-oriented. The management style is distinctive in being more egalitarian than in most other countries and in stressing cooperation and consensus. Employees are expected to make independent assessments of situations and issues, and one consequence of this is that management decisions are not automatically accepted and acted upon by lower levels. Thus, managers are required to explain, persuade, conduct meetings and cope with the questioning attitude of employees.

Swedish top managers in Nordea often portrayed Danes as 'merchants' who were always negotiating about everything. Among other things, this made the Swedes perceive the Danes as being less 'reliable' or 'trustworthy' than themselves or the Finns, as exemplified in the following Swedish quotes:

I believe Swedes and Finns feel that one does not only understand each other professionally, but one can also trust each other, so to speak. There is some kind of a Japanese honor mentality among the Finns, which says one cannot break one's promises. A Danish manager in the same position is more, if the expression is allowed, a merchant and it's like ... Well, I can say that you can reach an agreement with a Swede and a Finn saying let's do this and it stands, one does not change that decision. But, to make a caricature and this is how the talk is going in our organisation, when one meets a Danish colleague he says: 'I have changed this'. 'How the hell can you do that? We agreed we should...'. 'Well yes, but that was last week'.

Denmark has more or less a Latin negotiation culture. I mean in Sweden and Finland we built it up logically. 'This is what we want, this is how it is related, and if I let this go, then you will let that go, and then we get closer a solution. That is, in principle, the basic negotiation technique which is developed by the parties at the labor market. And it also works well in merger negotiations. In the Danish culture – or for that sake the Latin – one says 'this is the package we want.' 'OK, and where is the logic?' 'What kind of logic? I just want it that way.'

Apart from the images produced, it is interesting to note that the interviewees now constructed Finns as similar to the Swedes when talking about the Danes. In part, this may be explained by the fact that Swedes and Finns had worked together in MeritaNordbanken for 2.5 years before they merged with the Danes (see above). Finnish views of the Danes were often very similar to those produced by Swedes, as the following illustrates:

Well, I think that ... the Danes are always negotiating. It is shown in their everyday life that they used to be merchants when we (the Finns) were still producing tar. A thousand years of trade ... So negotiating with the Danes is never difficult, it just always begins anew.

In addition to the stereotyping of the Danish management style (see Schramm-Nielsen, 2000), it is interesting to note that the Finnish interviewee above makes an explicit linkage to the Danes' century-old trade tradition that distinguishes them significantly from the Finns in particular. At times, Finns could also make interesting linkages to the colonial past of the Swedes and Danes, which to some extent seems to strengthen the image of the Danes and the Swedes as taking their hegemonial role for granted:

> *The Danes and the Swedes have in a way a colonial attitude. They have somehow internalized that 'if I am a Dane I have specific importance' (which the Finns do not have).*

Finally, the Norwegians also tended to reconstruct Danes as negotiators who are quick to change their positions and views if that is needed to pursue their own specific goals. A Norwegian senior manager comments:

> *The big difference concerns management style, and the Danes are process oriented ... opportunistic and obsessed with power. As you can see, this is problematic ... You don't know if they mean yes or no or maybe or ...*

PRAGMATISM OR NATIONALISM? THE IMAGE OF STRAIGHTFORWARD NORWEGIANS

Finally, Norwegian senior executives in Nordea tended to describe themselves as 'straightforward' and quick decision-makers, as in the following:

> *We make decisions right away, and begin discussions after the decision has been taken. This sets off, in practice, creative processes in our organization, and we can see that quite clearly.*

Nation talk

Norwegian interviewees frequently positioned their approach to decision-making and management in the banking business as based on specific positive (Norwegian) capabilities and traits such as pragmatism. This is illustrated in the following self-description:

And the Norwegians manage well in this thing, that's my experience in general and internationally. Norwegians are bright, pragmatic, good at adjusting, funny, strong decision-makers, creative. I have a lot of nice things to say about Norwegians.

We can once more locate a widespread auto-stereotype on decision-making here. Grenness (2000: 299) describes the Norwegian management style as follows:

After the successful completion of the Lillehammer Olympic Games in 1994, the Norwegian prime minister at the time, Mrs Gro Harlem Brundtland, proclaimed that 'it is typically Norwegian to be good'. Whether she was referring to the Norwegian skiers, the organizers or both is not fully known. What is a fact, though, is that the top managers of the organization committee of the Lillehammer games were all experienced business managers, many of them with core competence from large projects related to the oil industry of Norway. [...] [P]ractical experience from the oil industry as well as the success of the Lillehammer Olympic Games has strengthened the self-confidence of Norwegian managers.

Swedish executives interviewed in Nordea perceived Norwegians as 'independence-driven' and 'particularly nationalistically oriented'.

80

Norwegians were, in fact, often presented similar to the Finns in the Swedish accounts:

And then you have the Norwegians, who have a Little Brother complex and who want to be independent. They are like the Finns.

Both Norwegians and Finns were described by Swedes as suffering from an inferiority complex vis-à-vis the Swedes. This may also produce an image of Norwegians' (and Finns') 'simplicity' in reaching decisions. This corresponds with the Norwegians' self-description as 'straightforward'. A more negatively framed ascription to the Norwegians emphasize their stubbornness.

Norwegians remained in many respects more alien in the Finnish accounts. Nevertheless, several Finnish interviewees expressed quite clearly that they experienced Norwegians as 'straightforward' – like the Finns themselves:

The Norwegians, they are most of all – Norwegians. For us, Finns and Norwegians, it is easy to discuss and talk very openly. We express ourselves without diplomacy. But they are much more nationalistically oriented.

The references to Norwegian 'nationalism' can be explained in several ways. The special role of sports in Norwegian society – reflected in the texts above – as well as the recent wealth accumulated by the oil business can help to understand such nationalistic tendencies. However, in the context of Nordea it is also important to bear in mind that the acquisition of Norwegian CBK was a complex process where Norwegian politicians and journalists debated whether Norwegian banks – as an essential part of the Norwegian financial system – could be given to foreign hands.

Further, it is interesting to note that in some of the Danish interviews, Norwegians were, in turn, seen as similar to the Danes. According to such views, the Danes' readiness to engage in direct confrontation is compatible with the straightforward approach of the Norwegians:

> *I've heard people say that it is always easier for Danes and Norwegians to talk and do business together. Clearly, this is where the interaction between cultures functions best. There are no problems. We can understand each other, so it's fine.*

ON THE ENACTMENT OF NATIONAL STEREOTYPES

The national stereotypes presented above have an interesting ontological status; their mere existence is dependent on their enactment. The images of the four nationalities illustrated above are particularly 'strong' national stereotypes that are articulated in many different situations. They tend to be shared both by the people representing the specific nationality and by the other national groups involved in our study. This particular strength of the stereotypes is due to several reasons. In the following, we will focus on their apparent 'truth value' and 'flexibility'.

The stereotypes can in many instances be traced back to the histories of the nations involved. These stereotypes have been told and retold in the literature and in the media. They also tend to cohere well with day-to-day experiences of social interaction with representatives of other nationalities. What is most important, these particular stereotypes are used to explain specific experiences encountered in Nordea. For example, several Finnish and Swedish interviewees described how the Swedish decision-making style differed significantly from the other national styles to be observed at top management meetings. When the Finns chaired these meetings, they talked less, and the meetings did not linger on. When the Swedes chaired, discussion took much longer time and often lasted several meetings before a decision was made. A story was told in the organization that when the Finns chaired the morning meetings, they had to call the restaurant to have the lunch served earlier than scheduled. When the Swedes chaired, the lunch was postponed. This is an example of stories based on experiences that tended to confirm the pragmatic truth value of Swedish 'consensus orientation' and Finnish 'action orientation'.

However, any absolute truth value of such stereotypes should be contested. For example, the Finns' reluctance to discuss issues at length in Nordic contexts could also be explained by the language used. Often, in Nordic encounters, 'Scandinavian' – a mixture of Swedish, Norwegian and Danish – is used. While for the Swedish, Norwegian and Danish this means an opportunity to use one's mother tongue, most Finns (excluding the small Swedish-speaking minority) have to cope with a foreign language. This makes it difficult to engage in – not to speak of leading – elaborate discussions. Consequently, in stories such as the one above, the apparently confirmed stereotype does not necessarily validate any 'real' characteristic.

These stereotypes are flexible in nature, which also often makes them ambiguous. The point is that rather abstract images make it possible to attach various kinds of positive and negative attributes to the different nationalities represented in the organization.

Consequently, in self-descriptions these auto-stereotypes are predominantly positively laden, which is important for the effective construction of self-esteem. In the descriptions of others, through hetero-stereotypes, these same images can be used in comparisons promoting, at the same time, the positive nature of one's self-image and the questionable (or even negative) aspects of the other. For example, consensus orientation is something that the Swedes seem to be proud of, and associate with democracy and empowerment. At the same time, Finns, Danes and Norwegians tended to describe this Swedish consensus-orientation as questionable (or negative) when compared to their own approaches to decision-making, which they find more 'quick', 'effective' or 'direct'.

CONCLUSION

In this chapter, we have argued that national stereotypes can function as an important part of the identity-building and sensemaking processes within multinational corporations. Especially in contexts such as international mergers and acquisitions, these stereotypes may serve as a means to make sense of the history, current status and future challenges of the merging organizations. They become taken-for-granted attributes that can be attached to people representing specific nationalities.

In our analysis, we have focused on some very strong stereotypes which were used by senior executives in narrative interviews when characterizing Swedes, Finns, Danes and Norwegians as decision-makers. According to these stereotypes in the Nordea context, Swedes are consensus-driven, Finns action-oriented, Danes are negotiators and Norwegians straightforward. Although many other interesting stereotypes could be traced in the interviews, these came out as particularly frequent and long-lasting images that were shared both by the representatives of the particular nation in question as well as the other nationalities involved in the making of Nordea.

On the basis of our analysis, we maintain that at least two things are characteristic of these kinds of strong stereotype. The first is that they have apparent 'truth value', which comes from linkages to the national histories of the specific countries and to the current experiences in the organization. In fact, some kind of 'explanatory power' vis-à-vis current organizational experiences is an apparently necessary condition for their widespread enactment. Such explanatory power is, however, not a guarantee of any absolute truth value of the stereotypes. The second is that these stereotypes are 'flexible'. They can be used in the construction of national uniqueness (and difference) in a way that promotes a positive self-image by the representatives of a particular nation. At the same time, the same basic images can be used by others in downgrading comparisons where the positive nature of their respective self-images is promoted. Ambiguity is thus an essential feature of stereotypes.

Why is it then important to pay attention to this stereotyping? The reason is that the produced auto-stereotypes and hetero-stereotypes also have political significance in organizations. As long as people use these stereotypes in their talk, the images in question are spread as representations of the groups of people involved. In mundane language use, people are not usually able to critically scrutinize these representations, question their validity or to offer other descriptions of the individuals or social groups in question (cf. Billig, 1995). The potential problem is that the stereotypes bring with them prejudices that may have long-standing social consequences.

REFERENCES

ANDERSON, B. (1983). *Imagined communities: Reflections on the origin and spread of nationalism.* London: Verso Editions and NLB.

BILLIG, M. (1995). *Banal nationalism.* Sage: London.

BRUUN, S. and WALLÉN, M. (1999). *Nokian valtatie.* Helsinki: Tammi. (Nokia's Highway).

GRENNESS, T. (2000). 'Management in Norway'. In Warner, M. (Ed). *Management in Europe.* UK: Thomson Learning Business Press.

GUNDELACH, P. (2000). 'Joking relationships and national identity in Scandinavia'. *Acta Sociologica* 43, 113-122.

LAURILA, J. (2000). 'Management in Finland'. In Warner, M. (Ed). *Management in Europe.* UK: Thomson Learning Business Press.

SACKMANN, S. A. (Ed) (1997). *Cultural complexity in organizations. Inherent contrasts and contradictions.* Thousand Oaks: Sage.

SCHRAMM-NIELSEN, J. (2000). 'Management in Denmark'. In Warner, M. (Ed). *Management in Europe.* UK: Thomson Learning Business Press.

SØDERBERG, A. - M. and HOLDEN, N. (2002). 'Rethinking cross-cultural management in a globalising business world'. *International Journal of Cross Cultural Management,* 2(1), 103-121.

SÄNTTI, R. (2001). *How cultures interact in an international merger: Case MeritaNordbanken.* Tampere: University of Tampere. Doctoral thesis.

TAJFEL, H. (1981). *Human groups and social categories.* Cambridge: Cambridge University Press.

VAARA, E., TIENARI, J. and SÄNTTI, R. (2003). 'The international match: Metaphors as vehicles of social identity building in cross-border mergers'. *Human Relations,* 56, 419-451.

WESTWOOD, R. (2001). 'Appropriating the other in discourses of comparative management'. In Linstead, S. and Westwood, R. (Eds.). *The language of organization.* London: Sage.

WODAK, R., de CILLIA, R., REISIGL, M. and LIEBHART, K. (1999). *The Discursive Construction of National Identity.* Edinburgh: Edinburgh University Press.

ZANDER, L. (2000). 'Management in Sweden'. In Warner, M. (Ed). *Management in Europe.* UK: Thomson Learning Business Press.

Chapter 5

THE 'BALANCE OF POWER' PRINCIPLE

NATIONALITY, POLITICS AND THE DISTRIBUTION OF ORGANIZATIONAL POSITIONS

Eero Vaara & Janne Tienari

INTRODUCTION

Studies on mergers and acquisitions have rarely focused on power or organizational politics (see, however, Hambrick and Cannella 1993; Vaara 2001). This is the case despite the fact that mergers and acquisitions tend to produce conflicts of interest at various levels of the post-merger or post-acquisition organization and among many different groups. International mergers and acquisitions are a special case in the sense that they also involve national confrontation, which is often closely linked with organizational divisions. In these cases, representatives of different nationalities are often found in two opposing camps.

From a political perspective, 'mergers' are specifically interesting because they involve the idea of 'balance of power'. This basic principle may on the one hand alleviate potential conflicts and prevent domination by any party over another. On the other hand, however, this 'balance of power' is in itself a frame that sustains power and politics because it implies a need to make sure that 'equality' or at least an image of 'equality' prevails.

Based on the extensive interview material and other information regarding three consecutive mergers leading to the creation of Nordea, we focus on the internal politics around top managerial positions. In our analysis, we illustrate how international mergers often involve a principle of 'balance of power' manifested and symbolized by an even distribution of important positions. This principle is effective, for example, in selling the merger idea to internal and external stakeholders unwilling to surrender control. It also seems to serve as a means to prevent 'unnecessary' politicking by committing and disciplining top decision-makers. The 'balance of power' principle, however, turns out to be problematic when new decisions and choices are made in the post-merger organization. In particular, this principle triggers and appropriates national confrontation. Over time, the balance of power principle also seems to reconstruct 'new inequality' as it conflicts with other key principles such as competence-based career development. Finally, the 'balance of power' principle seems to constrain the ability of top management to control and further develop the post-merger organization.

THE 'BALANCE OF POWER' PRINCIPLE IN MERGING ORGANIZATIONS

In social studies, 'power' has been conceptualized in many different ways (see e.g. Clegg, 1989). Organizational analyses have also made use of different power theories in the context of decision-making (e.g. Miller, Hickson and Wilson, 1996). Traditional organizational analyses have often conceptualized 'power' as a 'resource', meaning that power is something that the actors do or do not have but strive for. At best, these studies have provided in-depth contextual analyses of 'power games' and internal 'politicking' within organizations (Pettigrew, 1973; Mintzberg, 1983; Pfeffer, 1992). Taking a fundamentally different view, a number of recent studies have been inspired by 'post-structuralist' views where power is seen as something 'relational' or 'constructed', closely related to the discourses defining the identities of and relationships between specific actors. These studies have paid particular attention to discourses (re)creating and (re)producing power relationships in and around organizations. Such studies have most often been 'critical' analyses of the (re)construction and (re)production of power relationships and inequalities in the context of management and organizing (e.g. McKinlay and Starkey, 1998).

Several authors have also synthesized these different kinds of views on power in organizations. Clegg (1989), a sociologist and organization scholar, has put forward a framework of "circuits of power" where he integrates the different views – most notably the ideas that power involves resources and relationships – and further clarifies how specific instances of social interaction link with broader structures of domination. This kind of multidimensional understanding of power is the basis for our analysis.

Power and its exercise are always contextual. They are, to a significant extent, determined by the setting. In mergers, there is an interesting expectation of equality, fairness, justice and democracy between the parties, whereas in acquisitions the control or dominance relationship is more straightforward (Hambrick and Cannella, 1993;

Very et al., 1997; Meyer, 2001). Such 'balance of power' can thus be seen as a specific rationality characterizing mergers. It can also, however, be intentionally used as a top management control technique or solution to major questions in integration processes. It may also, if used as such and enacted though different decisions, grow to an ideology characterizing the decision-making of the post-merger organization.

What are then likely to be the most important issues in bringing up the 'balance of power' principle? Division of ownership and control, allocation of top managerial positions between the representatives of the previously separate organizations, location of headquarters and other units, division of roles and responsibilities, allocation of resources, focus of shutdowns and reductions, and the choice of corporate name and language are often likely to become significant 'issues' for the organization members in general and for the decision-makers of the post-merger organization in particular. Of these issues – which are naturally often linked with each other – we will focus on the struggle for positions as a key concrete and symbolic question in post-merger organizations.

For the top decision-makers, the distribution of top and other managerial positions is a key question that needs to be solved already at the outset of the merger. This is a particularly cumbersome question because the negotiators are usually themselves involved in an overt or more often behind-the-scene struggle for influence and prestige. The initial 'solution' is not, however, usually a 'complete solution' for a longer period of time. The initial 'solution' usually concerns only the very top positions, and new decisions concerning positions, roles and responsibilities are needed when the post-merger integration touches upon other layers and parts of the organization. Furthermore, the roles and responsibilities of the people holding different positions also tend to change over time. The people in question may also leave the organization, or other events may cause a need to make new decisions concerning positions. This means that the struggle of positions often becomes a more complicated process than initially assumed.

At the same time, the positions issue is likely to reinforce identification along the previous organizational and national border lines as it signifies the balance of power between the two – or in some cases several – parties. This identification may defy the levels of social stratification, leaving groups as disparate as upper level decision-makers and shop floor workers sharing a very similar view on these issues. The positions issue is then over time likely to become an inherent part of the sensemaking around the 'balance of power'. This means that various comparisons around 'justice' and 'equality' are likely to become a key part of the sensemaking processes of the top managers and other organizational actors (see also Very et al., 1997; Meyer, 2001). In such comparisons, the people representing the different parties are likely to view the issues from fundamentally different perspectives. These comparisons, especially when involving nationalism, are also often strongly emotionally laden (see e.g. Hellgren et al., 2002; Risberg et al., 2003). This means that the basis for the organizational division is often reinforced in the internal debates, even to the extent of reconstructing nationalism as a key social force and ideology in the merger context.

This national confrontation is obviously problematic for key decision-makers, if they want to pursue 'integration' and assume more clear-cut unilateral control of the organization in general. However, their role is difficult. On the one hand, they have to position themselves as 'beyond' the national confrontation while the expectation is that they represent specific nationalities and their interests. On the other, focusing on the balance of power principle may *per se* reproduce national divisions and confrontation.

THE 'BALANCE OF POWER' PRINCIPLE IN THE MAKING OF NORDEA

The Nordea case is a particularly interesting setting for an analysis of internal politics around the balance of power. This is because the organization was created through a series of cross-national mergers and acquisitions. The first cross-national merger was that between the Finnish Merita and the Swedish Nordbanken announced in October 1997. Important in this merger was the pronounced (national) equality manifested, for example, in positions in board and executive management. Hans Dalborg, a Swede and the CEO of Nordbanken since 1991, was appointed CEO of MeritaNordbanken. Vesa Vainio, a Finn (CEO of UBF in 1993-1995 and Merita Bank in 1995-1997), was appointed chairman of the board of directors. Vainio was, however, only to hold this position for the first full year following the merger. The position was then to be handed over to Jacob Palmstierna, a Swede, and Vainio was to become vice chairman. Otherwise, the positions in the executive management and board of directors were evenly split between the Finns and Swedes.

The second cross-national merger took place between MeritaNordbanken and the Danish Unidanmark. It was announced in March 2000. In this case, the issue of equality was more complex, but the rhetoric of 'merger of equals' was very central. On the one hand, the two merger parties were portrayed as equals. On the other, it was the three nationalities that were to be treated as equals. For example, a corporate governance model based on the equal representation of each nationality in the board of directors was developed.

The third cross-national manouevre was technically an acquisition. After complex negotiations, the Norwegian CBK was acquired in October 2000. The arrangement was not called a 'merger of equals', but ideas of equality and fair balance of power prevailed on different sides of the pan-Nordic organizations. Important from the Norwegian perspective was that the Norwegians were to develop a center of excellence around oil and shipping and that their CEO Tom Ruud was to gain a key position in the top management. After this acquisition, the group was renamed Nordea. For example, in external and internal corporate ad campaigns, the idea of equality between the nationalities was a central message (see chapter 7).

In the following, we will argue that 'balance of power' served as an initial political solution but that this principle later on turned out to be a problematic one. This is based on our analysis of the extensive interview material, company documents and more informal discussions with a few key informants. It should be noted that, although our interviewees are predominantly those who have succeeded in obtaining key positions, they also include several people who have 'lost' prestigious positions in the restructurings and those who have left the organization for one reason or another. We have, in fact, tried to place special emphasis on mapping out the reactions, views and coping strategies of those who have not been outright 'winners' in the organizational power games. Being critical towards the 'official truth' and paying attention to the voices of the 'marginalized' is actually a key requirement for this kind of analysis of power in organizations, a challenge which we have tried to take seriously.

The ` balance of power ´ principle

In this analysis, we are obviously 'biased' by our background, nationality, relationships with people in the organization and opinions of right and wrong. For example, our Finnish origin undoubtedly shows in our interpretations. However, its should be noted that what is important in the following is not whether it provides an 'accurate' or 'complete' historical description of the power and politics around top managerial positions – which we hope and believe it does – but that it reveals patterns and processes that are likely to characterize 'mergers of equals'.

'BALANCE OF POWER' AS A POLITICAL SOLUTION

In several senses, the 'balance of power' principle in Nordea apparently helped to conclude the merger or acquisition deals and to establish a working post-merger organization. In the next sections, we will focus on the following points: (1) how the 'balance of power' principle served to win the support of different stakeholders when making the deals, and (2) how this principle was used to justify the decisions concerning positions, to commit corporate decision-makers, and thus to a significant extent prevent individual power games.

SELLING THE DEALS TO INTERNAL AND EXTERNAL STAKEHOLDERS

In practice, many of the key political struggles in the making of Nordea took place during the negotiations. It was typical that, after having agreed upon an overall strategic vision and general financial principles concerning the merger or acquisition, key positions were distributed evenly or 'equally' between the different parties. This was an effective strategy in terms of 'selling' the merger idea, first to the negotiators themselves and, second, to the other stakeholders within and around the organizations.

Already in the merger of Merita and Nordbanken, it was apparent to the top managers negotiating the deal that a 'takeover' would have been unacceptable by either party. On the Swedish side, this would have been unthinkable due to the higher market value of Nordbanken. Furthermore, because the Swedish government had rescued Nordbanken with huge financial inputs during the Swedish banking crisis, it would have been unimaginable to surrender the control of this organization to foreign hands. On the Finnish side, due to its dominant market position and the historically significant position of its predecessors Kansallis and UBF in the Finnish society, Merita was not something either that could have been 'sold' to foreigners. A Finnish manager coined the situation as follows:

This was a cross-border situation where these mental questions, national questions, came to the fore because of the special role of Merita and its predecessors in the Finnish economy and society.

Consequently, for the benefit of both parties, the deal was constructed as a 'merger of equals'. This was shown, among other things, in an even distribution of positions in board and executive management.

In the merger of MeritaNordbanken and Unidanmark, the 'balance of power' had already been a key concern in the first contacts between the top managers a couple of years before the eventual merger decision. It was especially important for the Danes to gain a strong enough position vis-à-vis the Finnish-Swedish coalition. In fact, several Finns and Swedes claimed that the merger between Unibank and Tryg-Baltica creating Unidanmark – taking place just one year before the merger between Unidanmark and MeritaNordbanken – was, to a significant extent, motivated by a willingness to increase the size and weight of Unidanmark to match that of MeritaNordbanken. As a Swedish senior manager puts it:

It was to create a bigger unit, which could so to speak weigh more in the new context.

In any case, gaining sufficient influence and control was apparently very important for the top people on both sides. According to several key decision-makers, the fact that Thorleif Krarup became the new CEO was especially significant for the insurance part of Unidanmark. These people were hesitant to 'jump' to a new merger where insurance did not seem to be a core business. Appointing Krarup as the CEO was seen as a 'guarantee' that this part and its people would be given an important role in the new group.

In the case of CBK, negotiations were complicated by the central role of Norwegian politicians (see Tienari, Vaara and Björkman, forthcoming). In these complex negotiations, it became very important for the top managers of MeritaNordbanken-Unidanmark to convince not only the representatives of CBK but also the Norwegian politicians and the media that CBK would be given a significant role in the Nordic bank group. The equality rhetoric served as a key tool in this process. In this rhetoric, the acquisition was actually presented as a 'merger'. In the words of a Norwegian top manager:

So internally we speak about a merger, which is in itself a political choice of words, to avoid that Kreditkassen would be seen too much as a little brother or as an outsider.

Another Norwegian manager was more blunt when explaining what the balance of power principle meant in this case:

This balance of power thinking was clear in that (the CEO of CBK) had to be given a prominent position so that the Norwegians would feel welcome as partners.

DISCIPLINING THE CORPORATE DECISION-MAKERS

Defining the governance mechanisms and division of top management positions meant that the politics around major issues were thus to a significant degree guided and justified by the 'balance of power' principle. This implied a specific disciplinary power according to which the individuals had to accept and act according to the idea of 'balance'. The following is a description of how commitment was created on the Merita side of the organization before the merger with Nordbanken:

It was so that when the negotiations had proceeded pretty long Vesa (Vesa Vainio, the CEO of Merita) led the discussion in the executive management and asked each person separately whether he was willing to go forward. The whole team was behind the idea, so it was no use to criticize the deal afterwards.

For the people getting the most sought after positions, it was not difficult to accept and commit to this principle. For example, a Finn described his 'lucky' career development when MeritaNordbanken was created:

I was in a sense accidentally drawn into the executive top management when X left the organization three weeks after the

> *merger announcement. Then it was politically important to quickly appoint one more Finn as we had agreed upon these kinds of rules of the game where equality was the key principle. It was not a question of who was the best.*

Those who did not receive their favored positions, in turn, had to develop specific coping strategies. First, some decided to leave the organization when the opportunity arose. For example, several people left MeritaNordbanken at the time of the merger with Unidanmark when they no longer saw the career opportunities as lucrative. The following is a personal reflection on a decision not to accept the position offered:

> *I do not know, there are all these feelings, very little bitterness. It is in a sense the name of the game when you are at the top ... I was in fact little surprised that I made it there, became almost a Nordic champion ... So when I was offered a position below the executive management I said, hey, now I will develop my own competence instead.*

Second, some simply accepted the situation. For example, in the case of not achieving the positions they had aspired, they chose loyalty to the organization. This was naturally difficult both for the individuals and for the organization, as the following comment by a human resource specialist reflects:

> *Still you have to make sure that people in the organization are motivated ... When the size (both mergers and organizations) increases, the number of those who are left at the second level increases. Some of them say thank you, goodbye ... But others of course remain and we want them to remain. But how do you*

make sure that they are motivated? You have to say that OK, we are now at this stage, let's see and go forward. When we have passed this balance of power stage, new positions will open ...

Third, still others chose to actively promote their own agendas. For example, a Finnish top manager described his active engagement in the internal debates concerning the integration of MeritaNordbanken and Unidanmark:

We all have brains and the capacity to open our mouths. Or at least we should have this capacity to open our mouths and express clearly our own views, how we wish things to be. In this sense, I do not see Danes bringing in that big problems. You are supposed to build this (Nordea) in the spirit of cooperation, but if you see them favoring their own nationality, I at least will not keep my mouth shut.

THE EMERGING PRESSURES ON THE 'BALANCE OF POWER' PRINCIPLE

It is important to emphasize that only some key positions – the top of the iceberg – were fixed in the merger negotiations. As to the positions lower down the hierarchy, new appointments and justifications were needed when integration proceeded, and new organizational changes were introduced. This tended to create various types of internal discussions, which frequently led to the politicization of the issues at hand. In these debates, individuals were on the one hand fighting as a national group to secure 'national interests'. On the other, they fought among their own group when it was a question of particular organizational positions. The 'balance of power' principle was apparently frequently employed as a rhetorical weapon in these discussions.

Over time, the 'balance of power' principle, however, turned out as a problematic ideology in these internal decision-making processes. In the following sections, we will specifically argue that (1) the 'balance of power' principle triggered national identification and also appropriated nationalism, (2) created new inequalities by conflicting with principles such as 'competence-based' career progression, and (3) seemed to constrain corporate control when proceeding with post-merger integration.

REINFORCED NATIONAL CONFRONTATION

The 'balance of power' principle inevitably sustained and even reinforced national identification. This was manifested in tendencies to interpret most if not all decisions concerning key managerial positions from a nationalistic perspective. At times, this led to problems in the relationships between the representatives of the different nationalities due to experienced 'unfairness' or 'inequality' and tendencies to blame people on the other side for disappointments. For example, at the MeritaNordbanken stage, many Finns were complaining that the Swedes were dominating the merger:

In the merger of Merita, the Swedish CEO recruited only Swedes to his closest collaborators. This led to a situation where others, either left the company altogether or sought new jobs. The Finns were a bit immature in the sense that they did not want to fight all the way but simply left. It is interesting that only the three Finns (no Swedes) left the top management.

Many, in turn, criticized Danish dominance in the consequent creation of the Nordea organization. As a key Norwegian manager put it:

The Danes have managed to get a lot of positions, much more than they would have deserved.

In this context, it is important to point to the central role of the media in the sensemaking around balance of power. In fact, the media tended to frame issues as questions of 'winning' or 'losing', reinforcing national confrontation within the organization (see Risberg, Tienari and Vaara, 2003). A Finnish manager described the 'problems' with the Helsingin Sanomat, the leading Finnish daily newspaper, as follows:

We should not have these fixed (national) quotas. What I am saying is that Hesari (Helsingin Sanomat) is so childish – and others too – that they only count the number of managers, compare those to the number of Finnish managers ... (and conclude that) the percentage of old Merita is now only 23 while it should be 25 to be in balance. So this is childish, but it is going to be like this also in the future.

Consequently, enforcing the 'balance of power' thinking and restoring (national) equality became major challenges for top decision-makers. In these situations, the top management often consciously sought for a role beyond the national confrontation. A good example during the MeritaNordbanken merger was the work by the Swedish CEO Hans Dalborg. The Finns gave him a great deal of credit for enforcing the balance of power in personnel matters but also in other areas such as transfer of concepts and practices across the borders (see chapter 6). As a Finnish interviewee explains:

The ` balance of power ´ principle

> *The Swedes thought that Dalborg was actually too Finnish, that is, went too far in this direction. Here the role of the CEO is emphasized because if you are a Swede, the objectivity is tested, and the person knows that. Dalborg really wanted to emphasize the role of being beyond (his Swedishness) and wanted to stress the Finnish values, the Finnish language and the knowledge of Finnish culture ... But this was seen on the Swedish side (as a disappointment) because they could not get all the positions they would have wanted.*

In this sense, new mergers and acquisitions created specific problems because they implied a need to 'open old deals' – promises given to specific people concerning the future that could not be kept due to changing circumstances. At the same time, the new deals provided an opportunity to define the rules of the games anew, as the following comment by a Finnish interviewee describing the merger with Unidanmark illustrates:

> *Everyone basically understood that this was a new game and that now the team had to be gathered again. It had to be evaluated as to who would fit with which position and to continue (on that basis). It was a little bit like give and take. For some, it obviously meant that they had to give up some Nordic responsibility when a Dane came and took over. But for others it meant the same responsibility but even wider as Denmark came along. These are very personal issues that you cannot fight, it just is like this.*

However, most often, enforcing or restoring the 'balance of power' turned out to be difficult for the top managers. Many interviewees pointed to the inherent problems in making 'objective' or 'detached' decisions. A key manager explained the importance of the nationality of those making key appointments in different parts of the group:

You interpret it one way or another. In my view, it can never be equal. One reason of course is that the manager in the sense has the power, the manager in smaller companies, units and areas (within the group) makes the final decision ... In our case, it happened to be a Swede. Naturally, this was reflected in the ways of action. If it was a difficult spot ... No one can deny the experience that one gets being a Swede for 55 years. And suddenly you would have to be neutral. It is not possible.

Another referred to the practical possibilities of the people representing the four countries to participate in important meetings, due to the size and nature of their respective organizations as well as traditions in traveling and participation:

So I think that at an attitude level we do not want to discriminate against them (Norwegians). I think that we really genuinely talk about four countries but that in practice four Danes, one Swede, one Finn and no Norwegians participate in our meetings. This describes the fact that they (the Norwegians) have the smallest resources to participate in all these Nordic activities. And this easily leads to a situation where their opinions are not heard when they are not able to participate.

CREATION OF 'NEW INEQUALITY'

Like any grand principle, the principle of nationality-based 'balance of power' seemed to contradict other important business rationalities in

103

the merger context. In particular, people often considered 'national quotas' as contradictory to the principle of competence-based organizational advancement. As a Finnish senior manager put it:

This is an interesting question as we started with this balance of power principle. However, to remain a good and effective and attractive bank in the future, a financial institution, we cannot base our decisions on quotas. We have to rather start from evaluating which man or woman among the 38,000 people is the best, be it a Chinese, and he/she is then the one to get the job. So not by distributing numbers in a queue according to the nationalities.

A key Danish manager put it as follows:

Democracy – if that is the right expression – has been prioritized higher than competence. There are unbelievably many examples of choosing a person because he is of the right nationality rather than, perhaps, he has the right competencies.

Distinguishing 'competent' people without any reference to their (national) background, however, turned out to be difficult. This was because the managers responsible for making the appointments usually had long-terms relationships with their 'old colleagues' and knew the people from their 'old' organization relatively well. In contrast, people coming from the other parts of the merged organization were often only known from casual encounters, and evaluating their competence frequently involved consultation with their own superiors or colleagues. This, according to many senior managers, tended to reconstruct national juxtaposition even in cases where people explicitly wanted to avoid that.

From a top management perspective, the conflicting expectations and interpretations were very difficult to handle. In a sense, they often resulted in 'in-built' hypocrisy (cf. Brunsson, 1989) where the contradictions had to be explained away, especially in the public arena or in our narrative interviews. The following is a typical example of trying to explain things for the better in an interview situation:

Yes, there is in principle a contradiction. But if you think that in every organization there are good people, and the people are distributed ... according to the curve of Gauss. When we have a fixed number of positions, we find rather natural solutions by drawing the line so that those above just get the key positions.

Further, it may be that the national 'balance of power' also tended to overshadow attempts to work on other equality principles, such as equality between the sexes in management (see chapter 10). For example, this kind of thinking meant that competent female candidates in specific country organizations frequently had to compete with their colleagues in the same country for the increasingly scarce positions within their 'national quota' in the new organization.

IMPEDIMENTS TO CORPORATE CONTROL

The 'balance of power' principle also seems to have turned out somewhat controversial in terms of controlling and managing the post-merger organization. The constant negotiations between the different parties and the problems created by feelings of 'inequality' seemed to hamper the ability of the corporate managers to initiate new organizational changes and, in particular, to proceed with further integration. The nationality-based equality was, in fact, often seen as an impediment to 'efficiency', 'streamlining' and 'integration'. This seems to have made many top managers gradually abandon the 'merger of equals' rhetoric, especially after some time had passed since the acquisition of CBK. Building a business case where nationality was not significantly focused on was a strong message of the top management led by the CEO Thorleif Krarup when initiating the 'Second Wave' of integration in Nordea in the fall of 2001. As a senior manager put it:

No organization can live long if you select (the people) on the basis of balance of power from here and there. It is in the background that ... when we are really united, then the best person will be chosen to the job in question. Everyone knows that this stage will come sooner or later.

Another senior manager described the needed transition as follows:

Don't misunderstand me. I am quite sure that this (focusing on balance of power) was the right thing to do in the beginning. But now we have come so long in the merger that I think, and this is a general wish in the organization, that we must see that it is the right people, due to their competence, who are preferred over those that have the right nationality. So "the honeymoon period is over", as they say in English.

Underlying these kinds of reflections one could also detect a willingness to assume more control in the hands of the corporate management. This was overall seen as the appropriate model for corporate organizations and, in particular, a requirement for keeping up with international competition in the field of financial services. In this context, organizations such as the Nordic council or the airline

SAS were taken up as examples of what the top managers did not want to see Nordea develop into.

CONCLUSION

Power and politics have not received the attention that they deserve in research on mergers and acquisitions. In this chapter, we have attempted to understand the dynamics of power and politics around 'mergers of equals' by focusing on the principle of 'balance of power' in the making of Nordea. Our starting point has been that to make sense of these dynamics requires a contextual view where concrete issues – most notably decisions concerning top managerial positions – have complex power implications.

Although Nordea is in many ways a special case, in our view, it highlights the *inherent political instability* of cross-national mergers more generally. As described in the previous section, the 'balance of power' principle provided an effective means for selling the merger idea to internal and external stakeholders. It helped to alleviate resistance to the merger or acquisition deals and to specific changes related to them, and to 'freeze' internal conflicts in the merging organization. However, at the same time, it reinforced nationalism, which sustained confrontation and interpretations of 'inequality'. The 'balance of power' principle also turned out difficult to hold in the longer run – especially vis-à-vis competence-based career development. Finally, it also seemed to constrain the ability of the top management to pursue further integration in the post-merger organization.

By pointing to the instability of 'balance of power', this chapter shows how problematic and temporary specific political principles turn out to be in a complex multinational organization undergoing various kinds of post-merger changes. In particular, this instability helps to shed more light on three tendencies in mergers and acquisitions. First, like some previous analyses in the context of acquisitions (see Birkinshaw, Bresman and Håkanson, 2000), the present study seems to support the idea that post-merger or post-acquisition integration often proceeds in stages. In mergers, pursuing integration through a 'balance of power' principle seems to constitute a typical first stage – to be followed by new ones.

Second, similarly to Hambrick and Cannella (1993) and Very et al. (1997), our analysis illustrates the difficulties in maintaining a genuine balance in the power disposition in mergers. It thus helps to understand why mergers so often turn out to become 'acquisitions' where one party assumes a dominating position. Third, by illustrating the problems encountered when enforcing the national 'balance of power', our analysis also provides additional evidence to the discussion of why mergers and acquisitions so often turn out to be disappointments for the key decision-makers involved. In our analysis, we can point both to feelings of disappointment and unsatisfaction created when comparing the national 'balance of power' and to concrete problems of sacrificing efficiency in the name of equality.

What are then the managerial implications of this analysis? Clearly, 'balance of power' can be seen as a principle – or even a management tool – that works well for a specific period in a merging organization. In a sense, it seems an appropriate organizational principle for the first phases of integration in merging. However, in the long run, this principle seems difficult to hold on to. This means that being able to move from a 'balance of power' setting to another kind of political reality becomes a key challenge for managing post-merger integration. This requires specific skills in justifying the new 'rules of the game' – but also broad-mindedness to oversee that the new equality does not turn into new inequality.

REFERENCES

BIRKINSHAW, J., BRESMAN, H. and HÅKANSON, L. (2000). 'Managing the post-acquisition integration process: How the human integration and the task integration processes interact to foster value creation'. *Journal of Management Studies*, 37, 395-425.

BRUNSSON, N. (1989). *The organization of hypocrisy: talk, decision and actions in organizations*. Chichester: Wiley.

CLEGG, S. R. (1989). *Frameworks of power*. London: Sage.

DUTTON, J. E. and DUKERICH, J. M. (1991). 'Keeping an eye on the mirror: Image and identity in organizational adaptation'. *Academy of Management Journal*, 34, 517-54.

HAMBRICK, D. and CANNELLA, A. (1993). 'Relative standing: A framework for understanding departures of acquired executives'. *Academy of Management Journal*, 36, 733-62.

HELLGREN, B., LÖWSTEDT, J., PUTTONEN, L., TIENARI, J., VAARA, E. and WERR, A. 'How issues become constructed in the media: 'Winners' and 'Losers' in the AstraZeneca merger.' *British Journal of Management*, 2002, 13(2), 123-140.

MCKINLAY, A. and STARKEY, K. (1998). (Eds.). *Foucault, management and organization theory*. London: Sage.

MEYER, C. B. (2001). 'Allocation processes in mergers and acquisitions: An organizational justice perspective'. *British Journal of Management*, 12, 47-66.

MILLER, S. J., HICKSON, D. J. and WILSON, D. C. (1996). 'Decision-making in organizations'. In Clegg, S. R., Hardy, C. and Nord, W. R. (Eds.). *Handbook of Organization studies*. London: Sage.

MINTZBERG, H. (1983). *Power in and around organizations*. Englewood Cliffs, NJ: PrenticeHall.

PETTIGREW, A. M. (1973). *The politics of organizational decision-making*. London: Tavistock.

The` balance of power´principle

PFEFFER, J. (1992). *Power in organizations.* Boston, MA: Pitman.

OLIE, R. (1994). 'Shades of culture and institutions in international mergers'. *Organization Studies*, 15, 381-405.

RISBERG, A., TIENARI, J. and VAARA, E. (2003). 'Making sense of a transnational merger: Media texts and the (re)construction of power relations'. *Culture and Organization*, 9(2).

TIENARI, J., VAARA, E. and BJÖRKMAN, I. 'Global capitalism meets national spirit: Discourses in media texts on a cross-border acquisition'. *Journal of Management Inquiry*, forthcoming.

VAARA, E (2001). 'Role-bound actors in corporate combinations: A sociopolitical perspective on post-merger change processes'. *Scandinavian Journal of Management*, 17, 481-509.

VAARA, E. (2002). 'On the discursive construction of success/failure in narratives of post-merger integration'. *Organization Studies*, 23, 213-250

VERY, P., LUBATKIN, M., CALORI, R. and VEIGA, J. (1997). 'Relative standing and the performance of recently acquired European firms'. *Strategic Management Journal*, 18, 593-614.

Chapter 6

BEST PRACTICE IS WEST PRACTICE?

A SENSEMAKING PERSPECTIVE ON KNOWLEDGE TRANSFER[1]

Eero Vaara, Janne Tienari and Ingmar Björkman

INTRODUCTION

Mergers and acquisitions present a fruitful context for combining resources, knowledge and capabilities. It is therefore no wonder that 'knowledge transfer' has become one of the primary motives and justifications for contemporary merger or acquisition deals. At the same time, working on or managing knowledge transfer has grown into one of the key objectives and challenges of post-merger or post-acquisition integration (see e.g. Haspeslagh and Jemison, 1991). This post-merger knowledge transfer has, however, turned out to be far from unproblematic. Both academic studies and practical experience,

---

[1] This chapter is to a significant extent based on the article 'Best Practice is West Practice? A sensemaking perspective on knowledge transfer' by Vaara, Tienari and Björkman published in Nordic Organization Studies (1/2003).

in fact, suggest that social and cultural embeddedness often impedes effective transfer of knowledge (e.g. Ranft and Lord, 2002) and that people representing different organizations and units are not always 'committed to' but instead seem to resist such efforts (e.g. Empson, 2001).

In our view, this calls for studies analyzing the complex socio-political aspects involved in knowledge transfer. As a step in this direction, we outline in this chapter a 'sensemaking' perspective on the transfer of knowledge. We claim that Nordea is in this respect a particularly illuminative case because the concept of 'best practices' has been actively used at the different stages of building the organization. Drawing on extensive interview and archival material, we analyze corporate attempts to distinguish and make use of 'best practices' as a post-merger integration tool. In our analysis, we identify four specific sensemaking processes around the transfer of 'best practices': identification, evaluation, (re)contextualization, and (re)configuration. We argue that these sensemaking processes are characterized by inherent complexity, ambiguity and politics, and claim that uncovering these aspects helps us to understand the often-encountered problems and disappointments in post-merger knowledge transfer.

PRIOR RESEARCH ON KNOWLEDGE TRANSFER IN MERGERS AND ACQUISITIONS

Knowledge management and transfer have become increasingly popular perspectives in organization and management literature in recent years (Winter, 1987; Nonaka, 1994; Grant, 1996). Against this background, it is no wonder that models have been created to facilitate and manage knowledge transfer, especially to make tacit knowledge explicit and to create organizational structures and processes to encourage and motivate knowledge transfer. One of the concepts that have received a significant amount of attention is the idea of 'best practices', which has become widely used in connection with organizational learning and specifically benchmarking in knowledge transfer. As the term indicates, it is about identifying and spreading provably (most) successful organizational solutions, internally or externally. Naturally, the search, identification and implementation of such practices are far from straightforward. They are, for example, limited by the 'external' (e.g. industry dynamics and customer acceptance) and 'internal' (e.g. the nature of industrial relations as well as specificities concerning technology use and production) contexts (e.g. Martin and Beaumont, 1998).

Not surprisingly, knowledge transfer has become a key motive and justification for various types of industrial and organizational restructuring. Mergers and acquisitions in particular have been motivated by the possibility to acquire new knowledge, which is subsequently transferred to and recombined in other parts of the new corporation (Haspeslagh and Jemison, 1991; Laamanen, 1997; Bresman, Birkinshaw and Nobel, 1999; Ranft and Lord, 2002). The potential benefits of securing access to knowledge around new technologies, concepts, products, and practices have been viewed as especially important motives for mergers and acquisitions in high tech industries (e.g. Ahuja and Katila, 2001; Ranft and Lord, 2002).

Consequently, knowledge transfer has grown into an increasingly important managerial objective in post-merger integration (e.g. Haspeslagh and Jemison, 1991). This has also meant that concepts and management tools such as 'best practices' have been developed and used extensively for various purposes. These tools have, on the one hand, been used to reap the specific benefits of complementary knowledge and learning. On the other, they have been used to integrate, standardize, and homogenize the operations and cultures of the merging organizations, with uniform operations, standardized practices, rationalization of operations, and a joint culture as underlying managerial goals.

Results and outcomes of these post-merger knowledge transfer processes have, however, frequently been disappointing. Analyses have pointed to the significant impediments created by the embedded nature of knowledge (e.g. Ranft and Lord, 2002). Studies have also often showed how people representing different organizations and units are not committed to such knowledge transfer but instead, for various reasons, seem to often resist such projects (e.g. Empson, 2001).

The literature on knowledge transfer has been predominantly based on what could be called an 'essentialist' conception of knowledge. This is at odds with contemporary philosophical and sociological literature emphasizing the socially constructed nature of knowledge (e.g. Berger and Luckmann, 1966) and its linkages to identity and power (e.g. Clegg, 1989). In the specific context of knowledge transfer in mergers and acquisitions, this conception limits our understanding of the nature and dynamics of these processes in three important respects. First, an essentialist understanding tends to play down the social and cultural embeddedness of knowledge. In brief, if and when 'knowledge' is objectified, it is disentangled and detached from its social and cultural context. This often means that many of the linkages to ideas, beliefs, values, cultures, and identities at group and organizational levels are ignored. In consequence, complexities and ambiguities surrounding knowledge are tuned down and the transfer is portrayed as an overly simplistic process. This often results in surprises for top decision-makers in what seems like impediments to rational knowledge transfer (cf. Kostova, 1999; Andersson, Forsgren and Holm, 2002).

Second, and relatedly, an essentialist conception of knowledge is often closely associated with 'universalism' and 'one-best-wayism'. Especially concepts such as 'best practices' tend to encourage people to look for universally applicable solutions. The problem is, however, that organizations are in many ways unique due to their specific characteristics and contexts. It is therefore questionable whether the same practices, overall, 'create value' in different contexts (e.g. Martin and Beaumont, 1998). At worst, people may try to fit universal solutions into places requiring significant sensitivity to local circumstances and cultural heritage.

Third, a conception of objectified and neutral knowledge also easily leads to an inability to understand the complex socio-political aspects involved in knowledge transfer. This is unfortunate, given the numerous observations that the people involved in knowledge transfer processes are not motivated, encouraged or committed to such endeavors (e.g. Szulanski, 1996; Empson, 2001). They can, in fact, express strong fears of contamination or exploitation (Empson, 2001). There is also evidence that 'best practices' create disciplinary frameworks that force people to comply in ways that have unpredictable consequences (cf. Martin and Beaumont, 1998).

In order to better understand the complexities of knowledge transfer processes, there is consequently a need to move from a 'neutral' understanding of knowledge transfer to one, which allows us to see connections between knowledge, identity, and power. As a step towards that direction, we will now outline a sensemaking perspective on knowledge transfer.

KNOWLEDGE TRANSFER AROUND 'BEST PRACTICES': A SENSEMAKING PERSPECTIVE

The concept of sensemaking focuses on the complex socio-psychological processes through which organizational actors interpret organizational phenomena and thus socially construct or enact their 'realities' (Weick, 1995). While there are different definitions of sensemaking – and ambiguity concerning what should be included under the broad umbrella of sensemaking – most researchers seem to agree upon four points. First, sensemaking is grounded in identity construction. This entails that when people make sense of different events, issues, questions, problems, opportunities, threats, challenges, processes, or practices, they do it by constructing meanings for themselves. As Frost and Morgan put it, when people make sense they "read into things the meanings they wish to see; they vest [in[objects, utterances, actions and so forth subjective meaning which helps make their world intelligible for themselves" (1983: 207).

Second, sensemaking is linked with action. According to many scholars (e.g. Weick, 1995), most sensemaking is restrospective rather than prospective. This highlights the fact that the meaning or sense of specific phenomena usually becomes crystallized only retrospectively. In this article, however, we focus on sensemaking-in-action. We concentrate, in particular, on sensemaking as part of organizational action in the different phases of knowledge transfer processes.

Third, although sensemaking is essentially a socio-cognitive activity, it also involves emotional and political elements. These elements are obviously particularly important in contexts such as post-merger integration. Fourth, sensemaking is not only 'interpretation', but something that also 'enacts', 'creates' or 'constructs' organizational reality.

From a sensemaking perspective, emphasizing the continuous enactment of organizational reality, it is thus natural to explore the constructive and destructive processes involved in knowledge transfer. In brief, constructive processes, on which most of the previous literature has focused, include the identification and recontextualization of specific practices. Of these, recontextualization has received the least attention in prior research. Yet recontextualization is not a straightforward process of implementing the same practice in another context but rather involves a significant amount of knowledge creation in order for ideas and routines developed in a specific context to be effectively used in another. Deconstructive processes are, in turn, processes where specific ideas, traditions and routines are replaced by new ones and thereby (at least seemingly) destroyed. The deconstructive side of knowledge transfer has often been neglected in earlier research. In our view, it is, however, crucial for understanding the emotional and political aspects of knowledge transfer processes.

To understand how different organizational actors make sense of these constructive and destructive aspects, it is important to examine the identity-related 'lenses' and differences between them. In a corporate context, we must first pay attention to the inherent differences between corporate and local perspectives. In brief, according to the corporate perspective, priority is the 'corporate whole.' This means that, basically, any knowledge transfer that may foster learning and create synergy at the corporate level should be promoted. In the case of best practices, through internal benchmarking, transfer should be identified and the practices adopted that 'best' benefit the entire organization.

This may in most simple cases be relatively straightforward, in the sense that specific practices are more technologically advanced, less time-consuming, otherwise more effective, or simply result in better performance than others. As discussed above, however, this is often not the case. From a corporate perspective, nevertheless, integration, standardization and homogenization of processes and practices are also objectives *per se*. These may relate to a strong belief in the longer-term gains achieved by increased economies of scale or scope or benefits resulting from more effective coordination. On a more critical note, increasing control and power achieved by such processes may also be fundamental objectives *per se* for corporate managers. Consequently, concepts such as 'best practice' are an essential part of the disciplinary power imposed on members of corporate organizations (e.g. Martin and Beaumont, 1998).

From a local perspective, knowledge transfer may appear fundamentally different. It is important to understand that for a specific unit, for example, the replacement of a particular practice may also be destructive. This may weaken the ability to customize operations or to make use of specific local knowledge. Historical ties and connections may be violently dismantled. Considering emotional aspects on 'best practices', specific individuals and groups may have grown attached to particular ideas and values which they simply prefer to other alternatives, and find it frustrating or frightening to start adopting practices developed elsewhere (e.g. Empson, 2001). Problems related to 'not invented here' thinking are well known. Furthermore, from a political perspective, losing control of specific knowledge or practice may not be in the long-term interests of specific units in competition for internal resources, status, and even survival.

In the merger context, we must also emphasize the confrontation of the people representing previously separate organizations, different cultures, and social identities. In fact, in the merger context, these differences tend to be accentuated when people make sense of what they and the people on the side are like and what they represent. In international contexts, these sensemaking processes are likely to be especially significant due to the strength of national cultures and identities (see e.g. Vaara, 2000; Vaara, Tienari and Säntti, 2003). This means that, for example, attachment to one's own culture, ideas, and practices tends to be particularly strong in cross-border mergers. Furthermore, mergers are also often characterized by power plays and politicization of specific questions (see e.g. Vaara, 2001; Hellgren et al., 2002). Knowledge in general and 'best practices' in particular are also entangled in more general-level power games; choosing a practice identified with a specific unit or nationality may become a sign of their importance or even dominance. Choices may be made sense of through their anticipated future consequences.

In all, depending on the perspective taken, specific knowledge transfer projects may appear very different. Furthermore, the positions taken by different people may change over time, which adds to the complexity and ambiguity of knowledge transfer. To better understand these dynamics of the sensemaking processes, we now turn to our empirical case.

MAKING SENSE OF 'BEST PRACTICES' IN NORDEA

In the merger of the Finnish Merita and the Swedish Nordbanken, announced in October 1997, 'best practices' was a key concept that was frequently used in the integration of the various parts of the organizations – both as a general model for decision-making and as a practical tool to implement changes in the organizations. The experiences were in many ways positive, although some people also grew critical towards the tendency of 'best practices' thinking to reproduce organizational and national confrontation. In the subsequent merger of Merita-Nordbanken and the Danish Unidanmark, announced in March 2000, the concept of 'best practices' was also actively used. Because the integration now involved a considerably larger organization and three national sides, the application was less straightforward than in the preceding merger. It seems that the use of the concept of 'best practices' varied greatly in different parts of the organizations.

When the Norwegian CBK was acquired in October 2000, the situation shifted again. On the one hand, it seems that benchmarking increased in a number of units along with incorporating the Norwegian organization. On the other hand, in many ways practices identified as 'best' in the previous mergers were transferred to Norway without an extensive, new comparison.

In the autumn of 2001, corporate management in Nordea launched a campaign for a 'second wave of integration'. In part, this involved search, identification and implementation of 'best practices' with standardization as a pronounced objective. This endeavor focused especially on the centralization and rationalization of back-office operations.

For the purpose of this study, we examined our extensive interview material by focusing on the sensemaking processes and patterns surrounding what can broadly be termed knowledge transfer. This analysis was an inductive process where we developed ideas about the phases, patterns and dynamics of sensemaking as we dug deeper into the interview material. This eventually led us to distinguish different sensemaking processes around 'best practices': identification, evaluation, (re)contextualization, and (re)configuration. As the analysis proceeded, we gathered more material on specific cases of 'best practice' transfer to highlight our emerging points.

There are, however, three methodological points that should be noted. First, what we were essentially doing was seeking to understand sensemaking-in-action through interviews that were predominantly retrospective. This meant that especially for the processes that had taken place some time ago, we were unavoidably dealing with retrospective constructions, which in the case of sensemaking analysis should be taken seriously. The other material gathered, however, helped us to deal with this challenge.

Second, as interviewers, the members of the project group took part in constructing the interviewees' accounts. To overcome this problem, we have tried to engage in a very careful reading of the interview transcripts and discussed key issues with the other members of the project group. Third, all three authors of this article are Finnish. This may create a certain kind of 'bias' for our interpretations. However, discussing this analysis with the other members of the project group has arguably helped to balance our interpretations and conclusions. Furthermore, it should be emphasized that in this article we are not trying to create an 'objective' overview of knowledge transfer activities in the case company but trying to reveal specifically important processes, phases and patterns.

In the following, we will analytically distinguish and discuss four key sensemaking processes that characterize knowledge transfer around 'best practices'. These processes are complex and interrelated. Their distinction is thus first and foremost an analytical effort. For the sake of clarity, we have attempted to sketch the ways in which these sensemaking processes relate to different 'stages' in a traditional conceptualization of knowledge transfer. The table below summarizes the main characteristics of these processes.

Table: Sensemaking processes in knowledge transfer around 'best practices'

Stage	Type of sensemaking	Typical questions
Search for 'best practices'	Identification	What are the practices that can be transferred or replaced?
Selection of 'best practices'	Evaluation	What are the pros and cons of specific practices? Which are the 'best' practices?
Implementation of 'best practices'	(Re)contextualization	What are the impediments to the implementation of practices?
Evaluation of success/failure	(Re)configuration	What is the new organizational praxis like?

IDENTIFICATION

A key part of organizational sensemaking is the identification of potential 'best practices'. This is a process that involves focusing attention on specific practices, but also creative thinking when articulating and possibly codifying the knowledge around the practices in question. It should be noted that this process focuses both on those practices that are seen as relevant sources for learning and those that are possible targets for replacement.

From a corporate perspective, forcing or persuading people to look for and even compete in identifying potential 'best practices' fostered organizational learning. According to many key managers, the sheer reflection and discussion around different ways of doing things were valuable, even in cases that eventually did not lead to concrete implementation of specific practices. As a key Swedish member of the top management put it, describing the initial merger between Nordbanken (Sweden) and Merita (Finland):

The creation of so called best practices can partly be formalized by the corporate management by saying that this is the kind of behaviour that we have come to – it is most effective or otherwise to be hoped for. But this can also happen informally by contacting each other across the border and asking "how do you do things over there?". I remember that back in 1998-1999, when the MeritaNordbanken merger had taken place, the Finns responsible for the regional banks called their Swedish counterparts and said "listen, we want to have a look at how you do it over there," and vice versa. So there are a great deal of spontaneous activities going on enhancing learning.

Later, as part of the 'second wave of integration' in Nordea, one of the key aims of the corporate management was to foster learning by making people in different areas and units identify best practices on a continuous or 'automatic' basis. A key Danish manager summarized the corporate logic as follows: "*I think that even the fact that people are inspired and irritated by others' success is a good thing.*"

However, this identification process was often quite different for those in the midst of integration decision-making. For people that had been socialized into a specific social, cultural and institutional 'reality', it was often difficult to understand and appreciate the practices on the other side and their relations to the particular environment. People were also often emotionally attached to specific ideas and practices on their own side. Furthermore, the people involved tended to link the identification of potentially best practices with political decisions concerning investments, resource allocations, responsibilities and positions. As a Finnish interviewee put it:

As to the best practices, in my view, you have to accept the fact that if [dl] one party is strong and another weak. It tends to be a law of nature that the practice of the stronger becomes the best practice.

In Nordea, the identification of potentially best practices seems to have been clearly linked with the perceptions of balance of power between the different organizational and national sides. Especially in settings where the people involved were confronted with potentially threatening future scenarios involving dominance by another party, nationalism appeared to emerge as a particularly important sensemaking frame. For example, in the Merita-Nordbanken, the Finns – frequently presenting themselves as 'underdogs' – tended to associate the identification of 'best practices' with the historical Little Brother – Big Brother relationship between Finns and Swedes (cf. Risberg, Tienari and Vaara, 2003). For example, the slogan "Best practices are West practices" was frequently reflected upon on the Finnish side in the merger between Merita and Nordbanken. In this context, the Finns frequently felt that the Swedes were strongly dominating the identification of best practices. The following exemplifies the Finnish attitude:

We had a board meeting of X company, and the chairman of the Swedish unit came. That man, who is no longer working for us, started by saying "what we do in Sweden we are also planning to implement in Finland." Then the devil caught us (Finns), and

125

we said nothing. He started a sentence seven times by saying "what we do in Sweden we are also planning to implement in Finland." Only after that did we feel pity for him and said that the law is different here, that is simply illegal here.

In turn, when Unidanmark joined in, many Swedes and Finns felt that Danish practices were pushed on, as the following comments illustrate: *"The Danes think that best practice means Danish practice. If it is not invented in Denmark, it cannot be good"* (a Finnish interviewee), and *"Instead of best practice it has become Danish practice in all areas. And it is clear that this creates conflicts"* (a Swedish interviewee).

EVALUATION

Another key sensemaking process is the evaluation of alternative practices. From a corporate perspective, this evaluation can and should be based on concrete measures. A key top manager in Nordea explains corporate logic:

It is the responsibility of each manager to look him/herself in the mirror and understand that there are four countries where about the same kinds of things are done in perhaps four different ways and then see how much it costs in that country, how much it produces, what is the effectiveness, what is the bottom line. And when he/she looks and notices that one is two times more effective than the other, there is no need [sic] more additional benchmarking. Then he/she (the manager in charge) turns to the (country) manager who is responsible for managing the bad case and says OK, let's look through this, what it is that they do to be twice as effective. It may be that there is a natural explanation in the market (the specific features of the country in

question), but the burden of proof rests on the shoulders of the
one responsible for the bad case.

However, in practice, according to many interviewees, clear and uncontestable measures based on technological superiority, better organizational effectiveness or superior economic results were seldom available. It was rather a question of the corporate decision-makers or the managers responsible for specific business areas making the choices based on their "gut feeling" or own "preferences". While talking about the difficulties in making such decisions, many interviewees, adopting a corporate perspective, claimed that it was, in the end, better to make less than perfect decisions than to refrain from making any decisions at all. According to corporate logic, the other alternative would be no progress at all in terms of integration, harmonization, or standardization.

Nevertheless, people representing different sides had often fundamentally different views as to what was and should be seen as 'best'. In particular, people tended to value things on their own side and be suspicious of the others. Furthermore, political aspects of sensemaking were accentuated in this process leading to the labelling of particular practices as 'best' and stigmatization of others. In particular, best practices served as symbols of the balance of power in the sense that they were visible signs of superiority. In fact, even in situations of relatively insignificant operational importance, their symbolic value could be considerable.

It should be emphasized that evaluation leading to the labelling and selection of specific best practices also tended to reinforce national confrontation. Overall, this made many of the top managers sceptical towards the applicability of the 'best practice' concept. The following comments illustrate this:

Myself, I banned using the concept. I thought that it was simply ridiculous. There are no best ways to operate that fit all circumstances in every way. First of all, who determines what the best practice is? Here, I noticed that it had great (implications). If you choose a Finnish or Swedish (practice), then you automatically say that the other is second best.

I have this basic thesis – and I often find myself in opposition (to others). If you say that we are choosing the best practice, it is like declaring an open war because after that everyone feels a great responsibility to prove that he/she (and the country in question) has the best practice.

To alleviate the problems of confrontation, several key decision-makers called for open-mindedness in the identification and evaluation of best practices. As a key Finnish manager put it:

I have many times said that, of course, this so-called best practice means what is the best to be found in our house (Nordea). However, before adopting that, we should evaluate whether it still works (in different contexts), or should we search for an 'excellent practice' on a whole new basis and from a totally different environment than before.

(RE)CONTEXTUALIZATION

The contextualization and recontextualization – often called translation or editing – of the practice to be 'implemented' is yet another sensemaking process in knowledge transfer. This (re)contextualization is essentially a local process of making sense of specific practices, closely connected with concrete implementation efforts. It is therefore not surprising that this sensemaking most often focuses on problems. Characteristic of (re)contextualization is that the people involved – both those pushing and those initially resisting the transfer – discuss and debate the obstacles of implementation before, during and after concrete implementation efforts.

According to our interviews, it was often the case that people discovered problems of implementation or understood its nature and scope only when starting the serious efforts to actually 'implement' the new practices in a new location. A Norwegian manager expressed typical frustration when trying to adopt specific practices developed in Merita-Nordbanken:

You can have really great distribution chains in Sweden or Finland, but they are impossible to implement in Norway because of a different kind of legislation. You can find good elements ... but you cannot implement the whole value chain.

The following is, in turn, a typical example of the complexities encountered in trying to change specific practices in wider-scale information technology systems:

I think that one thing that we could not properly assess was this best practice and its dependence on the environment. If you choose a Swedish practice in Finland, our system does not necessarily deal with that information, and vice versa. This has caused many situations where, despite the fact that we are buying into (motivated to adopt) the practice, it is not the same in the technical sense, cannot be the same. So one can say that at this moment the computer center is operating pretty much as before.

However, apart from addressing 'real' obstacles to implementation, this (re)contextualization involved also emotional and political aspects. Apparently, it was most difficult when the transfer of practices was seen as imposing something that appeared 'alien' to the particular context. For example, in describing one of the first (ultimately successful) transfer projects involving the "Solo e-banking" practices developed in Finland, many Finns accused their Swedish counterparts of strange attitudes. A key Finnish manager explains:

In Finland we had this Solo (e-banking concept), and I remember telling them that this was a better practice, that we had used it for fifteen years without problems, that it is easy for the users, and that it is inexpensive for the bank. The answer (by the Swedes) was that we cannot move backwards ... Well, after a real fight we got it through there in six months. Now the market (the use of the concept) has risen to the same level as in Finland, and there are no problems. But the first reaction was, even after seeing the great advantages, that no way, it is going backwards.

It should be noted that obstacles such as cultural differences were also emphasized and put forth as justifications of what could then be termed resistance. For example, a Swedish interviewee explained the lack of success in implementing 'best practices' in back office operations as follows:

When we look at back office routines, we have different regulations in Sweden, Finland, Denmark and Norway. In this

*context, it is of no use to say that "hey, this is how they do it in
Denmark".*

The interviewees could also refer to examples where particular
managers had invented excuses for not being willing to implement the
identified 'best practices'. This had created frustration among those
who were pushing for the implementation of specific practices (top
managers) and those who felt that they had done their share in such
exchanges (managers in other countries).

(RE)CONFIGURATION

Finally, knowledge transfer around 'best practices' involves the
reconfiguration of the organizational praxis around the new practices.[2]
This creative process involving re-conceptualization and re-design of
existing operations around the new practices is crucial in successful
knowledge transfer. At best, people in the organizations are able to
take full advantage of the experience, concepts, technologies and ideas
developed elsewhere. Ideally, such practices thus become internalized
and normalized as part of everyday praxis in the organizations in
question. In the Nordea case, for example, the transfer of the Solo e-
banking concept developed in Merita (Finland), special mortgage and
customer concepts of Nordbanken (Sweden), and the asset
management practices of Unidanmark (Denmark) were seen as
positive examples of such transfer.

However, the people involved could also frequently describe how
it was difficult to abandon the old praxis due to the fact that the people
involved had grown attached to specific practices and associated

---

[2] 'Praxis' is here seen as a set of ideas, practices, capabilities and knowledge
linked with specific social or organizational activity.

traditions and values. The difficulties were accentuated, if the changes did not seem to lead to concrete or speedy improvements in the local contexts but rather tended to interfere with smooth everyday operations. In such circumstances, the old praxis could actually survive despite the 'official' adoption of new best practices. If they did not seem to invest in 'active unlearning' of old ideas, practices and habits, people could also be blamed for 'hypocrisy' by others. For example, a Norwegian manager described his experiences when working with the Danes:

> *In many meetings we (Norwegians) presented the case as it was (having done what was required). What we started to wonder about was that Unidanmark (the Danes) had not become fully committed to Nordea. They have a double organization where they see it [sic] necessary. They say that they participate in the Nordic organization but that they still retain the national system if they need it.*

What did seem to help in this reconfiguration was to link the 'best practices' with the step-wise creation of truly Nordic organization structures and processes. This was actually a key goal in the 'Second wave of integration' in Nordea, launched in late 2001. A Danish top manager explained the supportive role of the Nordic organization structures:

> *If you have two organizations, the problems arise when you have to put the managers of these organizations together to decide upon things. This requires construction of joint ventures. This requires construction of projects. So there is the problem of motivating the people. But if you have two colleagues (within a Nordic organization structure)[,] who work for the same*

organization goals and are compensated on the same basis, then the situation is the best possible.

It should also be noted that although specific practices had become essential parts of the new praxis in particular organizational units, these practices could still retain traces of 'dominance' in the sensemaking of the people involved. For example, people could still associate specific practices with superiority of a certain nationality, making it hard for some to fully embrace the new praxis. In this sense, slogans like "Best practice is West practice" or "Best practice is Danish practice" continued to live in the sedimented organizational memory (see Cooper et al., 1996). What could alleviate such labels was the construction of a pan-Nordic identity along with the pan-Nordic structures and processes. For instance, many interviewees pointed to the supportive role of a massive 'Nordic ideas' campaign, which promoted the view that all Nordic countries and the respective parts of Nordea have something distinctive to offer when constructing the Nordic whole.

CONCLUSION

A strategy of locating and transferring knowledge around 'best practices' can, at best, be an effective integration mechanism in merging multinational organizations. It focuses attention on concrete questions. Reflection around processes and practices can thereby become a key source of learning for the actors involved. This can also lead to innovations in terms of new 'best' ways of doing things. Experiences from mergers and acquisitions, however, tell a story of problems and disappointments. Knowledge transfer does not work out as planned by the merger strategists, people do not become committed, and all kinds of socio-cultural obstacles complicate the transfer of 'best practices' from one location to another.

In this chapter, we have suggested that a sensemaking perspective on 'best practices' helps to shed light on some of the aspects that have been hidden by an essentialist conception of knowledge dominating studies on knowledge transfer. We have identified four distinctive sensemaking processes – identification, evaluation, (re)contextualization, and (re)configuration – that can be seen as important parts of knowledge transfer around 'best practices'. By distinguishing these processes we have in particular attempted to illustrate the complex socio-political elements involved in transferring knowledge in a multinational organization.

While there are several interesting and important aspects that deserve special attention in sensemaking processes, our analysis highlights three important points. First, it illustrates the *complexities* of knowledge transfer. By pointing out how sensemaking is continuous and showing how 'official' decisions or choices are merely part of the sensemaking determining people's attitudes and responses, we can comprehend how problematic it is to believe in overly rationalistic models of knowledge transfer in post-merger or other contexts.

Second, our analysis shows how knowledge transfer around best practices is characterized by *ambiguity*. There is often uncertainty, disagreement and confusion about the merits of different organizational practices. The perspective adopted by actors at corporate level is often inherently different from national or local views. In addition, as can be expected in merger settings, the views of the people representing different organizations and nationalities are often fundamentally different, even contradictory. This is the case as people – *including the top decision-makers* – have been socialized into specific social, cultural and institutional 'reality'. Consequently, they have more intimate knowledge of, and become accustomed and attached to, some specific practices, traditions, ways of operation, ideas and values, but not to others.

Third, the analysis demonstrates the ways in which knowledge transfer is inherently *political*. As knowledge transfer is part of integration decision-making in the case studied, involving questions concerning the future of specific organizations, units, groups and individuals, it is no wonder that the people involved tended to interpret different propositions, questions, and problems in a political light. In most interesting instances, people could even link knowledge transfer to age-old national relationships. Such was the case, for example, when Finns linked Swedish suggestions with the historical colonial relationship between the two nations, and with Swedish dominance. It is noteworthy that by making explicit whose practice was the 'best', the concept of 'best' also tended to result in particularly clear distinguishing of 'winners' and 'losers'.

In all, highlighting complexities, ambiguity and political manouvering make it easier to understand why knowledge transfer often seems to result in unanticipated problems and disappointments in post-merger contexts. By illustrating how knowledge transfer processes involve elements and dynamics that are easily bypassed by researchers and practitioners, this analysis can also help to explain why plans concerning synergy or other gains turn out to be overly optimistic while integration problems are underestimated in merger or acquisition contexts (Haspeslagh and Jemison, 1991).

What are then the implications for the managers initiating, managing and leading these processes? It is likely that most knowledge transfer processes lead to such problematics as described here and that, therefore, it is very difficult for anyone to 'control' these processes. Therefore, the top decision-makers should critically scrutinize the most optimistic scenarios of the synergistic benefits coming from knowledge transfer and to try and foresee the major problems that are likely to arise with specific knowledge transfer projects.

It is also very important to see that structural changes in the post-merger organization and culture and identity projects support knowledge transfer. As this analysis points out, if and when people are made to see the rationale and benefits of specific knowledge transfer projects, they are usually very committed to such efforts. If, on the other hand, the immediate effects seem more negative than positive, it is very difficult to create the genuine enthusiasm that is often needed to create true new praxis. At the same time, the inherent problems of post-merger knowledge transfer should not discourage people in organizations – including top managers but also other organizational members – from trying to learn from one another and from creating ever better solutions and practices for specific operations. This learning has great potential, but it just seems to be less straightforward and take more time and effort than most people engaging in mergers and acquisitions realize.

REFERENCES

AHUJA, G. and KATILA, R. (2001). 'Technological acquisitions and the innovation performance of acquiring firms: A longitudinal study'. *Strategic Management Journal*, 22, 197-220.

ANDERSSON, U., FORSGREN, M. and HOLM, U. (2002). 'The strategic impact of external networks: Subsidiary performance and competence development in the multinational corporation'. *Strategic Management Journal*, 23, 979-996.

BERGER, P. L. and LUCKMANN, T. (1966). *The social construction of reality*. New York: Doubleday Anchor.

BRESMAN, H., BIRKINSHAW, J. and NOBEL, R. (1999). 'Knowledge transfer in international acquisitions'. *Journal of International Business Studies*, 30, 439-462.

CLEGG, S. R. (1989). *Frameworks of power*. London: Sage.

COOPER, D. J., HININGS, B., GREENWOOD, R. and BROWN, J. L. (1996). 'Sedimentation and transformation in organizational change: The case of Canadian law firms'. *Organization Studies*, 17, 623-647.

EMPSON, L. (2001). 'Fear of exploitation and fear of contamination: Impediments to knowledge transfer in mergers between professional service firms'. *Human Relations*, 54, 839-862.

GRANT, R. M. (1996). 'Toward a knowledge-based theory of the firm'. *Strategic Management Journal,* 17 (Winter Special Issue), 109-122.

HASPESLAGH, P. C. and JEMISON, D. B. (1991). *Managing acquisitions: Creating value through corporate renewal*. New York: The Free Press.

HELLGREN, B., LÖWSTEDT, L., PUTTONEN, L., TIENARI, J., VAARA, E. and WERR, A. (2002). 'How issues become constructed in the media: 'Winners' and 'Losers' in the AstraZeneca merger'. *British Journal of Management*, 13, 123-140.

KOSTOVA, T. (1999). 'Transnational transfer of strategic organizational practices: A contextual perspective". *Academy of Management Review*, 24, 308-324.

LAAMANEN, T. (1997). *The acquisition of technological competencies through the acquisition of new, technology-based companies*. Espoo: Helsinki University of Technology.

MARTIN, G. and BEAUMONT, P. (1998). 'Diffusing 'best practice' in multinational firms: Prospects, practice and contestation'. *International Journal of Human Resource Management*, 9, 671-695.

NONAKA, I. (1994). 'A dynamic model of organizational knowledge creation'. *Organization Science*, 5, 14-37.

RISBERG, A., TIENARI, J. and VAARA, E. (2003). 'Making sense of a transnational merger: Media texts and (re)construction of power relations'. *Culture and Organization*, 9(2).

RANFT, A. L. and LORD, M. D. (2002). 'Acquiring new technologies and capabilities: A grounded model of acquisition implementation'. *Organization Science*, 13, 420-441.

Best practice is West practice?

SZULANSKI, G. (1996). 'Exploring internal stickiness: Impediments to the transfer of best practice within the firm'. *Strategic Management Journal*, 17 (Winter Special Issue), 27-43.

VAARA, E. (2000). 'Constructions of cultural differences in postmerger change processes: A sensemaking perspective on Finnish-Swedish cases'. M@n@gement, 3, 81-110.

VAARA, E. (2001). 'Role-bound actors in corporate combination: A study of decision making in change processes following a merger'. *Scandinavian Journal of Management*, 17, 481-509.

VAARA, E., TIENARI, J. and SÄNTTI, R. (2003). 'The international match: Metaphors as vehicles of social identity building in cross-border mergers'. *Human Relations*, 56(4), 419-451.

WEICK, K. E. (1995). *Sensemaking in organizations*. London: Sage.

WINTER, S. (1987). 'Knowledge and competence as strategic assets'. In Teece, D. J. (Ed), *The Competitive Challenge*. Cambridge, MA: Ballinger.

Chapter 7

FROM WORDS TO ACTION?

SOCIO-CULTURAL INTEGRATION INITIATIVES IN A CROSS-BORDER MERGER

Anne-Marie Søderberg & Ingmar Björkman

INTRODUCTION

Today there is wide agreement among researchers and business consultants that a successful socio-cultural integration process is an important determinant of the success or failure of a merger or an acquisition (Buono and Bowditch, 1989; Mirvis and Marks, 1992; Stahl et al., 2002). Especially in mergers between companies where extensive integration is sought, it is important to facilitate the workforces' interaction and collaboration. Managers responsible for integration processes in such mergers will also have to cope with the employees' previous cultural identifications, which sometimes are even reinforced due to the merger (Kleppestø, 1998). In cross-border mergers and acquisitions, 'national' identification as well as delineation from other nationalities may play a crucial role, together with identifications with former corporate cultures, when employees try to make sense of events and actions following merger decisions (Calori, Lubatkin and Very, 1994; Gertsen, Søderberg and Torp, 1998; Olie, 1994; Søderberg, 2003). Such identification processes often turn into cultural stereotyping, at least in the initial phase after a merger has been announced, as described in chapter 4.

One way for management to cope with the negative perceptions of the merging partners may be to develop a new cultural platform (e.g. new corporate values and common symbols) in order to make the employees in the merging companies identify with the new company as an attractive community. But it is also important to go further linking the suggested cultural values with daily social practices, if the purpose is to enhance communication and collaboration across borders and strengthen the commitment among the employees to the corporate vision, mission and values.

The creation of Nordea as a multinational corporation and an integrated group of companies offering a wide range of financial services is hence an important managerial task, but, admittedly, also a very complex issue to cope with. Initiating a socio-cultural integration process in this context means building bridges over perceived differences between national cultures, corporate cultures as well as professional cultures involved in a multinational corporation, encompassing business units as diverse as Retail Banking, Corporate and Institutional Banking, and Asset Management and Life (insurance). This challenge was also acknowledged by Thorleif Krarup, CEO of Nordea from January 2001 to August 2002, when he took over the position from Hans Dalborg and publicly stated that

a precondition of success is an integrated company with common corporate values and branding. All core activities will be linked with these values and the Nordea brand, while the local brands will only be maintained as long as it can be justified from a commercial point of view. All employees have the right to be part of the company's culture and an obligation to live according to its values. The employees should know that Nordea stands for Nordic ideas which fulfill the customers' dreams and aspirations. (Nordea Annual Report 2000: 10).

Socio-cultural change processes must be acknowledged as a continuous challenge, and the ambitious cultural integration project launched by Krarup is not easily and quickly accomplished. In this chapter, we will look closer at some of the initiatives taken to manage the socio-cultural integration of the multinational workforce across the different business units. Focus will be on the period from spring 2000 – when the merger between Merita-Nordbanken and Unidanmark was announced and a set of new common values were presented – until spring 2002 – when the Nordea brand had been introduced to the employees in a process inviting them to discuss the suggested common values with their colleagues in their local work contexts.

Subsequent to a brief overview of research on corporate culture and identity management and on socio-cultural integration in mergers and acquisitions we will introduce and analyze some of the initiatives taken to manage socio-cultural integration. We start with the ambitious company-wide initiatives to develop a new common culture and a corporate brand, and contrast them with a more modest initiative taken by a cross-border business unit within the company. The guiding research questions to be answered in the empirical analyses in this chapter are the following: Which initiatives were taken to manage the announced socio-cultural integration process, and how were they communicated? Who took responsibility for these integration activities, and how were they received? And, finally, are there any indications that these initiatives have had the intended integrating effects among managers and employees in the merged companies?

PREVIOUS RESEARCH ON ORGANIZATIONAL CULTURE AND IDENTITY

There is evidently a lack of in-depth studies focusing on corporate culture and identity issues in post-merger integration processes. This means that the empirical study and the critical reflections on inherent problems in corporate culture building as part of socio-cultural integration initiatives is in fact our contribution to the research field. However, there are two areas of research of particular interest in relation to the issues we are dealing with in this chapter. Firstly, literature on the creation and maintenance of organizational cultures and identities; secondly, literature on socio-cultural integration processes in mergers and acquisitions.

More widespread interest in cultural perspectives on organizations did not emerge until the early 1980s when both national (see e.g. Hofstede, 1984) and organizational (see e.g. Pettigrew, 1979) level considerations started to interest organization and management scholars. This development was reflected in both more theoretically oriented research efforts (e.g. Ouchi and Wilkins, 1985) and more practically (Peters and Waterman, 1982; Deal and Kennedy, 1985). It is, however, our overwhelming impression that the international, cross-cultural management literature, in contrast to the literature on organizational cultures and identities, has not included reflection on the theoretical assumptions embedded in a certain concept of 'culture' (exceptions are Sackmann (1997) and Boyaciller et al. (forthcoming)). In international, cross-cultural management literature as well as in business consultants' culture interventions, culture has in many cases been seen as an area of interest, referring to something 'soft', human, unquantifiable, difficult to account for in rational terms and provided with a label of convenience, namely 'culture.'

This is in sheer contrast to the academic field of organizational culture and identity studies, where there have been fundamental disagreements and strong intellectual struggles about epistemology, methodology, theoretical categorisations and political orientations during the last two decades (for overviews, see Schultz, 1994; Martin and Frost, 1996; Whetten and Godfrey 1998). Consequently, there are many perspectives on and definitions of organizational cultures and identities, ranging from views on 'culture' and 'identity' as something objective and stable (culture as essence) to views on the multiplicity of cultures and identities as something negotiable and ever changing (culture as social construct).

Scholars within organization studies have even been involved in so called 'culture wars' (Martin and Frost, 1997) between different paradigmatic approaches to the study of organizational cultures and identities. Wars between 'functionalists' referring to cultural systems as 'essential' and looking for 'basic assumptions and beliefs (...) that operate unconsciously' (Schein, 1985), and 'interpretivists' understanding cultures and identities as constituted in social interaction (Smircich, 1983). Wars between scholars applying an 'integration perspective' when looking at the organization as an entity and assuming homogeneity and a unified culture as achievable, and other scholars emphasizing the multiple groups and cultural communities based on age, generation, occupation, gender that cross-cuts the organization and make the creation of a corporate culture illusive (differentiation perspective). Wars between 'culturalists' driven by a managerial interest in solving problems of the organization by building up a strong corporate culture through artefacts, rituals and story-telling (for example Deal and Kennedy 1985), and 'radical humanists' who take the power relations in the organization into account as well as the institutional and wider societal context of the organizations when they study cultural identifications in organizations (e.g. Parker, 2000).

However, the cultural and inter-organizational processes of international mergers and acquisitions may also be studied in different ways. And the choice of culture concept strongly influences the overall theoretical framework and the research design. Most importantly, it also seems to have a bearing on the results and implied recommendations to companies involved in cross-cultural co-operation.

CULTURE AND IDENTITY AS ESSENCE

The majority of the researchers in international business touching upon cultural issues seem to build upon the classic concept of culture, developed by Western anthropologists in the 1950s and 1960s. According to this essentialist understanding, culture is seen as a relatively stable, homogeneous, internally consistent system of assumptions, values, and norms transmitted by socialisation to the next generation. Moreover, culture is seen as something that members of a community – e.g. an organization or a nation – 'have' or 'belong to'. By virtue of the strong emphasis of sharedness – the assumption that all inhabitants in a nation and all managers and employees in an organization carry the same cultural value orientations – this view of culture also tends to entail blindness as regards social variation, diversity and power relations within a nation or an organization, or between nations and organizations.

Within this mainstream approach to the study of cross-cultural management issues, researchers tend to focus on cultural encounters between what they perceive as well-defined and homogeneous entities, for example, a parent company and its subsidiaries in foreign countries or two merger partners. They tend to see organizational integration problems as being caused by objective cultural differences both at an organizational and a national level. Often they also share the ambition to find out which national value orientations and organizational cultures can co-exist, for example, in international mergers and acquisitions, and how they can benefit from the collaboration. Their goal is normative – to advance general action instructions that may predict and thus minimize integration problems and promote more effective managerial action.

Much of the research on socio-cultural integration has started on from the assumption that cultural differences are major causes of problems in the integration of merging organizations rather than resources to build on. If merging companies do not pay attention to socio-cultural integration processes, but focus one-sidedly on strategic and financial issues, it is claimed that they may experience a decrease in employee productivity and reduced job satisfaction, severe communication difficulties between the companies, growing resistance to organizational change combined with the loss of key personnel (for reviews, see e.g. Buono and Bowditch, 1989; Cartwright and Cooper, 1993). Ultimately, a serious lack of socio-cultural integration initiatives may result in failures to reach the announced and expected synergy benefits of the merger.

From words to action?

In line with the essentialist conception, most cultural research on mergers see integration problems as being caused by objective cultural differences. In international settings, drawing on Hofstede's and Trompenaars' work, this has resulted in research arguing that mergers between culturally closer nations lead to better outcomes than those between more distant national cultures. The contrary argument that cultural differences may also be a source of value has received little attention until recent studies (Morosini, 1997).

Reflecting the essentialist conception of culture, most researchers in this field share an ambition to find out which organizational cultures can co-exist and how. A key argument presented in literature on pre-merger initiatives is that the decision to merge should be based on considerations of whether the organizational cultures of the two parties are compatible, which means whether there is a high degree of *cultural fit* (Cartwright and Cooper 1993). Both the *distance* between the home countries of the two organizations and their organizational cultures have been pointed to as potential sources of problems in merger implementation, and a large number of studies of pre-merger considerations have concentrated on the impact of organizational differences.

According to the 'cultural fit' or 'cultural compatibility' perspective (Cartwright and Cooper, 1992; Larsson, 1993), the most problematic situations are those where the beliefs and values of the organizational members are contradictory. According to this view, beliefs and values that do not conflict are not likely to create particular problems. Others, like Nahavandi and Malekzadeh (1988), Morosini and Singh (1994) and Calori, Lubatkin and Very (1994), have also developed the argument that the adopted integration strategies should be 'culturally compatible'.

146

There are several problems attached with the 'cultural fit' perspective. First, it is inherently difficult to identify and analyze differences between organizational cultures. This problem is partly due to difficulties in 'collecting data' on cultural issues prior to the decision to merge, partly because cultural specifics tend to come into existence or rather to be socially constructed only when the two organizations are into contact with each other, leading to identifications of 'us' versus 'them' (Janson 1994). Cultural identification is in this sense relational and moreover highly context-specific. Second, most organizational scholars agree today that organizational cultures are not monolithic. Although there may be some cultural consistency and homogeneity within the borders of a certain organization, organizational cultures can just as well be characterized and analyzed from a differentiation and an ambiguity perspective (Martin, 1992). It is the reason why we find that attention should rather be directed towards how socio-cultural issues are dealt with in the 'combination phase' (Mirvis and Marks 1992) after the merger has been decided.

CULTURE AND IDENTITY AS SOCIAL CONSTRUCTS

The classic, essentialist concept of culture, which has dominated the literature of international cross-cultural management, has been increasingly abandoned within the field of anthropology in which it originated. Many anthropologists, as well as media and organizational analysts, now regard culture as based on shared or partly shared patterns of meaning and interpretation. These are produced, reproduced, and continually changed by the people identifying with them and negotiating them in the course of social interaction. People's identifications with and affiliation to a multiplicity of different cultures, for example, national, ethnic, organizational, professional, gender and generation cultures, are thus subject to change, and boundaries between cultural communities become fluid and contingent (Hannerz, 1996).

Within this emergent dynamic approach to the conceptualisation of culture, culture is also seen as being made up of relations. This implies that for example national cultures, corporate cultures or professional cultures are seen as symbolic practices that only come into existence in relation to and in contrast to other cultural communities. People's cultural identity constructions and their social organizations of meaning are, in other words, contextual. This relational approach to culture and the idea of cultural complexity suggest that every individual embodies a unique combination of personal, cultural and social experiences, and thus that ultimately any communication and negotiation is intercultural.

This social constructionist approach to culture also implies that so called cultural 'data' are inevitably 'social constructs' made on the basis of the practitioners' and the researchers' own cultural thought patterns and the concepts and categories they are socialised into. One cannot make cultural analyses whose results can be applied in the form of general guidelines for managers. Nor can the outcome of collaboration and integration processes between organizations be predicted with any certainty. Unlike most research in the international business field, the social constructionist approach is neither normative, nor prognostic. Its scientific contributions to the study of cultural complexity (Sackmann, 1997) in the international management field are contextually sensitive, qualitative case studies focusing on the organizational actors' interpretations, identity-constructions and sensemaking processes (Weick, 1995). Parker (2000) and Gioia, Schultz and Corley (2000) are recent examples of this theoretical approach within the field of organizational culture and identity studies.

In this chapter, we will apply a perspective on the cultural change processes based on an understanding of cultures and identities as social constructs. We will analyze some managerial initiatives to achieve socio-cultural integration in Nordea, company-wide as well as in a cross-border business unit. The analysis will be based upon company documents as well as interviews conducted with both senior executives and HR and communications managers. The purpose is to convey an impression to the readers of how the key decision makers and the people responsible for the implementation of the culture change processes gave sense to and made sense of the integration initiatives, and how they reflected on the challenges met in the development of a new organizational culture and identity. If our empirical analyses of these integration initiatives tend to be rather critical, we would like to emphasize – once and for all – that the target of our criticism is not Nordea and the people responsible for the different integration initiatives. Our critical reflections are rather oriented towards the problems and limitations inherent in corporate-driven value and culture building programs.

COMPANY-WIDE INTEGRATION INITIATIVES

Planning of potential mergers, as well as negotiations and deals between merging companies are often dominated by managers' and consultants' strategic and financial considerations of synergies to be obtained. A strict focus on the activity segmentation and division of power positions and responsibilities often implies that cultural considerations are not given a prominent role by the people behind the strategic plans (e.g. Jemison and Sitkin, 1986). The Nordea case, however, shows how key people from Merita-Nordbanken and Unidanmark developed an approach where compatibility between the corporate cultures was also considered, and an exercise in creating a joint vision and new common values was conducted before the final merger decisions were made.

In the probing and negotiations leading up to the merger between Merita-Nordbanken and Unidenmark, the persons involved in the negotiations *"tried to present the two organizations to each other to get a deeper understanding of what kind of a vision, business model and corporate culture each company had, in order to see if the strategic plans would match each other as well as the soft values. We deliberately did that before we started investigating potential synergies and developing a business case"*, as a key figure put it. When the top managers of Merita-Nordbanken and Unidanmark announced their decision to merge in March 2000, they also presented a revised version of the joint document containing a brief statement of the mission and vision for the new organization, financial goals, business objectives and common values. This corporate statement was presented to the public as well as to the employees of the merging companies.

Top managers involved in the negotiations experienced the development and formulation of the shared corporate statement as a useful tool for making sure that they agreed on and were committed to a common understanding of what kind of organization would be created through the merger, both in terms of its cultural values, its internal functioning and its future direction. However, few efforts were made at communicating the content of the shared corporate statement throughout the organization.

At the outset of the merger of Merita-Nordbanken and Unidanmark, the new group executive management that was to be led by Thorleif Krarup, former CEO of Unidanmark, did not initiate any centrally orchestrated cultural training programs. Group Executive Management downplayed the perceived national differences in the new cross-border merger and instead focused on the set of negotiated corporate values as a basis for a development of corporate identity and branding which were to be the primary integrating instruments. In an interview, one of the key decision-makers argues for this values-based approach:

People always focus on the boundaries between the countries. But I feel that the cultural differences across business units are much bigger than the national differences within a specific business unit. And moreover, for me there is really nothing new in operating within and across many subcultures ... Of course, it is always a managerial challenge to avoid homogenizing and standardizing everything. It is not desirable or recommendable to create a homogenous organizational culture. But it is a good idea to aim at developing some corporate values that can function as an umbrella for the whole organization and afterwards be translated into specific procedures and practices within each of the business units. It means that for me the challenge is just as big, or even bigger to create an understanding in this company of how we can optimize our operations, in collaboration across business units and in interaction with the shared business functions such as IT.

151

NORDIC IDEAS

At the end of 2000, the next step was taken when the new company name, Nordea, was announced At the same time the new company logo was presented: a blue sail alluding to the Baltic Sea and the countries around it where Nordea was operating. According to its vision, this was going to be the leading company within the financial services sector. The company started to use the name Nordea on group level and in the cross-border Nordic operations in the business units Corporate and Institutional Banking as well as in Asset Management. In the more country-based retail banks a consistent change of signage and company name was postponed until an internal process around values, culture, identity and brand would ensure that the change of signage and company name would pave the way for the employees' emotional attachment to the new company.

Both the new company name and the new logo were introduced publicly in advertisements in Nordic and international newspapers and magazines, as well as in internal campaign material distributed during spring 2001. The main message of these campaigns was that the new company name, Nordea, derives from and refers to "Nordic ideas" which managers and employees within the merging companies have in common.

Nordea's Group Identity and Communications unit was responsible for the introduction of the new company in close cooperation with the Markets Support division. The advertisements were developed in collaboration with a Nordic communications agency. In Nordic newspapers the claimed Nordic *"innovative thinking"* was illustrated in advertisements showing world-famous Nordic design (the Finnish Aalto glass vase, the Danish Arne Jacobsen easy chair "The Egg", the Finnish studded tyre and the Norwegian Stokke high chair), created *"by individuals, entrepreneurs and organizations who dare break new ground"*.

In international newspapers and magazines the company name Nordea was introduced in an advertisement showing a man sitting in a winter landscape at a frozen lake fishing Nordic ideas:

> *Believe it or not, this man is busy harvesting our greatest natural resource, and it isn't fish - it's ideas. We love ideas, the wealth of our region is founded upon ideas and the ability to realize those ideas. The future will be built upon ideas and we encourage our customers and our employees to dream. We will partner with our customers, helping them to realize their ambitions and dream up new ideas.- We are a reflection of our region and its most important natural resource, ideas. We bring a clear Nordic outlook and approach to the market places of the world. – We are looking forward to doing business with you ...the Nordic way.*

Other advertisements referring to 'Nordic modesty' and 'Nordic clarity' showed beautiful pictures of deserted Nordic landscapes. According to studies conducted by the communications department, these advertisements increased the knowledge of the new Nordic company. The campaign thus played an important role in the external positioning of the company and its new corporate brand at an international market. Financial services are becoming generic, and therefore call for new and untraditional ways to attract customers' and other external stakeholders' attention.

As external communication about the company also functions as a kind of 'autocommunication' (Cheney and Christensen 2001), it is

153

important to know how managers and employees received and reflected on them as part of their identification with the new company. Some employees reported that they felt a certain pride because the company they were working for was now exposed so professionally in the media. Other employees did not find the Nordic ideas as such available as an identification tool. Also some of the top managers interviewed in the autumn 2001 expressed certain reservations about the campaign. One interviewee pointed to the misfit between the Nordic ideas campaign and the products and services that internationally oriented financial services institutions offer, whether they are Nordic or located in another country:

> *I think we should be a little bit careful when referring to our Nordic Ideas. We are operating in an internationalized industry, and it is hard to claim that a Nordic financial product is more unique than for example a German or a British. I prefer to use the concept of Nordic ideas about the exercise we are doing when the merging companies try to find out what is 'best practice' in different areas ... Personally I feel uncomfortable when we use words such as 'dreams' and 'aspirations' in the communication of our corporate statement. Perhaps I am too much down to earth ... and of course you can interpret it that way that a customer who want to acquire a summer cottage, can make this dream come true if we grant him a loan and offer him an insurance, but ....*

Another interviewee gives an example of how some people in the organization used this Nordic Ideas-campaign without reflecting on the need to translate it when communicating with new employees or with customers in retail banking:

Earlier today I met with an employee from our local communications department. We are going to recruit some trainees for retail banking. In the draft of a job announcement this man had written that we were' looking for people full of ideas'. I said to him that this was simply nonsense, while he defended his choice of words with reference to the Nordic Ideas-campaign. But imagine if we recruited 100 trainees to produce Nordic ideas in our branch offices ... Nordic Ideas is a theme and a somewhat fancy working title for top management. But our customers should never experience that we claim that we can offer them Nordic ideas. They want solutions. The Nordic ideas must therefore be transformed into concrete products and services. That's what our employees are going to sell the customers!

The two interview statements above point to the importance of linking ideas and values with the companies core activities and practices, and to the need of translation and local adaptation of these ideas and values; two issues that we will revert to in the following analyses.

Nordea's group executive management decided to follow this values-oriented approach both in external communication activities and new integration initiatives at the socio-cultural level. Nordea's corporate statement was further developed during the summer of 2001. This elaborated Corporate Statement contained the company's vision[1], its mission *"Making it possible"*, and the three corporate values:

---

[1] *"We will be valued as the leading financial services group in the Nordic and Baltic financial markets with a substantial growth potential. –We will be number one or number two or show superior profitable growth in every market and product area in which we choose to compete. We will have the leading multichannel distribution with a top world ranking in e-based financial solutions"*

'adding value', 'empowering' and 'being innovative'. This Corporate Statement was to serve as strategic guidance for the further business development.

The communications department was the driving force behind the book project. But all business areas as well as the communications and HR departments were involved in the process termed 'From words to Actions'. The core team responsible for this process explicitly stated in an internal company document that the objective of this process was to *'build a bridge from the existing corporate cultures to the new Nordea culture'*. It means that they acknowledged the existence of former corporate cultures as well as the challenge of 'building bridges' from the merging companies' past to a common future. The team wanted to ensure that all employees would first understand, then accept and finally act in alignment with the set of Nordea values. They decided that focus in this phase should be on (1) Nordea's values, (2) the interpretation of these values in practical work within the organization and (3) investigation of how these values were perceived and how they affected Nordea's employees, customers and shareholders.

In the same internal company document the HR team identified some critical factors for the process:

Management buy-in and ownership

- *"walk the talk"*
- *ensure open dialogue*

Involvement of all employees through

- *personal interaction*
- *forums for culture focused dialogue*

Values being translated into operational terms

How are they applied to my personal work, and how are they applied in my unit?

The interviews conducted in the autumn 2001 with senior executives in the four merged companies showed widespread reservation about the translation of the new set of corporate values into common standards and daily practices. In the interviews these top managers themselves displayed the fact that people do not only have one work identity, for example, an organizational identity as Nordea managers and employees. Dependent on the changing contexts and coalitions, people employed in a multinational matrix organizations certainly shift between an identification with the company and an identification with the nation, the business unit, the profession, the former corporate culture, the age group, the gender group etc. There are so to speak always both integrating and fragmenting forces at stake.

We will analyze the 'From Words to Action' process in more detail below. From our perspective the crucial issue is how the set of relatively abstract company values were communicated, and if they were understood and translated into organizational practices that in the long term could make a significant difference, for both employees and external stakeholders.

THE NORDEA BOOK

The next step in the corporate efforts at accomplishing socio-cultural integration was taken in December 2001 with a booklet titled *'Making it possible'* being distributed to all Nordea employees. This so-called 'Nordea book' introduced the new company's vision, mission, corporate values and corporate personality, and visualized these in pictures of, for example, Nordic landscapes and houses and persons with Nordic looks. The vision and the values were seen as the 'common ground' on which a new organizational culture could be built. The CEO, Thorleif Krarup, emphasized in a foreword to the Nordea book the need for a strong corporate brand, for both internal and external purposes. The booklet starts out by explaining to employees why the company has initiated an internal culture/value process:

This is why we are establishing an entirely new Nordic brand.

As Nordea, we are not only breaking new ground. We are creating something quite unique. Nordea is not a conventional organization spread throughout several countries and run from headquarters in Helsinki, Copenhagen. Oslo and Stockholm. (Nordea 2001: 19)

It is stated as an already accomplished fact that *"Nordea is an integrated group whose activities extend across national boundaries and business areas"*. At the same time the minor differences within the Nordea group were acknowledged as an asset: *"We are sufficiently similar to be able to cooperate and sufficiently dissimilar to inspire each other"*. The vague references in the Nordea book to the multinational company's past, the series of national mergers and acquisitions that the companies have already experienced probably represents a challenge to the integrating efforts of this internal culture/value project.

In the four merged companies forming the Nordea group we find many voices and many opinions on what the new company's tasks and problems are, and how they should be resolved. But the booklet *"Making it possible"* is univocal, and thus the text itself does not do much to engage its readers in a dialogue. Virtually no open questions can be found, only (managers' and employees') rhetorical questions such as: *"What can I do to increase the value of Nordea?"*. The focus is on *telling* the employees what top management has already decided concerning the company's personality and its corporate values.

Moreover, it may be seen as somewhat paradoxical that Nordea refers so much to the "Nordic ideas" of freedom, entrepreneurship, democracy and equal opportunities, both in the advertisements and in the Nordea book, and at the same time tells the employees who they are and how they are going to realize the managerial visions (*Become a realizer! - Live the Nordea!*). The employees are expected to accept an already fixed Nordic way of thinking and to act according to Nordea's personality in order to make the corporate vision possible, even though Nordea's espoused core values of 'being innovative' and 'empowering' obviously contradict this message.

Although the booklet lists some barriers or obstacles to the realization of Nordea's vision of being *"number one or number two or show superior profitable growth in every market and product areas in which we choose to compete"* (Nordea 2001: 67), the nature of such obstacles are not mentioned. The booklet makes several references to a journey: *"we must begin our journey together"* (Nordea 2001: 5) and *"a thousand-mile journey starts with one step. And we have already taken many"* (Nordea 2001: 65). But no references are made to possible hindrances or critical issues to be overcome through a joint effort; only vague allusions to a Nordic folk song about a ship that cannot sail without wind (Nordea 2001: 59). The story may appear as somewhat banal and flavorless because it is neither based on an identifiable conflict or challenge (Shaw 2000), nor does it contain any references to actions to be taken to overcome critical issues. It might therefore also risk being ignored by its audience as neither compelling nor appealing.

THE CASCADE PROCESS

The booklet *'Making it possible'* was planned to function as a platform for discussions in the different sections and business units of the company during the internal culture/value process. But as already mentioned, the overall communication style in the booklet does not necessarily stimulate the employees to become involved in a culture-focused dialogue with their managers about interpretations of the organization's present and future challenges.

However, we cannot tell from an analysis of booklet itself, if and how the internal process functioned. It was recognized by the planning group that involvement of the employees in a culture-focused dialogue was absolutely necessary. The potential success of the initiated cascade process was not only dependent on the ethos and trustworthiness of the CEO and the managers involved. The cascade process was also dependent on their concrete support to the internal culture/value implementation, their 'buy-in' and 'ownership' of the project, and their willingness to involve the employees in an open dialogue and a translation of the corporate values into operational terms within the specific business units and departments.

In interviews with some Communications and HR middle managers and employees during the summer 2002, we got some impressions of how the booklet had been distributed and received by different audiences throughout Nordea. The following statements give an impression of how this process was evaluated by some of these middle managers. Several of them had reservations concerning the top-down nature of this process. One of them states:

The CEO was right when he decided to start this internal branding process, but he did not succeed in making the other managing directors responsible as partners in the cascade process.

Another middle manager confirms this impression that in some business areas there was a lack of managerial support to the internal process. Furthermore top management did not speak in one voice:

Group Executive Management probably accepted all these fine words and the text in the brand book[2]. But they did not mix their blood; they did not create a common understanding of the Nordic ideas and the common values. And if the top managers do not go through such a branding process themselves, they cannot implement the ideas behind.

We do not know in detail how the cascade process was carried out in the different departments and business units, and how the booklet 'Making it possible' was used as part of a dialogue between managers and employees. The 'Nordea book' may have been welcomed as an initiative that would inspire practice. We have examples from a regional retail bank where some of the abstract values had been translated into local meanings that made good sense to a specific group of employees in this organizational context. But we have also heard about situations where some employees tried to deconstruct the story presented about the new company, either because it did not meet their

---

[2] In interviews top managers often referred to the Nordea book as our 'brand book', thus using a term originally borrowed form marketing

needs of sensegiving to the turbulent change processes they witnessed daily in their working life, or because the company story's inclusiveness obfuscated the divisions and potential antagonisms that can be found within every large corporation.

Some employees tell in interviews how the internal cascade process at their workplaces did take less than an hour. The Nordea book was distributed by the middle manager who then went through a series of pre-produced Power Point slides telling them about Nordea's vision, mission, values and ideas. But there was no discussion of the presentation or any attempt to translate the relatively abstract words and concepts into the department's own tasks. Furthermore some employees felt offended by the communication style and the simplistic presentation in the Nordea book, which they found did not match their intellectual level:

"Most of the employees in our department have a university degree, and if a message from top management should be taken seriously we expect it to be communicated to us in another format."

An electronic survey via the company's intranet was conducted by the Group HR development centre after the Nordea book had been distributed and the cascade process finished (Nordea 2002). Employees were asked to respond (agree/disagree) to statements regarding:

Their personal view on values in Nordea

Their personal view on the value dialogue conducted in their unit

Their personal view on the three Nordea values

Their personal view on values in general

162

Their personal view on the Nordea book

The results indicate a strong internal support both among managers and employees for Nordea's new values, *'we create value'*, *'we are innovative'*, and *'we are empowering'*, when it comes to *understanding* the values. The *acceptance* of the values is also high, although some have difficulties with 'empowering', which perhaps also is the value that demands most translation if behavioral patterns are expected to be changed. A large number of employees confirm that a value discussion has taken place and that the corporate values are taken seriously in their unit.

It is, however, still unclear, if the corporate values have also been translated in the different local contexts to be part of a sustainable change of thinking and behavior. If they have been implemented into common daily practices to such an extent that the employees in the future *'will be living Nordea'* (Nordea 2001) and not any longer use national stereotyping. The HR team responsible for the survey concludes soberly that *'we can make the values work'*, but *'sustainable change of behaviour can only be achieved gradually and it takes time'* (Nordea 2002).

CULTURE BUILDING IN A BUSINESS UNIT

There are examples of cross-border units in Nordea such as the business unit Markets which have agreed upon their 'own cultural values', in spite of the company-wide process described above. In this section we will describe how Nordea Markets, which is a unit within the business area 'Corporate and Institutional Banking', very early after the merger tried to develop its own new culture. This was done in a process starting with the creation of cultural awareness, then clarification of the different cultural assumptions and practices managers and employees brought with them from their national companies. This consciousness-raising process was then followed by attempts to promote mutual respect and to create a new common culture in a process involving several management layers.

The following description[3] and analysis of this culture-building process is made to give an example of a process driven by a top manager who felt committed and actively behaved as a change agent. At the same time this case describes how the layer of middle managers can be much more actively involved in discussions about a common culture. Finally, this case can be used to demonstrate how cultural values must be closely linked with daily social practices as well as with performance appraisal systems to be taken seriously by the employees as something integrated in their daily working lives.

Over the summer 2000, the top manager of the cross-border business unit Markets had reached the conclusion that it would be important to work on creating a common culture. His idea was to begin with the whole management group of 30 people. By getting them 'on board' he believed that a new culture and new ways to do things would then gravitate further down in the organization. He also discussed the actual process with, among others, the HR manager for Markets in Finland. They decided to organize a series of culture seminars that would provide an opportunity for the invited middle managers to reflect on perceived cultural differences at a national and

---

[3] This description is based on a case written by Ingmar Björkman together with Eero Vaara. Ingmar Björkman was involved as external facilitator in the process described.

organizational level related to the three different banks, and then to build a new common ground for the cross-border Markets unit.

At this stage, little attention had been paid to cultural issues and cultural integration projects in the new bank's executive management group. The senior executive of Nordea Markets described his ideas and plans about the culture seminars to the head of Corporate and Investment Banking, and he raised no objections. No similar process was initiated at the level of Corporate and Investment Banking.

Since the organization of Nordea Markets had been announced in May 2000, each of the three country-based management groups had convened face-to-face weekly. Although these weekly meetings were seen as time-consuming, expensive and the constant travelling was felt as strenuous, the meetings were also perceived as important, both to promote a good flow of information and to further contact between the merging management groups. The crucial role of getting people to know each other and informing each other of plans and on-going projects was also widely stressed. Many managers had been surprised by the apparent information need that people had at all hierarchical levels in the merging organization. However, communication in general mostly took place within each business unit. Integration across the different units had so far mainly taken place at the level of the executive management group.

The first 'common culture' seminar took place in October 2000 at the Swedish School of Economics in Helsinki. Apart from a handful of short business meetings, this was the first time that the whole management group in Markets of some thirty persons convened and spent more time together discussing issues not directly related to business operations. The one-day seminar began with a presentation by the top manager of Markets on 'The management of Markets'. In his presentation he outlined four challenges facing the unit: (1) their strategic orientation, (2) the Nordic versus national dimensions in terms of how the business unit was functioning, (3) the significant increase in size and complexity as an outcome of the cross-border merger, and (4) the business culture. He presented his view that while Markets was doing well in terms of strategic orientation, the other three issues were still challenges to be faced.

The participants were then divided into groups of national teams. The groups first discussed and then presented to the whole Management Group how they experienced people from the two other countries, how they viewed themselves, and, finally, how they thought others perceived people from their own country. Subsequently, each group was given the task of constructing two metaphors for each of the other two banks and two for their own.[4] The people in the groups made drawings and created names for the kind of organization that they perceived both their own and the other banks to constitute. The group tasks revealed that several managers had considerable artistic talent, and the metaphors indicated with a considerable amount of humor how the people in the groups viewed their own organization and those of the others.

In the discussion following each group presentation, the focal bank representatives were encouraged to comment on how they viewed the metaphors and how they corresponded to the way their banks had been functioning. In spite of the implicit critique of parts of the corporate culture of each bank and the fact that sensitive and critical issues were brought up, the discussion took place in a positive atmosphere with people laughing and joking about the different

---

[4] This method had been used also in the MeritaNordbanken merger (see Säntti, 2001)

metaphors. Reflecting on the first seminar the top manager of Markets comments:

The first cultural seminar marked a major breakthrough in terms of what we were able to talk about. Even today, some of the features are talked about as in the metaphors. Everything from the spider [Nordbanken], to the complicated space rocket that doesn't take off the ground [Unibank]. These are now becoming things that have facilitated our talking about the past. We are able to talk about the political issues in Stockholm, we have some words about it, it's a spider web ... And when someone from Copenhagen comes with [a large complicated plan that] would cost a 'gazillion' and it would be very grand. Yeah, fine, but let's do a simpler piece of machinery that will do the same thing, and at least lift off. And when we have a tiny Finnish something – we say: remember that you are not coming directly from the woods, you have attended school, so how do we do this? These are issues that we have learned to talk about.

The second cultural seminar, a two-day gathering, was organized in November 2000. In the meantime, the new bank had been granted a permission to acquire CBK in Norway, but no one from CBK was present as the acquisition had not yet been completed. Prior to the seminar, each of the business units had been given the task of defining what they thought should be the guiding values for Markets. The objective of the seminar was to arrive at key values through a collective process. The senior executive in Markets began the seminar with a presentation of the corporate values of the largest and most successful international investment banks.

From words to action?

The focus of the rest of the seminar was on the creation of a set of core values for Markets. Each of the business units began by presenting their own suggestion, followed by a general discussion. Then the groups were told to re-iterate what they thought would be suitable, based on the other groups' presentations. At the end of the second day 'the 4 Cs' had been defined and each participant in the seminar had individually agreed on them: (1) *Customer orientation,* (2) *Communication,* (3) *Competence and* (4) *Credibility.* Each manager was to be responsible for *'living the 4 Cs'* and for negotiating the values with his subordinates and 'translating' them. Additionally, it was decided that the HR manager in Markets carried the main responsibility for developing a form to be used in the appraisal reviews in the whole Markets organization with a focus on these four new values.

According to interviews with the senior executive of Markets, he found the second seminar constructive in the sense that the management group here started to discuss how the organization was to function in the future in accordance with the negotiated values regardless of in which country they were working. The 4 Cs meant *"that we are sending much more clear and homogenous signals about what we want in terms of behavior."* These values were explicitly referred to when letting a few employees go. In these cases, although their financial performance was good, the people apparently did not respect these organizational norms. The senior executive saw this as a strong signal to the employees that these organizational values were to be taken seriously.

During winter and spring of 2001 efforts were made to continue to work with the organizational values. Performance appraisal reviews were carried out based on the new appraisal form in which the 4 Cs

168

were the main focus. Additionally, the HR team in Markets carried out a Management Review in which individual interviews were conducted with all line managers. The interviews covered, among other things, general job satisfaction and attitudes in the focal unit, the working of the management group in terms of the 4 Cs, and status concerning the culture-building process in Markets. Finally, each business unit was to prepare answers to the following questions for a third culture seminar in May 2001: (1) *How have the values been implemented in your part of the organization?* (2) *How has the appraisal tool been used in your part of the organization?* and (3) *List the strong and weak sides – in your experience – of the effects of the values so far.*

Most participants viewed the third culture seminar as less significant than the two first seminars; the discussion was also less lively. The participants stated that it was still somewhat unclear which impact the values had had on daily operations within each of the country based units, although considerable efforts had been made to implement the 4 Cs and *'some progress in their implementation'* had been made. Some pointed to the difficulties in measuring the values. Furthermore, it was mentioned that the values were perceived and interpreted somewhat differently by different people and by different country-based units. Eventually some argued that the new values would only influence the behavior of people in Markets, if the managers succeeded in explicitly linking compensation with the extent to which employees adhered to the values in their daily work. It was generally agreed that a key to the implementation of values was that the managers would 'enact' the values themselves.

CONCLUSIONS

This chapter has revolved around a few managerial initiatives aimed at promoting socio-cultural integration in the four merging companies. Initially socio-cultural integration – as a process of long standing – was given relatively limited attention, even though top management had established a task force responsible for socio-cultural integration efforts. It should ne noted that some of the initiatives described in this chapter are only short-period initiatives, such as the communication of the new company name through advertisements, or the 'From words to Action' process.

The interviews conducted during the autumn 2001 in the four merging companies indicated that socio-cultural integration was not an issue given very high priority within top management. These interviews displayed two struggling perspectives: On the one hand, the top managers acknowledged that some initiatives had to be taken to integrate the merged companies and create commitment among employees toward the corporate vision and the new set of values. Top managers thus articulated a 'One Company' discourse emphasizing that Nordea *is* or must become an integrated corporation. They argued – in a very rational tone – for the need for merging, cooperating, and acquiring new and better competencies to secure growth in the internationalized financial services sector.

On the other hand, the same interviews revealed a certain ambivalence, even among the top managers, towards this integration project. The harmonious perspective incorporated in the integrating and unifying discourse that we found in the booklet *'Making it possible'* was thus challenged by other voices and perspectives favoring local and national communities and identities. Therefore, it

170

could not be expected that these top managers would all play a forceful and consistent role as organizational change agents in the socio-cultural integration process.

The Nordea Markets case shows that socio-cultural change processes may be initiated and followed up in a less top-driven way, at least in organizational subunits, where a larger group of people can be involved in negotiating new values and developing a new organizational culture. In this case 30 managers' and employees' past experiences, values and the values and practices they had developed in a certain historical and cultural context, were explicitly acknowledged as the platform on which cultural changes could be based on.

A first step might hence be to transform perceived differences between nationalities and corporate cultures into more 'joking relationships' (Gundelach 2000) where the exchange of cultural metaphors paves the way for better understanding and collaboration across borders. The next step may be to discuss former values, then develop new values and finally consider how these values can be linked with daily social practices so that 'superficial' or 'empty' rhetoric is avoided. The challenges met in the Nordea Markets case also show that managers must take their role as change agents seriously in such a process and wholeheartedly 'enact' the common values themselves. And their performance, as well as the performance of the employees, must be evaluated to ensure that this new organizational culture is living and lived by all organizational members.

To what extent should corporate top management give more room for distinctive business area/unit cultures within a common company frame of reference? Official corporate cultures can certainly provide a 'value' umbrella for the people involved, support some kind of identification with the new company, and guide strategic action based on future visions. However, in multinational organizations as large and complex as Nordea it may be difficult to create something common – and unique – for everyone independent of age, gender, nationality, educational background and professional interest. And the result of such culture building attempts might be a superficial and – harmless – organizational rhetoric that provides relatively little guidance for strategic action. At worst such initiatives might create contradictions, if for example claimed ideas of democracy and individualism and values such as 'being innovative' and 'empowering' are confronted with social practices that contradict these ideas and values.

A final message to managers aiming at ambitious socio-cultural integration projects between merging companies is therefore that organizational cultures do not exist, if they are not made sense of and discussed by those who should feel attached to and identify with them. Rather than focusing on abstract ideas and values, managerial efforts should therefore be put into aligning ideas, values and norms around concrete organizational practices. Reflections on perceived practical and cultural differences, concrete changes in practices and conscious cultural development should support each other. In such a culture building process strong linkages between corporate vision and strategy, integrated communications and HR management are crucial.

REFERENCES

BOYACILLER, N.A., KLEINBERG, M.J., PHILLIPS, M.E. and SACKMANN, S.A. (2003). 'Conceptualizing Culture: Elucidating the streams of research in international cross-cultural management'. In Punnett, B. J. and Shenkar, O. (Eds.). *Handbook for International Management Research*. Ann Arbor: University of Michigan Press.

BUONO, A. F. and BOWDITCH, J. L. (1989). *The human side of mergers and acquisitions. Managing collisions between people, cultures, and organizations.* San Francisco: Jossey-Bass.

CALORI, R., LUBATKIN, M. and VERY, P. (1994). 'Control mechanisms in cross-border acquisitions: An international comparison'. *Organization Studies,* 15, 361-379

CARTWRIGHT, S. and COOPER, C.L. (1992). *Mergers and Acquisitions: The Human Factor.* Oxford: Butterworth-Heinemann Ltd.

CARTWRIGHT, S. and COOPER, C. L. (1993). 'The role of culture compatibility in successful organizational marriage'. *Academy of Management Review,* 7, 57-70.

CHENEY, G. and CHRISTENSEN, L. T. (2001). 'Organizational Identity - Linkages between Internal and External Communication'. In Jablin, F. and Putnam, L. (Eds.). *The New Handbook of Organizational Communication. Advances in Theory, Research and Methods.* Thousand Oaks, CA.: Sage.

DEAL, T. AND KENNEDY, G. (1988). *Corporate Cultures.* Harmondsworth: Penguin.

GERTSEN, M., SØDERBERG, A.-M. and TORP, J.P. (1998). *Cultural Dimensions of International Mergers and Acquisitions.* Berlin: Walter de Gruyter.

GIOIA, D., SCHULTZ, M. and CORLEY, K. (2000). 'Organizational Identity, Image and Adaptive Instability'. *Academy of Management Review,* 25, 63-81.

GUNDELACH, P. (2000). 'Joking relationships and national identity in Scandinavia'. *Acta Sociologica* 43, 113-122.

HANNERZ, U. (1996). *Transnational Connections. Culture, People, Places,* London: Routledge.

HOFSTEDE, G. (1991). *Cultures and organizations: Software of the mind.* New York: McGraw-Hill.

JANSON, L. (1994). 'Towards a dynamic model of post-acquisition cultural integration'. In A. Sjögren and L. Janson (Eds.). *Culture and Management.* Stockholm: Multicultural Centre and IIB, pp. 127-152.

JEMISON, D.B. and SITKIN, S.B. (1986). 'Corporate acquisitions: A process perspective'. *Academy of Management Review,* 11, 145-163.

KLEPPESTØ, S. (1993). *Kultur och identitet vid företagsuppköp och fusioner.* Stockholm: Nerenius and Santérus förlag.

LARSSON, R. (1993). 'Barriers to acculturation in mergers and acquisitions: Strategic human resource implications'. *Journal of European Business Education*, 2, 1-18.

MARTIN, J. (1992). *Cultures in organizations: Three perspectives.* New York: Oxford University Press.

MARTIN, J. and FROST, P. (1997). 'The Organizational Culture War Games: a Struggle for Intellectual Dominance'. In Clegg, S., Hardy, C. and Nord, W. (Eds). *Handbook of Organization Studies.* London: Sage, pp. 599-621.

MIRVIS, P.H. and MARKS, M.L. (1992). *Managing the merger: Making it work.* Paramus New Jersey: Prentice Hall.

MOROSINI, P. (1997). *Managing cultural differences - effective strategy and execution across cultures in global corporate alliances.* Oxford: Pergamon Press.

MOROSINI, P. and SINGH, H. (1994). 'Post-cross-border acquisitions: Implementing national-culture-compatible strategies to improve performance'. *European Management Journal* 12, 390-400.

NAHAVANDI, A. and MALEKZADEH, A. R. (1988). 'Acculturation in mergers and acquisitions'. *Academy of Management Review,* 13, 79-90.

NORDEA (2000). *Annual Report* 2000.

NORDEA (2001). *Making it possible.*

NORDEA (2002). *From Words to Action. Results from Electronic Survey.* (CD rom).

OLIE, R. (1994). 'Shades of culture and institutions in international mergers'. *Organization Studies,* 15, 381-405

OUCHI, W. and WILKINS, A. (1985). 'Organizational culture'. *Annual Review of Sociology,* 11, 457-483.

PARKER, M. (2000). *Organizational Culture and Identity.* London: Sage.

PETERS, T. J. and WATERMAN, R. H. (1982). *In search of excellence: Lessons from America's best run companies.* New York: Harper and Row.

PETTIGREW, A. (1979). 'On studying organizational cultures'. *Administrative Science Quarterly,* 24, 570-581.

SACKMANN S.A. (1997) (Ed.). *Cultural Complexity in Organizations: Inherent Contrasts and Contradictions.* Thousand Oaks: Sage.

SCHEIN, E. (1985). *Organizational culture and leadership*. San Francisco: Jossey-Bass.

SCHULTZ, M. (1994). *On studying organizational cultures: Diagnosis and understanding*. Berlin: Walter de Gruyter.

SHAW, G. (2000). 'Planning and Communicating Using Stories'. In Schultz, M., Hatch, M. J. and Larsen, M. H. (Eds.). *The Expressive Organization*. Oxford: Oxford University Press.

SMIRCICH, L. (1983). 'Concepts of culture and organizational analysis'. *Administrative Science Quarterly*, 28, 339-58.

SÄNTTI, R. (2001). *How cultures interact in an international merger: Case MeritaNordbanken*. Tampere: University of Tampere. Doctoral thesis.

WEICK, K. (1995). *Sensemaking in Organizations*. Thousand Oaks: Sage.

WHETTEN, D. A. and GODFREY, P. C. (1998). *Identity in Organizations – building theory through conversations*. Thousand Oaks, CA: Sage.

Chapter 8

QUO VADIS, HR?

AN ANALYSIS OF THE ROLES PLAYED BY THE HR FUNCTION DURING THE POST-MERGER PROCESS

Ingmar Björkman & Anne-Marie Søderberg

INTRODUCTION

The human resource (HR) function is frequently encouraged by academics, consultants and practitioners to play a more 'strategic' role in their organization. This is the case particularly in connection with dramatic organizational changes such as cross-border mergers and acquisitions. Given the apparent significance of people management in post-merger processes, it is, however, unfortunate that we know only little about how the HR function develops and implements interventions, policies and procedures that contribute to the integration of workforces and cultures. At present, especially little is known about the activities and contributions of the HR function during large-scale merger processes.

In this chapter, we will explore the roles that the HR function plays in post-merger change processes. This will help us uncover the inherent problems in managing HR issues in the post-merger organization and will specifically highlight the difficulties in giving HR issues a 'strategic' status. For this purpose, we will draw on specific insights of role theory (Katz and Kahn, 1978) in general and studies on the role of HR in particular (Ulrich, 1997). Our key starting point is that the roles of the HR function are shaped not only by the initiatives of the HR people themselves, but that the expectations and actions of top executives and line managers are essential in determining the strategic or non-strategic status of the HR function (cf. Truss et al., 2002). For this analysis, Nordea is a particularly illustrative case. On the one hand, it reveals typical problems in organizing and managing HR issues. On the other hand, it also illustrates how the HR function is easily left with a secondary, non-strategic role in these processes.

Based on interviews with HR managers and top executives in Nordea, we will first describe the roles played by the HR function and examine the effects of the roles enacted by the HR function on how the workforces were managed and integrated in the post-merger processes. Secondly, we will analyze issues that influence the changing roles played by the HR function in Nordea during the period from the merger of MeritaNordbanken and Unidanmark in the spring of 2000 to the situation in the early fall of 2002. We focus on the question why HR has not been given a more strategic role in the integration process.

THE ROLES PLAYED BY THE HR FUNCTION

Beginning in the mid-1980s and gaining force during the 1990s, the concept of human resource management (HRM) has taken the center stage in discussions of how to manage people in corporations. HRM is presented as a

> *distinctive approach to employment management which seeks to achieve competitive advantage through the strategic deployment of a highly committed and capable workforce, using an integrated array of cultural, structural and personnel techniques.* (Storey, 1995: 5)

The basic assumption is that human resources constitute an important source of competitive advantage for the organization (e.g. Wright and McMahan, 1992; Pfeffer, 1994; Storey, 1995). Hence, HR practitioners need to evaluate the economic consequences of the firm's HRM practices, assess how human resources and their management compare to those in competing firms, and understand HR's role in building organizational capabilities for the future (Barney and Wright, 1998). In contrast to the 1970s, when the personnel function was associated with labor negotiations and the administration of policies and procedures, the HR function is now being exhorted to take on a strategic and business role. At the same time as the HR function is supposed to become more strategic, the responsibility for people management is also to be at least partly shifted back to line management (Storey, 1995). It has been argued that the distribution of responsibilities for HR issues needs to be clarified and agreed upon between HR professionals and line managers (Ulrich, 1997).

Scholars have suggested various ways of classifying the different roles played by the HR function in large firms (see e.g. Legge, 1989; Schuler, 1990; Storey, 1992; Tyson, 1995; Evans, Pucik and Barsoux, 2002). An influential conceptual model is the one developed by Ulrich (1997). Ulrich proposes a model where HR practitioners are seen as somebody adding value to their organization in various and at times potentially conflicting ways. Ulrich's framework is based on two main dimensions. The first axis reflects the demands of a current/operational/tactical versus a future-oriented/strategic orientation. The second axis consists of a focus on people at the one end of the axis, and a focus on process at the other. It is suggested that HR professionals are at least in part responsible for the following four roles in the organization: (1) management of infrastructure of the personnel basics (the HR function as 'administrative expert'), (2) management of employee contribution (HR as 'employee champion'), (3) management of strategic human resources issues (HR as 'strategic partner'), and (4) management of change and transformation (HR as 'change agent'). The two latter roles are strategic in their nature.

There is some indication that the HR function is becoming more strategically oriented than before (Hope-Hailey et al., 1997; Sisson, 2001). However, available empirical evidence suggests that most HR functions still play a predominately tactical role (Truss et al., 2002) and that HR professionals have low status and influence in many companies (Berglund, 2002).

Handling both tactical and strategic HR issues well seems particularly important in mergers and acquisitions. Several studies have indicated that financial and strategic issues tend to receive the most attention in connection with mergers and acquisitions (e.g. Jemison and Sitkin, 1986), and there have been urgent calls for more attention to be paid to the people side during the integration process (e.g. Buono and Bowditch, 1989; Cartwright and Cooper 1992; Schuler and Jackson, 2001; Stahl et al., 2002). Against this background, it is very important to explore how HR issues are, in fact, dealt with and managed in the post-merger processes.

To the best of our knowledge, there is no published research on the roles played by the HR function in international post-merger processes. However, some work has been conducted on factors that influence the roles played by HR functions in large firms in general. First, the roles played by the HR function are contingent on the expectations held by top and line managers – key actors in the role set (Katz and Kahn, 1978) of the HR organization – towards the function. These expectations are in turn likely to be deeply rooted in the administrative heritage of the organization (Truss et al., 2002). As organizational roles are at least partly socially constructed, an HR function that is perceived by key actors in the corporation to already have a high degree of 'reputational effectiveness' (Tsui, 1984), is more likely to succeed in enacting more strategic roles (Truss et al., 2002). Outside the organization, the diffusion of notions of what constitutes 'appropriate' ways to handling HRM issues may also shape top and line managers' expectations vis-à-vis the HR function (DiMaggio and Powell, 1983; Purcell, 2001). It can be expected that the organizational roles played by the HR function in general will influence the roles it is expected to play also in specific contexts, such as in merger processes.

Second, to change existing roles requires awareness of a need for change and agreement of the direction in which the HR function would like to develop its activities (Flood, 1998). Third, the power, social capital and political skills of the HR managers are likely to facilitate the expansion of the roles of HR in the corporation (Ferris and Judge, 1991; Galang and Ferris 1997). Fourth, sufficient resources, appropriate support systems, and an absence of 'corporate chocks' (Truss et al, 2002) help HR managers free enough time to focus on the development of their function. Fifth, the size and complexity of the corporation has been found to influence the HR function's ability to operate in a strategic and well-coordinated manner (Truss et al., 2002).

Following a brief description of how the HR functions in Merita, Nordbanken, Unidanmark, and CBK operated before the establishment of Nordea, we will describe and analyze the roles played by Nordea's HR function during the post-merger processes. We will also analyze how the enactment of the different organizational roles influenced the management of people in the integration process. The analysis builds partly on data collected during interviews with the top management of Nordea in 2001. Among the managers interviewed in 2001, four worked within the HR function. We carried out a second round of interviews with two of these managers during the summer and fall of 2002, when we also interviewed five other HR managers working within three of Nordea's business areas. Our interviewees included employees from Denmark, Sweden, Finland, and Norway. Furthermore, we were provided access to company-internal material concerning the HR function.

BACKGROUND: THE HR FUNCTIONS IN THE MERGING ORGANIZATIONS

Compared to the other parties in the merger, *Merita* had an HR function that was relatively small, centralized and heavily focused on executing traditional HRM processes like pay systems and labor relations. There was only limited interaction between the line organization and the HR function. Merita had a separate central competence development unit that organized courses and also played a central role in how the bank during the 1990s worked with the cultural integration of the merging Union Bank of Finland and Kansallis, the previous archrivals. Also in *Nordbanken*, the HR function was largely centralized, but the regional banks also had their own HR personnel. The Swedish HR unit mainly focused on traditional personnel management processes that were highly standardized across business units. Few resources were allocated to directly supporting the line units. However, according to some Swedish interviewees, competence development was viewed as *"more business oriented and less theoretically based"* than in Merita.

When Merita and Nordbanken merged, the two country-based HR organizations first remained separate, but in 1999 a cross-border HR organization was established consisting of one unit for competence and management development, and another for HR administration. The managers of these units had offices both in Sweden and Finland and commuted regularly between the two locations. In the HR administration unit, little integration took place. More joint activities across the Swedish-Finnish border took place in the competence development unit. Notably, during 1999 the HR function organized 20 cultural seminars for more than 300 Swedish and Finnish employees (see Säntti, 2001).

Compared with MeritaNordbanken, *Unidanmark* had invested many more resources in the HR function, and the Danish unit also seems to have taken more initiatives across a broader scope of HR issues. In 1996, Unibank introduced a system of 'HR partners' who were to function as change agents and sparring partners in HR issues within the different organizational units. Within this system, the HR professionals were employed centrally in the HR function, but were assigned their own line unit to work with, in particular its management. The HR function had also developed a detailed pay system and a standardized procedure for performance and appraisal interviews and competence development discussions that were used throughout the bank. The head of the Danish HR function was also involved in the process leading to the establishment of the bank's corporate values. When Unibank merged with the Danish insurance company Tryg-Baltica in 1998, the HR units continued to operate separately.

Towards the end of the 1990s, the HR function of *CBK* went through a process of decentralization from a central HR team in the mid-1990s to the HR professionals gradually being transferred to the business units. In 2000, each business unit had an HR unit of its own, and some of the business units had developed unique HR solutions. In some units, HR managers were involved in strategic HR issues, in others they worked mostly on administrative processes. CBK had a central corporate management development unit responsible for running a career management system for the top echelons of the bank, and this unit also conducted a corporate management training program. In terms of number of staff, CBK's HR function was well resourced.

ORGANIZING THE NEW HR FUNCTION

When the merger of MeritaNordbanken and Unidanmark was negotiated in 1999-2000, the HR function as such was apparently not given much attention, and few issues related to the management of human resources were debated apart from the question of who would fill the top management positions in the merged bank. Neither was the organizational placement of the HR function much discussed. In the end, it was decided that the person who had worked as the secretary of MeritaNordbanken's Executive Management Group would be in charge of the Group HR function. When taking up the job a few months after the merger, the head of Group HR was to report directly to the CEO of the new bank. However, he would neither be a member of Group Executive Management consisting of seven members nor of the larger Group Management, which included another eight senior executives. But Nordea is not unique in this respect. Research carried out on other large European corporations indicates that only in few cases is the HR director member of the corporate executive management.

Subsequent to the merger of MeritaNordbanken and Unidanmark, it was decided in discussions involving the national HR executives that a country-based HR organization would be established. In essence, it meant that there would, at least initially, be little integration of HR functions across the country borders. With a few exceptions, people employed within the HR function were still part of the national HR units rather than the line organizations. Based on Unidanmark's experiences with an HR partner model, there were also ideas to appoint HR professionals based in the national HR units 'HR Partners' for the different business line units, but during 2000 and 2001 this model was only implemented in selected parts of the Nordea group.

The country-based HR units operated until January 1, 2002, when a new cross-border organization was implemented (see the figure in the appendix). At that stage, a decision had been made to create a new position as responsible for Group Staffs, including IT, HR, Identity & Communications, and Legal services. The former CEO of the Norwegian CBK, who after the acquisition had been made responsible for Nordea Securities, was appointed as head of this new cross-national organizational unit.

The background for the internal restructuring of the HR function will be described and discussed below, whereafter Nordea's HR function will be presented and analyzed in terms of the four roles of the HR function put forward in Ulrich's (1997) conceptual model.

HR AS 'ADMINISTRATIVE EXPERT'

The administrative role of the HR function covers the way the function designs and performs the processes of staffing, training, appraising, compensating and rewarding, promoting and otherwise managing the flow of employees through the organization (Ulrich, 1997). One of the challenges for Nordea' HR management in the transition process from four domestic institutions to one multinational financial services institution was to deal with the task of developing an HRM infrastructure that would ensure efficient, equitable and high quality HRM processes and practices while at the same time paying sufficient attention to the national and business unit differences within this complex multinational organization. This crucial question was the subject of continuous debate among Nordea's HR managers. Collective agreements, union relations and legal requirements obviously differed across the Nordic countries. The merging country-based organizations had different HR systems and concepts, and the differences across business units were also considerable.

Initiatives were taken both in 2000 and 2001 to collect data to get an overview of how the different HRM activities were carried out in the various countries. Efforts were also made to align job titles in different countries as well as to coordinate the timing of salary negotiations across borders and different job functions, so that managers only once a year had to spend time on such negotiations for the whole group or department.

However, in most areas less than perfect agreement existed as to what constituted 'best HRM practices', and consequently only relatively few changes and adjustments were made at the group level in the administrative HRM processes during 2000 and 2001. An HR senior executive among the interviewees even described the country-based HR functions as a 'brake block' to cross-border integration initiatives:

If you maintain national HR organizations, they will tend to emphasize the national rules, highlight difficulties due to national differences and propose national solutions and thus develop impediments to joint solutions.

The decision finally made in 2002 to invest in a group-wide IT-based platform for HRM data was intended primarily to provide cross-border HR data but would also contribute to the alignment of HRM practices and processes across borders and business areas.

After the merger between MeritaNordbanken and Unidanmark, some of the 'cross-national' business areas and units claimed to get little support from the corporate HR professionals in handling issues such as staffing. There were particularly strong reactions to the delays in finalizing an employment contract for a senior manager in one of the cross-border business areas. The head of this unit eventually described his frustration in a letter to Nordea's CEO. The HR function in the country in question explained that the delay was due both to an overall lack of resources and to an established national tradition according to which management positions had to be negotiated with and accepted by the unions. This clashed with the expectation within the business area of much more expedient decision-making in headhunting and recruitment. The perceived slowness in handling staffing issues thus indicated that the HR function, from the point of view of the business area, failed to live up to the demanding needs of a cross-border financial services institution in a highly competitive labor market.

In the fall of 2001, a consulting firm was then hired to examine the functioning and organization of the HR organization. A reorganization of the HR function into three main units – Group HR Administration, Group HR Partner and Group HR Centre – was one of the concrete results of the report, which was prepared by the consultants in cooperation with Nordea's own HR executives. Group HR Administration would be responsible for administrative HRM processes, a responsible Head of HR was to be appointed within each business area with HR partners in the subordinate business units, and Group HR Centre would be responsible for developing corporate tools for staffing, training, leadership development and remuneration.

This case illustrates the complexities and challenges involved in changing existing HRM procedures and practices in cross-border mergers. One the one hand, the decision-makers who had been in charge of the national HR functions differed in their perceptions of how to handle a number of HRM issues. The following view was held by several of our interviewees: *"The fact that our points of departure have been so different has been a barrier for the Nordic HRM work."*

For instance, Unidanmark had an elaborate salary system where each position in the bank had been classified and clear rules developed on how to determine individual salaries. In Nordbanken (Sweden), the person's superior and the superior's superior were largely setting salaries themselves, while in Merita (Finland) the central HR unit played a decisive role in the negotiation process and was even evaluated on the basis of how well it was able to keep salary hikes under control. The perceptions held by the national HR managers about 'best practices' that could be used as a basis for increased standardization of Nordea-wide policies were rooted in both national HRM practices and in how HR issues had been handled in their own organization. The differences in views led to prolonged discussions and arguably to a lack of attention to the new HRM needs in the integration of and the further functioning of the new cross-national organization.

On the other hand, the expectations of the line managers in the cross-border business areas and units on the HR function clearly differed from the services provided by the function. The letter sent to Nordea's CEO (see above) constituted an extreme example of how the expectations and demands of line managers were communicated to the HR function.

HR AS 'EMPLOYEE CHAMPION'

The 'employee champion' role has to do with the way in which the HR function helps enhance employee contributions (for example commitment) to the firm by paying attention to employee needs (Ulrich, 1997). In 2000, the extent to which HR professionals had a close and trusting relationship with employees and, hence, were well-positioned to understand and address their concerns, seemed to vary considerably across units and countries. In most parts of Nordea, HR units had a tradition of operating as a centralized and rather bureaucratic organization that mostly dealt with administrative HRM issues such as employment contracts and salaries. For most employees, it was not a natural thing to approach the HR professionals with their grievances and concerns.

Quo vadis HR?

The importance of professional counseling and support for employees and proactive actions to ensure employee commitment are particularly important during periods of great upheaval such as large-scale mergers (Cartwright and Cooper, 1992). For example, a more clearly defined employee champion role might have prevented the loss of some employees with key competences during the merger processes. One HR professional admits:

I could have prevented people from leaving the company. If my own role had been well-defined ... I could have persuaded them to calm down. Often the importance of HR is forgotten.

Another HR professional tells how much time he spent convincing employees that they will benefit from staying in the company instead of being tempted by higher salaries in other international companies abroad:

We have experienced that foreign financial companies have tried to attract whole teams of employees who could almost set their own salary levels... But the recipe is not to offer a higher salary, but to elucidate how many other benefits you have as employee in one of the four Nordic countries in contrast to for example London. We are able to retain many of our employees and attract unsolicited job applications due to the whole range of welfare services offered in the Nordic societies.

The group-wide HR partner model – established in 2002 – with HR professionals being physically and organizationally part of the focal line organization may over time contribute to closer relationships between HR professionals and employees. As pointed out by a manager in the HR partner organization:

If people can come to me to openly discuss their problems, this will help me do a better job in helping management to deal with the situation.

Whether or not this actually materializes, will depend not only on the initiatives and the competencies of the HR partners, but perhaps even more on the role expectations communicated by line managers and employees.

HR AS 'STRATEGIC PARTNER'

The 'strategic partner' role focuses on the alignment of HR strategies and practices with business strategy (Ulrich, 1997). Whereas the organizational representation of the HR function in the hierarchy of the corporation can be viewed as an indicator of its corporate status and its possibility to participate in decision-making in formal meetings, a more valid indicator of its real strategic impact is the extent to which the function influences the outcome of strategic decision-making (Purcell, 2001). Previous research indicates that the HR function, rather than being centrally involved in strategy formation, is most often called upon to advise on the people issues after the strategies have been formulated (Truss et al., 1997).

As mentioned earlier, the HR function did not have a permanent 'seat at the table' in Nordea's Group Management. Up till late 2001 there was a direct reporting line between the head of Group HR and the CEO of Nordea, but according to interviews with both of them, corporate strategy-making took place without much influence from the HR unit, and few issues related with human resources were discussed in depth within the executive management group.

However, in May 2001, Nordea's CEO and a senior HR manager met with Nokia's top HR executive, a meeting that was to influence the attitude towards HR within Nordea's top management:

[It was then] understood how much time Nokia's CEO and HR executive spend on every top manager, what they did, where they should be next time, what the whole pool of potential top managers is, and what kind of feedback each person gets.

From being a function that was largely neglected by Nordea's corporate top management, HR now became a factor that had to be dealt with. During the latter half of 2001 and continuing during 2002, extensive efforts were made within the HR function with the help of consultants to agree on the distribution of responsibilities within the HR organization and to develop objectives, strategies, policies and procedures. But although the HR function gradually received some more attention from top management, HR professionals were still not intimately involved in corporate strategy discussions. With the proposal of a new stock option program for senior executives as the main exception and top management's approval of a company-wide management training program as another issue, it also seems as if the group executive management board rarely discussed issues that were specifically related to the HR implications of the corporate strategies.

The establishment and gradual roll-out of a group-wide HR partner concept in 2002 was intended to enhance the strategic contributions of HR professionals within each business area/unit. Interviews conducted with line managers by the consulting firm in 2001 had revealed that the line managers felt a strong need of HR services that were directly adapted toward the particular needs of each business area. As a business area manager expressed it in the fall of 2001:

I have a growth strategy, we want to be four times the size we have today in order to be one of the biggest in Europe. Therefore I need a HR strategy in all areas: recruitment, training, incentives etc.... but I cannot get this kind of service from the four country based HR organizations. They can hardly deliver me transparent information about my employees' salaries ... Therefore it is urgent to develop a Nordic HR organization in the Nordic bank.

In line with consultants' suggestions and reflecting the practice in many other corporations, HR professionals were now to be 'hired and fired' by the line organization. Each of the three business areas, Retail Banking, Asset Management and Life, and Corporate and Institutional Banking, now had a Head of HR, who was, however, typically excluded from membership in the top management group of the business area he or she was in charge of. Most business areas had HR partners responsible for each business unit within the business area. For example, the business area Asset Management and Life would consistently employ HR partners that were responsible for each of the business units: Investment Management, Investment Funds, Long-Term Savings and Life, Nordic Private Banking, European Private Banking, and Life and Pensions. In most instances, except in retail banking, the HR partner function was organized in cross-national teams, typically with one HR partner appointed country responsible but also with a responsibility for either some function within HR (e.g. competence assessment and development) or a sub-unit within the larger business area/unit.

Quo vadis HR?

The organizational change of the HR department seemed to lead to other changes fairly quickly. First, it led to more interaction across borders within the focal business unit rather than domestically across business units. Second, according to line managers, HR professionals who had previously been employed by the central HR organization gradually shifted focus and began: *"to understand what we [in the line organization] had been fighting for all these years"*.

The Heads of HR in the different business areas only had a 'dotted line' to the Group Head of HR and only participated in formal meetings with him four times a year. Therefore, they developed a stronger loyalty and commitment towards their own business area. However, this was done at the expense of potentially dynamic interaction within a board of HR directors joined in dealing with strategic HR tasks at the corporate level.

Third, according to a HR manager in one of the business areas, the reorganization had the implication that it had become less feasible for top management just to launch an initiative or present a new HR tool such as a standard for performance appraisal interviews and make it mandatory for all business areas and units:

If associating the HR function with the different areas is to be taken seriously, initiatives must grow from the bottom. And when you realize that there are some issues where it is reasonable to harmonize and coordinate in order to be able to offer something to the whole company, you can of course do it. But with this reorganization of the HR function top management cannot continue managing HR issues in a top-down process.

As a consequence, the adaptation and contribution of the HR function to the performance of the focal business unit was more emphasized, and a more reserved attitude emerged within the HR partner organization towards corporate policies, standard procedures and joint processes developed in the Group HR centre:

We run the risk – and I have already experienced this – that for example common strategies and tools are developed in relation to recruitment, but there are no customers to buy them… But out of necessity recruitment is carried out in different ways in retail banking and asset management, and therefore we must have the initiative and express a demand for specific tools and administrative services which the Group HR center afterwards can develop and perhaps coordinate at a group level.

Some Heads of HR in the different business areas also voiced skepticism concerning the added value of a corporate management development program organized by the Group HR Centre:

that would focus too much on general leadership rather than on the business skills needed in our unit.

However, it is still too early to tell whether the reorganization of the HR department will lead to a HR partner function exerting more influence on strategy making and implementation both at business area and unit levels. Some interviewees at least mentioned that it was also a challenge to ensure that the HR partners currently employed had the competencies needed to fulfill a more strategic role:

Looking at my own HR organization, I believe I will have to replace several people who don't have the necessary competencies and recruit new persons from the outside instead. And then furthermore we will have to develop those we have already employed.

Another future challenge will be to engage HR managers from business areas and units in a dialogue concerning the kinds of tool that on the one hand serve to integrate personnel and business practices across units, and on the other hand are sufficiently adaptable to the needs of each unit. Networking and exchange of experiences across units are likely to be important in the processes of both clarifying the roles to be played by HR professionals at different organizational levels and further developing the way in which strategic HRM issues are handled throughout the corporation.

HR AS 'CHANGE AGENT'

The second strategic role in Ulrich's (1997) conceptual model is that of the HR function as a change agent. Based on normative literature, this role could be expected to be particularly important in integrating cultures in the merged corporation during the post-merger period. However, the picture emerging from the interviews is that the HR organization had limited influence on the transformation and integration process following directly after the mergers and acquisitions in 2000.

Overall, socio-cultural issues were given little attention in the integration process following the merger between MeritaNordbanken and Unidanmark and, later, the acquisition of CBK. As described in detail in the chapter 7 on socio-cultural integration management, the corporate HR function played only a secondary role in the cultural integration process which was driven forward primarily by Nordea's Identity and Communications department (GIC). Top management's lack of expectations vis-à-vis the HR department probably made it difficult for the people responsible for HR – in spite of the fact that the HR function in the MeritaNordbanken had played an active role in the cultural integration process – to take center stage. Additionally, the fact that a cross-border HR department was not established until January 2002 may also have shifted influence in favor of the GIC. Consequently, in the initial phase of the integration process, corporate communications and branding was emphasized at the expense of a stronger HR focus on internal change management.

Compared with the interviews that we did in 2001, our interviews conducted during the summer and fall of 2002 revealed a more positive perception among HR managers of the two strategic roles played by the HR function. However, in terms of Ulrich's model of the different roles played by the HR organization, the focus of Nordea's HR function still seems to be more on HRM processes than on people issues.

DISCUSSION AND CONCLUSIONS

In this chapter we have examined the roles of the HR function in the processes following the merger between MeritaNordbanken and Unidanmark and the acquisition of CBK up to the summer of 2002. In this two-year period, the HR organization went through considerable changes. Especially in the initial post-merger period, the emphasis was clearly on integrating, rationalizing and developing the administrative HRM policies and procedures, while there is little evidence of the HR function playing roles as employee champions, strategic partners or change agents. Based on our analysis we suggest that the organizational roles played by the HR function influence how the workforce is, in fact, managed in cross-border mergers. Top management's low expectations as regards the strategic contributions of the HR function seem to have contributed to the limited attention given to people management and cultural change issues in the integration process.

A number of factors appear to have influenced the largely non-strategic roles played by the HR function. First, from the initial merger negotiations processes onwards there is little evidence of top management having high expectations to any strategic contribution of the HR function. As a consequence, the HR function was not invited to play any central role in the post-merger integration process.

Second, it was clearly difficult to identify one way in which to organize the HR function and its work in order to satisfy the demands and expectations both of different cross-border business areas and business units, and the more country based retail banks. The national HR organizations and HRM systems in place before the quadruple cross-border merger had largely been developed so as to support retail banking. As there were limited changes in the operations of retail banking in 2000-01, there was still a reasonable fit between the national HR systems and the local needs of this business area. According to one HR manager

[It] was completely natural since the majority of the personnel were in the retail banks. As [the retail banks] were to continue to operate locally, HR could also continue to be handled domestically.

However, the establishment of cross-border organizations in other business areas led to a misfit between the expectations and needs of these areas and the services offered by the national, retail-oriented HR organizations. Early experiences with establishing an HR partner organization in 2002 indicate that the reorganization of the HR function may lead to the HR function getting a more significant strategic role, at least at the individual business area and/or business unit level. However, a too strong pendulum swing towards a business area/unit focus may in the long term create a risk of failed synergies across business areas and units.

Third, the merger situation itself seems – at least during the initial phase of post-merger integration – to have diverted the attention of the HR managers from the function's potential contribution to the strategic development of the rest of the organization to decisions concerning how to organize their own work. There were disagreements on how to develop the function, and there were a large number of decisions that had to be taken concerning how to deal with the transactional elements of HRM in the new cross-border HR organization. The attention of Nordea's top management also appears to have been more focused on the financial outcomes of the integration process than on how to deal with people management, including the input and activities of the HR function. Previous research on merger processes provides evidence that this often tends to be the case (Jemison and Sitkin, 1986). Furthermore, the emphasis on reaping integration benefits in terms of cost reductions meant that it was difficult to obtain support for investments in IT-based HRM systems needed for the cross-border HR organization.

Fourth, when more significant changes were initiated in the HR organization in 2001 and further developed during 2002, models were sought from the outside. External business consultants played a key role in developing a new model for the HR organization, and examples of how to handle HR issues successfully were sought from other large multinational corporations like Nokia, IBM, Citicorp and British Telecom. This benchmarking exercise also appears to have played an important role in convincing both the Head of Group Staffs and the Group Executive Management about the need to invest considerably in IT as support for the corporate HR system. At the same time, HR managers held to the idea that a decentralized 'HR Partner model' was the "right way" to organize HR support to add value in the business areas and units.

This piece of research has been an attempt at exploring and analyzing the organizational roles played by the HR function during the post-merger period. The empirical analysis in this chapter has primarily been based on interviews with HR managers, while few of the line managers interviewed directly commented on how they perceived the HR function. Future research should collect empirical material from members playing different HR roles within the HR department, but also from top managers, line managers and other employees. The Nordea case indicates that the communication of role expectations both to and from the HR function may be particularly important in clarifying the roles this function is to play in the post-merger process. Additional research is clearly needed both on the enablers and constraints of the organizational roles played by the HR function, and on how these roles relate with how people are managed in large-scale cross-border mergers.

REFERENCES

BARNEY, J. and WRIGHT, P.W. (1998). 'On becoming a strategic partner: the role of human resources in gaining competitive advantage'. *Human Resource Management*, 37, 31-46.

BERGLUND, J. (2002) *De otillräckliga: En studie av personalspecialisternas kamp för erkännande och status*. Stockholm: EFI. Doktorsavhandling.

BUONO, A.F. and BOWDITCH, J.L. (1989). *The Human Side of Mergers and Acquisitions*. San Francisco: Jossey-Bass.

CARTWRIGHT, S. and COOPER, C.L. (1992). *Mergers and Acquisitions: The Human Factor*. Oxford: Butterworth-Heinemann Ltd.

DiMAGGIO, P. and POWELL, W. (1983). 'The iron cage revisited: institutional isomorphism and collective rationality in organizational fields'. *American Sociological Review*, 48, 147-160.

EVANS, P., PUCIK, V. and BARSOUX, J.-L. (2002). *The Global Challenge: Frameworks for International Human Resource Management*. Boston: McGraw-Hill.

FERRIS, G.R. and JUDGE, T.A. (1991). 'Personnel/Human Resources Management: A Political Influence Perspective'. *Journal of Management*, 17, 447-488.

FLOOD, P. (1998). 'Is HRM dead? What will happen to HRM when traditional methods are gone?' In P. Sparrow and Marchinton, M. (Eds.). *Human Resource Management: The New Agenda*. London: FT Pitman.

GALANG, M.C. and FERRIS, G.R. (1997). 'Human Resource Department Power and Influence through Symbolic Action'. *Human Relations*, 50, 1403-1426.

HOPE-HAILEY, V., GRATTON, L., MCGOVERN, P., STILES, P. and TRUSS, C. (1997). 'A chameleon function? HRM in the 1990s'. *Human Resource Management Journal*, 7(3), 5-18.

JEMISON, D.B. and SITKIN, S.B. (1986). 'Corporate Acquisitions: A Process Perspective'. *Academy of Management Review*, 11, 145-163.

KATZ, D. and KAHN, R.L. (1978). *The social psychology of organizations*. New York: John Wiley. Second edition.

LEGGE, K. (1989). 'Human resource management: A critical analysis'. In J. Storey (ed.). *New Perspectives in Human Resource Management*. London: Routledge.

PFEFFER, J. (1994). *Competitive Advantage Through People: Unleashing the Power of the Workforce*. Boston: Harvard Business School Press.

PURCELL, J. (2001). 'The meaning of strategy in human resource management'. In J. Storey (ed.): *Human Resource Management: A Critical Agenda*. London: Thomson Learning.

SCHULER, R. S. (1990). 'Repositioning the human resource function; Transformation or demise. *Academy of Management Executive*, 4(3), 49-60.

SCHULER, R. S. and JACKSON, S. (2001). 'HR Issues and Activities in Mergers and Acquisitions'. *European Journal Management*, 19, 239-253.

SISSON, K. (2001). 'Human resource management and the personnel function: a case of partial impact?' In J. Storey (Ed.). *Human Resource Management: A Critical Agenda.* London: Thomson Learning.

STAHL, G.K., EVANS, P.E., PUCIK, V. and MENDENHALL, M. (2002). 'Human resource management in cross-border mergers and acquisitions'. In A.-W- Harzing and J. van Ruysseveldt (Eds.). *International Human Resource Management: An Integrated Approach.* London: Sage.

STOREY, J. (1995). 'Human resource management: Still marching on, or marching out?' In J. Storey (ed.). *Human Resource Management: A Critical Text.* London: International Thomson Business Press.

SÄNTTI, R. (2001). *How cultures interact in an international merger: Case MeritaNordbanken.* Tampere: University of Tampere. Doctoral thesis.

TRUSS, C., GRATTON, L., HOPE-HAILEY, V., STILES, P. and ZALESKA, J. (2002). 'Paying the piper: Choice and constraint in change of HR functional roles'. *Human Resource Management Journal,* 12, 39-63.

TYSON, S. (1995). *Human resource strategy.* London: Pitman.

TSUI, A. (1984). 'A multiple constituency framework of managerial reputational effectiveness'. In J. Hunt, C. Hoskin, C. Schriesheim and R. Stewart (eds.). *Leadership.* New York: Pergamon.

ULRICH, D. (1997). *Human Resource Champions: The Next Agenda for Adding Value and Delivering Results.* Boston: Harvard Business School Press.

WRIGHT, P.W. and MCMAHAN, G.C. (1992). 'Theoretical Perspectives for Strategic Human Resource Management'. *Journal of Management Studies,* 18, 295-320.

CHAPTER 9

TRAPPED IN THE PAST OR MAKING USE OF EXPERIENCE?

ON LEARNING IN POST-MERGER INTEGRATION

Ingmar Björkman, Janne Tienari & Eero Vaara

How does previous merger experience influence subsequent merger processes? Apparently, the lessons learnt are likely to guide decisions concerning the new merger integration process and they may, if adequately applied, also result in improved performance. However, past learning experiences do not always have positive effects in another context. This is often the case in cross-border settings where the social and cultural contexts tend to change significantly when companies move from one merger to another.

Studying learning in mergers and acquisitions has usually meant analyses of how previous experiences affect the performance of subsequent mergers or acquisitions in large samples of cases (Haleblian and Finkelstein, 1999; Finkelstein and Halablian, 2002; Hayward, 2002). These have frequently resulted in relatively simplistic models concerning organizational learning and its management.

However, few studies have examined how previous experiences influence concrete organizational decisions on how to integrate organizations in specific merger or acquisition cases (Leroy and Ramanantsoa, 1997). This is a severe deficiency because it tends to undermine the inherent complexities in organizational learning processes.

Therefore, we focus in this chapter on learning around socio-cultural integration when organizations move from one cross-border merger to another. We concentrate on the problems and challenges related to making sense and use of previous experiences when dealing with socio-cultural integration. For this purpose, we focus on four ideas that played a major role in the Merita-Nordbanken and MeritaNordbanken-Unidanmark mergers. These are: (1) working on shared corporate visions as a means to create commitment, (2) the idea of virtual headquarters as a sign of balance of power, (3) the need to outline a corporate language policy, and (4) the need for cultural awareness programs.

In these contexts, we describe the emerging learning experiences in the MeritaNordbanken merger, consider their effects on new actions when MeritaNordbanken merged with Unidanmark, and outline the subsequent new interpretations of success/failure. In our analysis, we point out that such learning is inherently context-specific, that it often involves ambiguity, and that the significance attributed to specific learning experiences depends on the dominant coalition. Based on this reflection, we offer suggestions as to how to avoid the most simplistic ideas about learning but foster effective exploitation of past experiences in cross-border mergers.

ON ORGANIZATIONAL LEARNING

Many learning theorists characterize organizations as systems that adapt to interpretations of the relationship between previous action and their effects (Cyert and March, 1963; Levitt and March, 1988). According to this organizational learning perspective, adopted in this chapter, organization members engage in interpretations of the success/failure of actions, routines, procedures and strategies. If central organization members – sometimes referred to as the 'dominant coalition' (Duncan and Weiss, 1979) – interpret a certain historical action as having been successful, these insights are coded in cognitive structures that mirror the causal relationship that has been inferred. Hence, interpretations shared among top managers of what has constituted successful versus unsuccessful actions are likely to influence decision-making and to be translated into strategies, processes, procedures and structures (Levitt and March, 1998; Crossan, Lane and White, 1999). In this study, we analyze decisions made by top management on how to integrate the merging organizations; hence, in the empirical part of the chapter we focus on examples of the role of individual and collective learning in integration decision-making.

Although organizations tend to learn from experience, researchers have identified a number of factors influencing the inferences that are drawn from history. First, a range of *socio-psychological factors* influence the inferences that managers make based on history. For instance, managers' commitment to a certain strategy or procedure makes it difficult for them not to retain the existing course of action, especially if their support to current activities has been stated publicly (Staw, McKechnie and Puffer, 1983). The ambiguity about cause-effect relationships that often exists may mean that managers misread information and engage in superstitious learning (March and Olsen, 1976). It has also been shown that managers often attribute good organizational performance to their own actions, further strengthening existing routines and strategies (Fiske and Taylor, 1991). In short, existing cognitive structures and organizational strategies are likely to exhibit some degree of inertia.

Second, interpretations of success or failure are *social constructions*. In this perspective, there is a need for members of the top management group to perceive and present the outcome of their own previous actions as successful to both themselves and others so as to protect their self-esteem and their own identity as successful professionals. In fact, within the context of mergers and acquisitions it has been shown that managers often reframe and reinterpret as successes what had previously been considered failures (Vaara, 2002). This can, for example, be done by shifting measures of success from a focus on profitability or synergy to one of socio-cultural integration of the two units.

Third, learning depends on the *focus of attention* of the learners (Cyert and March, 1963; Levinthal and March, 1993). Hence, depending on the kind of issues that the top management team focuses on in the organization and its environment, different learning outcomes result. For example, if top managers focus on the competitive environment of the firm, the management group is more likely to develop insightful interpretations of the effects of a merger on the competitive situation of the merged firm than to consider the effects of the socio-cultural integration process on organizational performance. In this case, managers are unlikely to critically examine whether or not previous experience from socio-cultural integration also might work under other conditions.

Fourth, the question of *who learns* is central to the learning perspective. Not only do different groups in the firm have access to different information and focus on different issues and, therefore, tend to learn about different things. They may also evaluate the outcome of a certain action differently and have different interpretations of the factors that led to the outcome. For example, new managers are more likely to define previous outcomes more negatively than their predecessors (Hedberg, 1981). Further, the learning that takes place within the management group of one organizational unit does not necessarily impact the activities of others (Levitt and March, 1988). Hence, the vertical and hierarchical structure of the organization influences the implementation of the learning experience.

Fifth, as pointed out by Huber (1991), *political behavior* may cause problems in organizations. Politicking tends to be associated with suppression and distortion of information. In the case of organizational actors deliberately manipulating the information that constitutes the basis for the interpretation of success versus failure, the outcome of the learning process is distorted accordingly. Organizational actors who pursue their own individual interests are also likely to be selective in terms of the learning points that they share with others in the organization.

Finally, organizational learning can be said to depend on the *memory* of the organization (Levitt and March, 1988; Walsh and Ungson, 1991). Learning at a certain point in time may not be available for retrieval at a later stage. Although the inferences that managers draw from history may be codified and recorded in written manuals, procedures, and reports, these may not be widely known.

207

Learning to merge

Consequently, they are not sought and retrieved by organization members at later moments. Retrieving the outcome of learning tends to be even less likely when the 'organizational memory' mainly resides with the memory of individuals. Reorganizations and turnover of personnel may further aggravate the availability of historical insights about what works and what does not.

Previous research taking a learning perspective on mergers and acquisitions has mostly examined the statistical relationship between (quantitative measures of) the organization's merger or acquisition experience and the performance of the focal merger or acquisition (Haleblian and Finkelstein, 1999; Finkelstein and Haleblian, 2002; Hayward, 2002). These studies have shown that experience does not necessarily lead to improvements in performance. For instance, the insights gained from one merger may be applied in a subsequent merger that appears superficially similar but where the differences are big enough to make the lessons from the first merger wrong or even dangerous (Finkelstein and Haleblian, 2002). There is also research on the learning that takes place in the processes of merging two companies pointing to the complex interrelationships between cognitive and behavioral factors in decision-making, but in-depth analyses of specific cases are rare (Leroy and Ramanantsoa, 1997).

Of the many areas of post-merger or post-acquisition integration, socio-cultural integration arguably represents a particularly cumbersome challenge. As argued in the different chapters of this book, the phenomena around socio-cultural integration are context-specific, ambiguous and difficult to control by management. In fact, even the conceptualization of what constitutes socio-cultural integration is difficult, and outlining key managerial activities and tasks in this context is not at all straightforward. Furthermore, agreeing upon what are the most appropriate and effective integration strategies is likely to be difficult in organizations where the actors, due to their different backgrounds, positions, roles and identities, are likely to look at issues in different ways.

This means that learning concerning socio-cultural integration is likely to involve specifically complicated social processes. To outline some of the key problematics of these processes, we now turn to the Nordea case.

LEARNING TO MERGE: LESSONS FROM THE MAKING OF NORDEA

The Nordea case is a particularly fruitful setting for an analysis of organizational learning around socio-cultural integration. This is because the organization has been created through a series of cross-national mergers or acquisitions within a relatively short time period, allowing one to examine emerging learning experiences and their impact on subsequent actions. Furthermore, as illustrated in the previous chapters of this book, socio-cultural integration has been seen as a specifically important managerial challenge in the different merger processes, providing us with plenty of examples of more or less successful decisions, strategies and practices in this area.

We decided to focus on the learning experiences gathered in the merger between Merita and Nordbanken (1997) and to then examine their impact on subsequent decisions in the merger between MeritaNordbanken and Unidanmark (2000). For this purpose, we examined our extensive interview material by focusing on the decision-making processes around socio-cultural integration.[1] However, we could also draw from our previous work on this case and the material gathered in these earlier analyses (Vaara, Tienari and Säntti, 2003; Vaara et al., 2001). This eventually led us to focus on four ideas that were extensively dealt with both in the Merita-Nordbanken and MeritaNordbanken-Unidanmark mergers. We chose to concentrate on these ideas because they are clearly articulated learning experiences derived from the Merita-Nordbanken merger and because they provide us with different kinds of examples of the complexities surrounding organizational learning.

There are two methodological points that should be noted here. First, what we were essentially doing was to try to reconstruct organizational decision-making processes and examine the role of learning experiences in these processes. This was a very difficult task, especially when dealing with phenomena that are not easy to define and by their very nature ambiguous. This meant that especially for the processes that had taken place some time ago, we were unavoidably dealing with retrospective constructions. What helped in this process was the material and knowledge gathered elsewhere.

Second, while our focus on the Merita-Nordbanken merger is justified from the perspective that this was the first cross-border merger case and thus the 'original' source of cross-border merger experiences, this meant that we were probably not paying 'adequate' attention on experiences gathered elsewhere. This is a problematic limitation especially since all of us three authors are Finnish and thus

---

[1] In this context, we want to emphasize that we are not concentrating on learning concerning specific methods of carrying out, for example, merger negotiations nor the development of such skills. In these respects, the Nordea case is full of excellent examples of personal and social learning as well as less successful experiences.

inclined to emphasize the experiences of the Finns. However, it should be stressed that we were not trying to reconstruct one 'truth' around these complex decision-making and learning processes, but rather aimed at uncovering and illustrating complexities that are often likely to characterize organizational learning in cross-border merger settings.

SHARED CORPORATE VISION

One of the key questions in socio-cultural integration is to be able to tackle challenges related to cultural confrontation as early as possible. However, this is often not the case as planning and negotiation processes tend to be dominated by strategic and financial considerations. Furthermore, division of responsibilities and activity segmentation often imply that specific cultural projects are not initiated by the people behind the strategic plans and given special attention by top management (e.g. Jemison and Sitkin, 1986). In this respect, our case is an interesting exception. In fact, creating a shared corporate vision was one of the key issues that top management focused on both in the Merita-Nordbanken and MNB-Unidanmark mergers.

Apparently, key representatives of Nordbanken had focused on outlining a shared corporate vision already in their previous domestic acquisition of Gota Bank in 1993. In particular, top managers had started acquisition negotiations with a focus on a joint vision statement to ensure that the expectations of both parties would fit together. This vision statement later then also provided the basis for the actual integration of the new organization. A Swedish top manager who played a central role in this process stressed the positive experience of this exercise as follows: *"If there is something that I've learnt it is that it is much more important to share a vision for the bank than to mechanistically estimate the synergy savings"*. It seems that the Finnish managers coming from Merita had similar kinds of ideas concerning the importance of focusing attention on a joint future as a means to avoid cultural confrontation and the politicization of specific questions.

In any case, working on a shared corporate vision was a key managerial objective in the Merita-Nordbanken merger. When the negotiations started, the representatives of Nordbanken and Merita deliberately focused on outlining a positive but realistic vision for the new bank. Only after that did they turn to those questions that are usually seen as critical in merger negotiations such as the valuation of the companies or distribution of top management positions. This first shared vision provided the preliminary guidelines for future decisions to be made. However, for the new top management of Merita-Nordbanken, working on shared future visions also served as an overall method in solving problems in the following organizational change processes. In general, this idea was seen as a key learning experience by the top managers of MeritaNordbanken. As a Finnish executive put it:

What was important in this process, and what I then learnt and used later, was not at all to discuss critical issues concerning the merger deal itself, but rather, through the business concept, [to discuss] our vision concerning the development of the industry and the business concept of the new, merged bank.

Not particularly surprising in view of the positive experiences of the Swedish and Finnish executives, they insisted on starting the negotiations between MeritaNordbanken and Unidanmark in a similar way. *"We used the same mode"l*, put one representative of MeritaNordbanken it bluntly. Apparently, the Danish representatives had nothing against this, as they had themselves seen the importance of clear-cut corporate messages in their previous domestic merger between Unibank and Tryg-Baltica in 1999.

The discussions between these two parties resulted in a document providing the basis for the operations of the organization after the merger. When the top managers of MeritaNordbanken and Unidanmark announced their decision to merge in March 2000, they also presented a revised version of the joint document containing a brief statement of the mission, the vision and the overall values for the new organization. This corporate statement was presented to the public as well as to the employees of the merging companies. Work on this corporate vision continued also after the announcement of the merger; for example, revised versions of the corporate statement were drafted in the following year. The extensive corporate value programs could also be seen as logical follow-up steps in this process (see chapter 7).

On the whole, the top managers saw this focus on shared visions as 'the right approach' to avoid unnecessary cultural confrontation and organizational politics often characterizing such international settings. In fact, the idea of starting any negotiations with a future vision has thereafter been presented as a key learning experience in various internal and external forums by the senior managers of the new banking group.

However, on a more critical note, many people speculated that this focus on corporate statements made the corporate management rely too much on this method as a means of solving problems related to cultural confrontation. In this context, especially the lack of active dialogue with organizational members was often criticized and seen as undermining the value of these corporate visions (see chapter 7). This success with the corporate visions was apparently also one reason behind the decision not to engage in specific cultural training programs – an issue that we will return to later.

VIRTUAL HEADQUARTERS

Comparisons between the two merger parties regarding such issues as ownership, distribution of managerial positions, location of headquarters, and – in international settings – choice of the corporate language appear to be inherent parts of socio-cultural integration. These questions obviously involve concrete decisions, but it is the symbolic aspects that are crucial in terms of understanding internal divisions and cultural confrontation. The Nordea case illustrates particularly well challenges related to headquarter location and the choice of the corporate language.

In the negotiations concerning the Merita-Nordbanken merger, it soon became apparent that this would have to be perceived as a 'merger of equals'; otherwise it would be very difficult to accept the merger in Finland and Sweden. This posed specific challenges as to the division of ownership and creation of balance of power within the post-merger organization (see also chapter 5). The location of headquarters was a particularly difficult issue. However, the negotiators came up with an innovative decision to place the official domicile of the firm in Helsinki (Finland) but to move the actual corporate management headquarters to Stockholm (Sweden). The management of MeritaNordbanken noticed quickly that the location of headquarters was a sensitive issue. Instead of concentrating top management work in one location, top managers were to spend time both in Sweden and Finland. This was viewed as symbolically important. The extensive travels by executives were also intended at improving the personal relationships between Swedes and Finns. Although these efforts did not prevent the relationships between the Swedish and Finnish parts of the organization to be strenuous at times, the common interpretation among top management was that the decisions concerning headquarters and mobile managers had been correct.

When MeritaNordbanken and Unidanmark merged, the issue of headquarter location was also on the table. Apparently strongly influenced by the positive experiences gathered in MeritaNordbanken, it was decided that the new company would have no formal headquarters. Instead, there would be a 'virtual headquarters' – a term later frequently used to denote this innovative idea. Top managers would retain their offices in their home country organizations but travel extensively in all the Nordic countries. Group executive meetings were to take place once a week either in Denmark (Copenhagen), Finland (Helsinki), Sweden (Stockholm) or later Norway (Oslo). This was a choice that effectively promoted the idea of equality between the different country organizations and nationalities.

However, after some time had elapsed, the problems of this approach became apparent. The difficulties that had been seen as minor in the Merita-Nordbanken merger grew into severe problems due to the increased size, geographical dispersion and larger operational scope of the new pan-Nordic organization. The absence of a geographical center in the Nordic financial services group led to inflated travel costs and much valuable time spent traveling. In addition, the rare co-location of the top managers – with few opportunities for spontaneous informal face-to-face discussions between representatives of different nationalities – was viewed as problematic for effective decision-making. A senior manager coined the general learning experience as follows: *"What has received too little attention here is that the management does not spend enough time together"*. From an individual perspective, the constant travelling had negative effects on the 'life balance' (see chapter 11).

As a result of such experience, without making a big issue out of it, the top executive group agreed during the fall of 2001 to try to spend two days a week in Stockholm, geographically the most centrally located of the Nordic capitals. A senior manager explained this solution as follows:

> *This model that we now have (virtual headquarters) was probably chosen to prove ourselves, our colleagues, or the reporters of Helsingin Sanomat (the leading daily newspaper in Finland) that this is a Nordic bank. But it cannot function like that, it has to establish one headquarters, and Stockholm is the only option.*

LANGUAGE POLICY

At the last stretch of the negotiations between Merita and Nordbanken, there were several key issues on the table concerning, for example, positions in the board of directors and executive management. The question of the language of the top management of the new bank was also discussed, though not seen as particularly important at the time. Somewhat ironically, it was the Finn Vesa Vainio, the CEO of Merita, who suggested that the new top management would use Swedish. The reasons for this were apparently pragmatic; the Swedes had Swedish as their mother tongue and the entire Finnish top management team spoke Swedish, most fluently. As Swedish is the second official language of Finland, all Finnish employees supposedly knew at least some Swedish. This decision was later described as something that just *"happened by accident"*, as one Finnish negotiator put it.

The corporate representatives of the new post-merger organization made public their decision to introduce Swedish as the working language of the corporate management of MeritaNordbanken. This policy became a major issue of debate within the new organization and attracted considerable media coverage, especially in Finland (see Risberg, Tienari and Vaara, 2003). As a result, corporate management had to justify the decision made, for example, by referring to pragmatic needs, to the proficiency of the Finns in Swedish, and to the inadequate English skills of Nordbanken (and Merita) staff. Later, it was also specified that this language policy would apply only in areas where it was meaningful, that is, in top management meetings and those business operations where interaction between Finns and Swedes was the liveliest.

The choice of Swedish as corporate language created various internal problems on the Finnish side of the organization. For example, many Finnish managers and members of staff felt handicapped by their limited skills in Swedish. They perceived a power imbalance and felt inferior in their social interaction within the bank. The language choice also created a sense of professional incompetence and was psychologically strenuous for some. For example, top Finnish experts had frequently considerable difficulty in communicating their views and expertise in meetings where Swedish was used. It has also been speculated that the choice of Swedish as the working language was a reason for several key individuals leaving the Finnish part of

MeritaNordbanken. At a symbolic level, on the Finnish side, the choice also involved a reconstruction of a history-laden Finnish-Swedish confrontation. In fact, not only the people within the bank but also the Finnish media framed this issue as (yet another) example of Swedish dominance, linked with the historical colonial relationship between the two nations.

Interestingly, it was not an issue frequently discussed in Sweden. In fact, it was a 'no issue' for many Swedes who could continue speaking Swedish as before the merger and for whom the symbolic aspects of this language choice were not obvious. In this context, it should be noted that while the Finnish media focused on this issue, this was a very minor question in the Swedish media (see Risberg, Tienari and Vaara, 2003).

Even after some time had elapsed, some key decision makers stuck to the rationale of the initial decision and justified the decisions, for example, in the interviews, as in the following:

Yes, it is important to note that it (Swedish) was intended as the language for the management and the board of directors. When this caused discussion I said that just go ahead and speak any language that all the people around the table understand. It doesn't matter as long as people understand each other and we speak the language of the customer, if we just can.

However, most Finnish and Swedish managers, including the members of the top executive management, saw the initial decision as a mistake, as the following reflections of two key persons illustrate:

One can see this language issue as a strategic mistake, which was made a bit carelessly at some point in the merger negotiations.

I'd say it [the choice of Swedish] was a mistake. This might be a bit difficult for the Swedes to admit. For us [Finns], it is perhaps a little easier.

When the merger of MeritaNordbanken and Unidanmark was planned, the top managers had several choices as to how to handle language policy issues. In the Nordic context, 'Scandinavian' – a mixture of Swedish, Danish and Norwegian – is widely used. English has, however, become an increasingly dominating language in most Nordic corporations, not only to be used externally but also internally.

In this situation, the previous problematic experiences in MeritaNordbanken had, according to many interviewees, a fundamental impact on the language policy issue – not only on the eventual choice of English but also on the careful formulation of an explicit language policy.[2] Especially the Finnish interviewees could in this context talk about "correcting a mistake." According to the language policy, English would become the new corporate language, but in all locations one would be encouraged to use the language preferred by the customers.

Within the merged organizations, the explicit choice of English as the corporate language was widely interpreted as the right one. Among most Finns, the change from Swedish to English as working language was particularly welcomed. Almost all of the internal corporate communication is now carried out in English. Customers continue to be served in their own language in the four countries but most meetings

---

[2] English became the language for the board, executive management teams and some of the wholesale banking units (working internationally where the language is English) whereas local languages remained the primary means of communication for most employees, among whom not least Retail Banking employees.

among top management in Nordea are held in English, at least if there is a native Finnish speaker among the participants. This has created a situation where everybody in professional interactions has to use a neutral, non-native language. In everyday work-related and social interaction in the organization, however, 'Scandinavian' is still widely used. Therefore, in many concrete situations the Finns may still find themselves in inferior positions vis-à-vis native speakers.

This policy did not, however, turn out to be unproblematic. Although the choice of English solved the apparent question of inequality among the merger parties, it also meant that all organizational members had to communicate in a foreign language, creating problems in terms of clarity of expression as well as impoverished internal communication. This has made some people view the language policy decision as unsuccessful. People have also questioned whether this language policy is consistent with the distinctive 'Nordic' image of the Nordea organization.

CULTURAL AWARENESS

Awareness of cultural differences is an issue that frequently comes up in cross-border mergers (see also chapter 7). In brief, cultural awareness can reduce unexpected post-merger problems, help to map out potential areas of conflict, and to avoid misunderstanding and confusion. Explicit discussions of cultural differences might also allow people in merging organizations to raise and deal with issues concerning 'us' versus 'them' that would be too contentious to confront directly. However, discussions on cultural differences may also be counter-productive in that they may strengthen nationalism and belief in the existence of 'fundamental' cultural differences across countries and organizations as obstacles to integration. It has also been suggested that one should focus on the development of the new corporate culture instead of concentrating on the differences between the merging organizations. Our case provides an interesting illustration of how specific efforts aimed at increasing cultural awareness had a prominent role in Merita-Nordbanken but not in the following merger with Unidanmark.

On the Finnish side, there was extensive experience with cultural training already before the Merita-Nordbanken merger. The domestic merger between Kansallis and the Union Bank of Finland in 1995 had involved a cultural training program where hundreds of managers and employees were brought together to discuss differences between the merging organizations and challenges in the integration of the banks (see Tienari, 2000). In the Merita-Nordbanken merger, based on their previous successful experience, it was the Finns in particular who pushed for cultural training (see Säntti, 2001).

Key parts of this cultural training were numerous cultural seminars run by the Human Resource Development unit in MeritaNordbanken. These concentrated on cultural differences between Swedes and Finns, and Nordbanken and Merita. Approximately 330 managers and specialists took part in these seminars. The participants were encouraged to identify ways in which to develop cooperation in the new organization. Within MeritaNordbanken, the seminars were generally viewed as useful and interesting. It was seen as specifically important to acknowledge and openly discuss the historical and cultural background of the merger parties and to develop suggestions concerning how to further develop the organization. On a more critical note, some experienced the seminars to be somewhat detached from their daily work.

The domestic Danish merger involving Unibank and Tryg-Baltica in 1999 was in many ways different. The merger involved very limited integration of the actual operations of the banking and insurance parts of the merged organization. The need for specific socio-cultural training programs was thus not obvious. Instead, the corporate management of the merged company relied extensively on communicating the strategy and values of the merger company to internal and external stakeholders.

When MeritaNordbanken and Unidanmark merged, the new corporate management, led by Thorleif Krarup, the ex-CEO of Unidanmark, decided not to initiate any centrally orchestrated cultural training programs. In fact, national cultural differences were deliberately downplayed by top management, and very few organized efforts were made to address issues related to organizational or national differences in culture. One of the key reasons for this approach was apparently a conviction among the Danish members of the corporate management that one should focus on the future and not spend too much time on "irrelevant" cultural differences. The successful experiences with working on shared vision statement also made the other members of the corporate management confident that "things were moving to the right direction" (see the discussion above). It should be noted that the joint corporate statement published when the merger was announced emphasized that the group would build on common Nordic values. Dwelling on differences between the Nordic countries could thus be seen as contradicting this message.

Most interestingly, as in the previous merger between Unibank and Tryg-Baltica, the Group Identity and Communication unit was given a prominent role in socio-cultural integration initiatives (see also chapters 7 and 8). These efforts focused on the branding of Nordea. National or organizational cultural differences were not paid specific attention to in this process. The Human Resource Development unit, which had been responsible for organizing cultural seminars in MeritaNordbanken, was not actively involved. Neither Finnish nor Swedish executives, who had experience from the cultural seminars in MeritaNordbanken, had any overall responsibility for the socio-cultural integration in Nordea.

Overall, this lack of specific cultural training programs got mixed responses. Some viewed it as the right choice given other priorities. Others, especially those who had been involved in the cultural seminars organized in MeritaNordbanken, saw a need to reflect on the real or imaginary differences across the different countries and organizations. Interestingly, some managers recognized this need only after some time had elapsed since the first integration efforts. As a Danish senior manager in charge of a major unit put it: "*I have learnt that one should be more aware of the cultural differences before starting this kind of process.*"

DISCUSSION AND CONCLUSIONS

In this analysis, we have focused on the problematics in making sense and use of previous experiences in socio-cultural integration when moving from one merger to another. Our four examples serve as an illustration of the complexities surrounding organizational learning. As such, they thus cast doubt on the most simplistic ideas concerning learning or its 'management'. Based on our analysis of the four examples, we can, however, in particular point out that such learning is inherently context-specific, that it often involves ambiguity, and that the significance attributed to specific learning experiences depends on the dominant coalition.

Our case highlights the *context-specificity of learning experiences*. Due to the fact that the nature of socio-cultural integration problems and challenges vary from case to case, the learning experiences tend to be closely linked with specific cases. This means that specific learning experiences, in particular ideas as to how to manage socio-cultural integration, do not necessarily make sense in others. This does not imply that organizations and managers could not develop ideas that would be useful in changing circumstances. On the contrary, as exemplified by the positive experiences in using corporate vision statements, such learning is clearly possible. However, as illustrated by the experiences around 'virtual headquarters', ideas developed in specific contexts can and often do produce unintended consequences when applied in a new context. In this case, the complexity of the new situation created such problems that the corporate management decided to abandon this idea after some time had passed after the merger.

Our analysis also points to the *inherent ambiguity of learning experiences*. Indeed, one can in all our cases point to significant ambiguity concerning the success/failure of specific integration efforts. This was the case with the learning experiences around the corporate language policies. Both the initial decision to introduce Swedish as the corporate language for MeritaNordbanken and the subsequent decision to make English the official language could be seen in a positive or negative light depending on the person and perspective in question. The idea of investing in extensive training programs to increase cultural awareness is another example full of ambiguity.

Our analysis also illustrates how the *significance of specific learning experiences depends on the dominant coalition*. This means that whether or not a particular idea about socio-cultural integration is at all recognized or paid attention to depends on who is in charge of the specific activities. In merger settings, it is particularly notable that the representatives of the two merger parties may have quite different backgrounds and learning experiences. This was the case also here as the MeritaNordbanken people had already gone through a cross-border merger while the experience of those coming from Unidanmark came primarily from their recent domestic merger. In all our examples, except for the idea of promoting cultural awareness by specific programs, the experiences gathered in MeritaNordbanken had a fundamental effect on subsequent decisions and actions. One reason for this was that in these questions people coming from MeritaNordbanken were actively involved as key decision-makers. However, cultural training was not seen as a particularly important idea by the key decision-makers, involving in this case primarily people from Unidanmark.

In this context, one should not discard the specific ideas developed in the Merita-Nordbanken merger and the subsequent merger with Unidanmark as trivial. On the contrary, all four ideas can be seen as methods or solutions that other companies going through mergers and acquisitions could take advantage of. Focusing on shared visions as a means to create commitment, promoting balance of power by not establishing one headquarters, outlining language policies that ensure equality, and increasing cultural awareness by specific programs make great sense in many circumstances. However, as vividly illustrated by our examples, while these ideas can in many ways promote socio-cultural integration in cross-border merger settings, they can also create surprising and unintended consequences when applied in new contexts.

What are then the implications for practitioners? On the one hand, experience offers opportunities for enhanced performance in subsequent merger processes. On the other, however, there are a number of challenges involved in learning from the past. We want to emphasize three points. First, one should invest in systematic evaluation of the success of socio-cultural integration efforts. Learning requires actions, observations of outcomes and interpretations of the relationships between the two. Making someone responsible for such an evaluation and gathering of experiences would be an ideal solution to ensure that decision-makers are kept informed about the emerging problems and challenges.

Second, one should also make sure that the past experience and existing pools of knowledge are teased out and used when new strategies and actions are outlined. In this context, a particular problem is the ability to make explicit and externalize knowledge that resides in individuals and isolated groups. Even though the explicit responsibility for different integration activities would rest with particular units and individuals, it is important to collectively engage in a process of explicitly sharing and then critically discussing and articulating what worked and what did not (Zollo and Singh, 2002).

Third, and most importantly, one should take the contextual nature of socio-cultural integration seriously. The actions that led to positive outcomes in one merger process may or may not have positive performance effects in another context. Previous experience must therefore be scrutinized critically from the point of view of being able to see the differences in the previous and the new circumstances. The end result could be an enhanced understanding of what kind of integration approach works in what kind of situation. For this to materialize, it is crucial for the people involved to develop an understanding of *why* a certain approach works in a specific context.

REFERENCES

CYERT, R. D. and MARCH, J. G. (1963). *The Behavioral Theory of the Firm*. Englewood Cliffs, NJ: Prentice Hall.

CROSSAN, M., LANE, H. and WHITE, R. (1999). 'An organizational learning framework: From intuition to institution'. *Academy of Management Review*, 24, 522-537.

DUNCAN, R.B. and WEISS, A. (1979). 'Organizational learning: Implications for organizational design'. In Staw, B. (Ed.): *Research in Organizational Behavior*. Greenwich, CT: Jai Press.

FINKELSTEIN, S. and HALEBLIAN, J. (2002). 'Understanding acquisition performance: The role of transfer effects'. *Organization Science*, 13, 36-47.

FISKE, S. T. and TAYLOR, S. E. (1991). *Social cognition*. New York: Random House. 2nd edition.

HALABLIAN, J. and FINKELSTEIN, S. (1999). 'The influence of organizational acquisition performance on acquisition performance: A behavioral learning perspective'. *Administrative Science Quarterly*, 44, 29-56.

HAYWARD, M. L. A. (2002). 'When do firms learn from their acquisition experience? Evidence from 1990-1995'. *Strategic Management Journal*, 23, 21-39.

HEDBERG, B. (1981). How organizations learn and unlearn. In Nystrom, P.C. and Starbuck, W. H. (Eds.). *Handbook of organizational design*. New York: Oxford University Press.

HUBER, G. (1991). 'Organizational learning: The contributing processes and the literatures'. *Organization Science*, 2, 88-115.

JEMISON, D. and SITKIN, S. (1986). 'Corporate acquisitions: A process perspective'. *Academy of Management Review*, 11, 145-163.

LEROY, F. and RAMANANTSOA, B. (1997). 'The cognitive and behavioural dimensions of organizational learning in a merger: An empirical study'. *Journal of Management Studies*, 34, 871-894.

LEVINTHAL, D. A. and MARCH, J. G. (1993). 'The myopia of learning.' *Strategic Management Journal*, 14: 95-112.

LEVITT, B. and MARCH, J. G. (1988). 'Organizational Learning'. *Annual Review in Sociology*, 14, 319-340.

MARCH, J. G. and OLSEN, J. P. (1976). *Ambiguity and choice in organizations*. Bergen, Norway: Universitetsforlaget.

RISBERG, A., TIENARI, J. and VAARA, E. (2003). 'Making sense of a transnational merger: Media texts and the (re)construction of power relations'. *Culture and Organization*, 9 (2).

STAW, B. M., McKECHNIE, P. I. and PUFFER, S. M. (1983). 'The justification of organizational performance'. *Administrative Science Quarterly*, 28, 582-600.

SÄNTTI, R. (2001). *How cultures interact in an international merger: Case MeritaNordbanken*. Tampere: University of Tampere. Doctoral thesis.

TIENARI, J. (2000). 'Gender segregation in the making of a merger'. *Scandinavian Journal of Management*, 16, 111-144.

VAARA, E. (2002). 'On the discursive construction of success/failure in narratives of post-merger integration'. *Organization Studies*, 23, 213-250.

VAARA, E., TIENARI, J. and SÄNTTI, R. (2003). 'The international match: Metaphors as vehicles of social identity building in cross-border mergers'. *Human Relations*, 56, 419-451.

VAARA, E., TIENARI, J., MARSCHAN-PIEKKARI, R. and SÄNTTI, R. (2001). 'Does your Swedish cut the mustard? The power of corporate language in a Nordic post-merger integration'. Paper presented at the annual meeting of the Academy of International Business, Sydney, Australia, November 16-19, 2001.

WALSH, J. P. and UNGSON, G. R. (1991). 'Organizational memory'. *Academy of Management Review*, 16, 57-91.

ZOLLO, M. and WINTER, S. G. (2002). 'Deliberate learning and the evolution of dynamic capabilities'. *Organization Science*, 13, 339-351.

Chapter 10

AN UNEASY COUPLING

REFLECTIONS ON WOMEN AND MANAGEMENT IN A MERGING ORGANIZATION

Janne Tienari, Charlotte Holgersson[1], Anne-Marie Søderberg & Eero Vaara

This chapter maps out reflections on what we term the uneasy coupling between women and management. We discuss trends in organizational life in general, and take up the making of Nordea as an example to illustrate some of the gendered problematics in the contemporary 'globalizing' business. We ask the question: '*Why are there so few women in the top management of multinationals such as Nordea?*' Our findings suggest that organizational legacies, persistent perceptions of family obligations, and specific notions of managing change and transformation play a crucial role in the ways in which top management is constructed and reconstructed as a male terrain. In the context of Nordea, national stereotyping brings an additional flavour to this construction.

Mergers and acquisitions are characterized by competition between key individuals for top organizational positions. When the

---

[1] The three last authors are listed in alphabetical order.

going gets tough, the tough gets even tougher. And this usually involves men. This is, of course, not something specific to mergers. There is a substantial body of literature to show that organizations are not gender-neutral. Rather, they are dominated by men, masculinities and male ways of being. This is also the case in Nordic societies, which on a general level carry a gender egalitarian image.

GENDER MATTERS

In its Corporate Statement for 2001, Nordea declares that it *adheres to a Nordic heritage of freedom, equal opportunity, care for the environment and good citizenship*. Apart from this one reference, however, the gender equality question did not make the text in the annual report, while care for the environment and good citizenship were discussed elaborately. In the section on human resources in the report, a table shows the distribution of men and women in management. However, there are no explicit distinctions between different layers of managerial responsibility. It is evident that there are a number of women in managerial positions in Nordea. It can also be concluded from the list of senior executives – provided in the last pages of the annual report – that the top echelons of the company consist almost exclusively of men.

The lack of women in the top echelons of the organization is not something that goes unnoticed in Nordea. It is an issue that surfaces occasionally in debates in and around the bank group. It is something that is, for example, raised by owners' representatives at the shareholders' meeting. It is a topic that is also discussed in public by journalists. For example, some time ago a journalist from *Talouselämä*, the major Finnish business weekly, interviewed Vesa

Vainio, who was at the time the chairman of the board in Nordea. The present state and future plans of the company were discussed. The journalist dedicated a short section in the article to equal opportunities for the sexes. When questioned about the lack of women on the board and in the group executive management of Nordea, Vainio replied: *It is just a matter of time until the situation in the top management will become more balanced.* Women have since been appointed to the board of the bank group but not to the group executive management.

With a dominantly male senior executive management, Nordea is by no means an exception in the Nordic context. Although Denmark, Finland, Norway and Sweden have a gender egalitarian image, the labor markets in these countries are segregated. Horizontal segregation prevails as a relatively high percentage of women in the Nordic countries work in female-dominated caring and household-related occupations. Vertical segregation is also prominent as the upper echelons in organizations continue to be a particularly clear example of a male-dominated terrain, especially in the private sector (Vanhala, 1999; Statistics Sweden, 2000; Højgaard, 2002). Even in service industries where women dominate numerically – such as retailing and financial services – the top levels in organizations consist almost exclusively of men (Sundin, 2000; Tienari, 2000).

Equality is, of course, not merely about the distribution of sexes in top management. The gender equality question is also addressed more broadly in Nordea. In the Danish staff newsletter Unifact, for example, a column entitled *More women to managerial jobs* was published in August 2001. The text presents a point: *There are simply too few women who seek vacant managerial positions* in the company. The message in the text is that *we want to change this*. Accordingly, the human resources unit of the Danish retail bank has launched a process whereby human resources experts and line managers locate competent female candidates for managerial positions.

Further, it is important to note that gender equality concerns each and every organizational member. Management represents in this sense just one aspect of the issue – albeit a visible one (and one which we will concentrate on in this chapter). In Nordea, initiatives have been taken in relation to equality between the sexes. In Finland, for example, over a number of years, efforts have been made to correct historically-constituted pay differentials. Questions of the training and development of human resources have also been identified as important. Solutions for 'life balance' represent a relatively new area in this respect; flexible working time arrangements are worked on especially from a gender equality perspective. In Sweden and Denmark, mentoring programmes tailored for women have been launched. These examples are by no means exhaustive, but demonstrate the timeliness of the equality and equal opportunities issue.

Equal opportunities versus diversity management are currently the subject of intensive debate in gender studies and feminist theory. Whereas equal opportunities for the sexes has been the traditional approach for companies in the Nordic context, with particular focus on improving the position of women, the concept of diversity management, originating from Anglo-American contexts, has gained ground in recent years. Diversity management refers to policies and initiatives through which the company recognizes that their employees are not a homogeneous mass, but differ in terms of gender, race, physical ability and sexual orientation (Foldy, 2002). Today, diversity is also the subject of popular how-to-do-it books for corporate managers (see e.g. Johnson and Redmond, 2000).

For us, the crucial issue is that women are not a 'minority' at Nordea. We therefore prefer the concept of equal opportunities for women as individuals and as a group over the concept of diversity management, where equality questions become overly individualized. Whether, at one extreme, one sees equality as a question of optimal use of corporate human resources or, at the other, a fundamental principle in human existence, the message is clear. Gender matters, and no organizational decision-maker in the Nordic countries can ignore this.

GENDER IN THE NORDIC CONTEXT

In cross-national comparisons on the labor market position of women in relation to men, Nordic countries typically enjoy a gender egalitarian status. This is grounded in specific arrangements in society that enable large-scale participation of women in the labor force. For example, there has been a gradual extension of public childcare facilities to enable combinations of child rearing and participation in the labour market for both sexes. This is often perceived as an indication of gender equity. In such a 'Nordic Ideal', state policies are based on an egalitarian-individualistic, double earner family model where men and women are considered as individual breadwinners (Duncan, 1998; Åström, 1995; Melkas and Anker, 1998; Meriläinen, 2000).

Consequently, there are societal and institutional normative pressures towards equality and equal opportunities between the sexes in the Nordic countries. Specific outcomes are also clear. In contrast to societies marked by more conservative male dominance (Duncan, 1998), women have made significant advances in the labor markets of Nordic welfare society (Aaltio-Marjosola, 2001). Balancing work and family life, for example, has increasingly become a question of individual solutions for women aspiring to succeed in the public sphere of life (Meriläinen 2000; Jacobson and Aaltio-Marjosola, 2001). This is in contrast to 'male breadwinner societies' such as Germany where women in practice are forced to choose between a business career and having children (Tienari et al., 2002).

Hand in hand with these societal material advancements, it seems, the overall discursive framework on men and women has shifted in the Nordic countries over the past decades. The public discourse in the Nordic context nurtures equality and equal opportunities (cf. Bergquist et al., 1999; Borchorst et al., 2002). This is perhaps most notable in Sweden. In public discussion, it has therefore become increasingly suspicious to utter opinions and viewpoints that question the basic ideal of equality between the sexes, that is opportunities for all members of the society to fulfil themselves as individuals. It has been pointed out that this is the case especially in times of strong economic growth (Anttonen, 1997). Why is equality between the sexes then still problematic in organizational practice and especially in management? We set out to answer this question with reference to Nordea.

GENDER IN INTERVIEW SITUATIONS

What intrigues us especially is how male senior executives account for, or justify, inequality between the sexes. Our focus is on accounts produced in interviews conducted in a specific local, organizational and societal context (cf. Alvesson and Kärreman, 2000); fragmented, emergent, temporary accounts of how things just happen to be. These accounts reflect and (re)produce a particular gendered organizational subtext (Benschop and Doorewaard, 1998). This subtext or gendered order informs the ways in which women become marginalized in and excluded from the organization through specific speech acts and discursive practices (Calás and Smircich, 1999). We attempt to reconstruct and critically discuss such situated knowledge on gendered organizational order. Nordea, with its recent history of domestic and cross-border mergers and acquisitions, provides a particularly interesting context for addressing this. Two questions on equality between the sexes were included in the standard interview guide in our research project: '*Has equality between the sexes emerged as an issue in the negotiations or integration decision-making?*' and '*How has the cross-border dimension changed views and policies concerning equality*'. The questions on gender brought about specific reactions in the interview situations.

As researchers, we are a team of women and men. Some of the executives talked to a woman, some to a man, some to an interview team of a man and a woman or to a team of two men. The way in which the questions on equality between the sexes were posed in the interview situation varied. One of the female researchers in our project carried out the interviews alone. An experienced senior academic, she reflects that *I sometimes felt almost embarrassed asking questions on gender in this specific context because it seemed to totally break the flux of storytelling and sensemaking about the merger integration process.* She decided to abandon the original questions and found other ways to inquire about equality between the sexes. She noticed that *the actors' more spontaneous stories about their role in the negotiations and the integration processes did not touch the gender issue at all.* One of the male researchers, who carried out most of his interviews alone, says that he felt that he had to "*re-frame*" gender-related questions in order to try to fit them in the flow of each interview. Also other researchers in our project had similar experiences.

It is thus important to note that we, as interviewers, have to a significant extent taken part in the particular constructions of management and gender that are presented in the following. The crucial point here is that *questions on gender equality did not fit in*. Interviewers sensed this. The interviewees were typically surprised by the questions.

This is, of course, not a unique experience. A number of researchers have pointed out how (talk about) sex or gender often feels out of place in the public sphere of life. In the Finnish context, Korvajärvi (1998) has explored ways in which gender is often distanced from everyday organizational life by organizational members. Gender and questions of equality and inequality are, for example, distanced spatially or temporally. In spatial distancing, the basic message is that 'in other organizations there are problems, but in our organization the situation is alright'. Distancing can also be accomplished temporally, in the vein that 'things used to be bad here, but now they are alright' (cf. Hearn, 1998). With the interview experiences, *distancing* emerged as a core concept for us to make sense of gender and top management in Nordea. In this kind of talk, inequality is 'elsewhere'.

WOMEN AND MANAGEMENT: THE UNEASY COUPLING

With particular reference to managers, managing and management in organizations, the question of inequality can be approached through several perspectives. We discuss Nordea in the light of four perspectives: historical continuity, managerial work and family (public-private divide), organizational change, and perceived national differences.

HISTORICAL CONTINUITY

It is evident that accounting for the lack of women in top management can be accomplished through historical reflection where the past is explicitly drawn from to make sense of and justify the present situation. Lack of women becomes justified by the fact that there were no suitable female candidates available for top management positions when decisions had to be made. In this sense, *there hasn't been a problem*, as a Finnish executive puts it. The definition of management competence is presented as gender neutral, not as something shaped according to a specific interpretation of maleness or masculinity. The concept of competence is not problematized. In order to have a chance to be chosen for a particular managerial position, you have to be at the right place at the right time and with the right formal qualifications.

'Formal justice' according to criteria such as seniority and track record – attained through experience – is the cornerstone of this account. A somewhat artificial light is shed on attempts by female employees to make an upwardly mobile career in the organization. A Danish senior executive commented on the apparent difficulties of recruiting up-and-aspiring women: *I can see the problem, but I don't have an answer to it.*

The crux of the matter is that you see what you are looking for. Male executives can easily rule out women as lacking the necessary competencies, because they conceptualize choosing candidates for top positions as first and foremost a question of individuals. When the equality issue is considered as a question of individuals, the excuse for ignoring women is readily at hand; seniority and qualifications attained through experience determine the most competent candidates for managerial positions. On this account, senior executives can readily conclude that there are no women available. The cycle of gender segregation is self-fulfilling; women are never able to obtain the necessary qualifications (Tienari, 2000; Tienari et al., 2002).

This account of historical continuity, with its elements of 'formal justice', is not entirely surprising. In the Nordic labour markets and working life in general, segregation according to gender persists in terms of access to different areas of activities. Several explanations have been suggested for this. Despite claims for gender equality, for example, male executives have been reported to acknowledge that they feel comfortable working with other men. They also have a tendency to rationalize such preferences in recruitment; in other words, privileges are turned into merits (Asplund, 1988; Holgersson, 2001).

Earlier studies of the perceptions of women and management held by Swedish male top managers also indicate that it is common for male managers not to see the lack of women in top positions as a problem; if they do perceive the lack of women as a problem, it is a problem for women, not for the company (e.g. Wahl, 1995, Holgersson 2001). This is also the experience that Czarniawska-Joerges (1994) reports from her field studies in Sweden; the attitude among male managers seems to be that equality programmes will effectively take care of the 'problems of women' as a minority in management.

MANAGERIAL WORK AND FAMILY OBLIGATIONS

The lack of women in top management can also be grounded in people's perceptions of the separation of different spheres of life. This discourse constructs relatively traditional views on the distinction and separation between public and private spheres. It reflects a point of view where, at the end of the day, it is the woman's responsibility to take care of the private sphere: home and family. In this thinking, women deviate from the managerial norm, which calls for total commitment; women cannot deliver (because women deliver and take care of babies). This discursive construction prevails parallel to the egalitarian public discourse in Nordic societies.

A Danish senior executive reflected on this:

I experience more frequently that the woman stays at home and is absent due to illness in the family, more so than the man. And it is definitely not because we in any way push her to do so. Also, we are at times confronted with a request from the women here to get a part-time position. I have never heard a man ask for that sort of thing. And as the saying goes 'out of sight, out of mind'; when some of the women go on maternity leave, and, after that, on parental leave, this means that it takes 1-1½ years before you see them again. And the vacuum they left will disappear, and in the meantime some of their male colleagues will continue to make their careers.

On this account, it is evident that women themselves are discursively constructed as actively contributing to segregation. They are portrayed to value family over work when the time for building and nurturing a family comes. A reflection on women being reluctant to make an upwardly mobile career in the organization and turning down more challenging jobs is that they *prefer to have a kind of package,* as a Norwegian senior executive puts it, including interesting work, sufficient pay and *some time left for family life.* In this way, *women are sort of smarter.*

It has been argued in a number of earlier studies that managers and management continues to be constructed according to the 'classic' core family and male breadwinner model in the Nordic context, in spite of the egalitarian public discourse (e.g. Wahl, 1995; Andersson, 1997; Holgersson, 2001; Højgaard, 2002). This is an all too familiar story. Kanter (1977) argues that a male manager requires the emotional and practical work contributions of a wife. Management thereby consists of the work of two people; the man at work and the wife at home. Relatedly, segregation is a question of parenthood. For women attempting to pursue a career, family and motherhood continue to be a drawback. Conceptions of parenthood and motherhood are embedded in the 'cultures' of companies (Eriksson, 2000) as well as in the mythical management archetypes in society (Aaltio-Marjosola, 2001). Against this background it is interesting to note that an extremely high proportion of top executives in the Nordic context are married men with children.

Importantly, this kind of cultural and material construction of top management is as much about expectations of motherhood as about being a mother. According to Höök's (2001) study in the Swedish context, motherhood is constructed as a biological process. To have children is something that concerns women only. Fatherhood, however, is socially constructed as a one-time event. In comparison with the mother, the father is not perceived to be affected by any of the practical or emotional consequences of parenthood. The implications of this are, for example, that women who have children and who also want to pursue a career are seen as doing so at the expense of her children. A father, however, is seen pursuing his career for the sake of the children since he is the breadwinner. In sum, the constructions of fatherhood and management are mutually reinforcing, while the constructions of motherhood and management undermine each other. (Höök 2001; Hearn and Parkin, 1987; Aaltio-Marjosola, 2001)

To put it crudely, up to a certain age, every woman is a potential mother. And, as a Finnish executive puts it: *no man can replace the mother in the family.* Such accounts enable senior executives to repudiate gender inequality as something company-specific. If there is a 'problem', it transcends the boundaries of the firm. Inequality is distanced to the societal level. Also in the Nordic context, it is the women that are expected to take the main responsibility for children.

The managers' ability to make sacrifices for the benefit of the company is the nucleus of this account (cf. Acker, 1990). Management is constructed as extremely time-consuming. It demands total commitment and willingness to be continuously mobile. The burden of giving birth to and nurturing a child then becomes the foundation of the different gender roles. Women are marginalized and excluded from management if they are not able or willing to give higher priority to work than to family when necessary. This, in the minds of the male senior executives, they often cannot do. Catch 22.

ORGANIZATIONAL CHANGE

In line with the above, it is evident that male domination in management is not a static phenomenon. Gender distinctions and relations are embedded in practices and structures, which are in constant flux. Relatedly, gender equality and inequality can be approached in the light of managerial strive for, and legitimization of, constant change and transformation in organizational structures and practices (Tienari, 2000; Tienari et al, 2002). For example, it has been argued that an instance of organizational change such as a merger is likely to result in a reconstitution of gender segregation; when the relative number of managerial positions decreases, competition for the remaining positions intensifies, also among the otherwise privileged, that is, men. In Abrahamson's (2000) words, the dominant gender order is restored in the organization even when it becomes subject to change efforts such as mergers. There is, in this sense, stability in change.

In a world of ever-tougher business, the question of equality between the sexes often becomes 'automatically' downplayed. According to a Swedish senior executive, in a merger situation *a large number of managerial positions disappear. And then, unfortunately, if it is not the 'principle of senility' that is in force, then it is in any case the 'principle of seniority'. So men of fifty or over will prevail.* It is clear that the self-fulfilling aspects of segregation become accentuated when the cross-national element enters the stage. *In a merged company such as ours where you put people together according to their nationality and the business units they represent, then you will inevitably end up with a group of men ...,* as a Norwegian senior executive puts it. In these kinds of account, inequality is distanced as gender concerns are alien to the 'normal' flow of organizational life. At the same time, however, concerns about equality between the merging companies and their representatives attract a lot of attention.

Discourse on motherhood, discussed above, also gains specific strength when the cross-border, transnational element is brought to the fore in organizational change (Connell, 2001). Family obligations are constructed by the senior executives as an increasing burden in the context of managing corporate growth, particularly in the cross-border management of a multinational company. This relates to Calás and Smircich's (1993) ideas about how, in an apparently globalizing world, "the household is extended up to the national border".

As a Finnish senior executive puts it:...*this is the way it is. Take me, for example; for the past three weeks ... I've been away for four days* [every week]. *And it doesn't work out if you don't have total freedom, well, from all family responsibilities.* He continues to state that *now it is a question of real commitments* and *you don't carry out this work as a mother of a family, that doesn't work, one must give up something, and it is still so that it is easier for a man to take that step.* It is notable that while motherhood is talked about elaborately, fatherhood is absent from this discourse. Fatherhood seems to go naturally hand-in-hand with management.

Under rubrics such as extensive need for travelling, the gendered subtext in the transnational organization is discursively reproduced. In the male top executives' perception, women are not able to travel as much as is required of executives, due to their family obligations. They are unable to meet the challenges of the international or 'global' playing field that has become ever more prominent in the company through the cross-border, Nordic dimension. Senior executive management remains reserved for men whose wives take care of the home.

'NATIONAL DIFFERENCES'

In an organization built on cross-national mergers and acquisitions, questions of the lack of women in top management are further complicated by the potentially different understandings of gender equality between representatives of different countries. The Danish, Finnish, Norwegian and Swedish male executives interviewed in Nordea talked about a number of differences between themselves and representatives of other Nordic nationalities (see chapter 4 on national stereotypes). This was also the case in relation to gender and (in)equality. Differences were accomplished through essentialist notions of distinct national collectives. The basic theoretical point here is that in constructions of national collectives, the ways of 'Us' (e.g. as Danes or Swedes) are rendered normal and the ways of 'Them' (e.g. as Norwegians or Finns) are estranged.

The extent to which there are 'real' similarities and differences in cultures – for example, vis-à-vis gender relations and equality between the sexes – in Denmark, Finland, Norway and Sweden is not a focal point here. Rather, it is assumptions of similarities and differences that people utter about themselves and representatives of other nationalities that are interesting. Here, male senior executives position 'Us' and 'Them' as national collective identities (Billig, 1995; DeCillia et al., 1999) to make sense of gender equality and inequality. These identities are embedded in a complex constellation of national relations and 'cultural' perceptions in the Nordic context, discussed in more detail in other chapters of this book.

The prevalent male self-image constructed by Danish senior executives seems to be what we call a 'relaxed tough guy'. *The weak point of the women is that they are not able to just sit down and have a beer with their colleagues,* as one of the Danish executives said. A key message of male Danishness vis-à-vis the (in)equality question is flexibility. Formal systems are looked upon suspiciously. *We have a different culture in Denmark from that in Sweden and Finland. They have made it a criterion of managerial success to get a better balance. In these countries, gender really has a bearing. To be quite honest, I feel that it is a rather odd way to look upon these things.*

A different kind of prevalent image of man is constructed by Finnish senior executives. This can be best described as a 'pragmatic man of action' (Berglund and Werr, 2000). The key message of male Finnishness is that action speaks louder than words. *On the Finnish side, we don't so much talk for the sake of talk. We do something about it,* as a Finnish executive stated about equality work. His colleague noted: *so that's the difference. In Sweden it is talked through whereas in Finland one does something about it.*

It seems that the Norwegian male self-image is that of a 'sensible individualist', who constructs equality as a question of individuals and emphasizes that women themselves may be reluctant to make a career in the company. *We are still trying really hard to find some women who will go for the right jobs,* a Norwegian executive commented. *Many of them are more competent than those who eventually get the jobs, but they do not apply. And we can't just say 'this job is yours, and that's final'.*

A prevalent self-image of a 'responsible man' is constructed by many Swedish senior executives, conscious of the need for equality between the sexes. A key message of male Swedishness here is that a structured and well-planned approach is the appropriate way forward. *I think that we in Sweden have reason to be proud, because these issues have been placed on top of the agenda,* stated a Swedish executive. *In our company plan we have an account of how equality and environmental issues have to be carried out. This was something totally new to our Finnish colleagues.* He went on to observe: *But I have the feeling that in practice equality has a much higher priority in*

Finland, although it has not been debated so much. In Finland, you don't talk so much, you simply make it work.

Although conceptions of culture as essence are in many ways problematic (Søderberg and Holden, 2002), they provide an avenue to analyze perceptions of similarity and difference (Vaara, 2000). 'National' culture is no exception here. Although viewed from the outside the Nordic countries would appear a relatively monolithic block, literature on cross-cultural management insists on differences between cultures in the Nordic context (e.g. Laine-Sveiby, 1987; 1991). As described above, these may also reflect somewhat different conceptions of equality between the sexes. In all, however, it seems that notions of the 'others' (as national collectives) provide male executives with ways to distance gender inequality in space, if not in time (cf. Hearn, 1998; Korvajärvi, 1998); the basic point is that 'we would do something about inequality if it wasn't for the other nationalities'.

DISCUSSION

In this chapter, we set out to answer the question why there are so few women in the top management of multinationals such as Nordea. We briefly outlined the popular gender-egalitarian image of the Nordic countries. With particular reference to the making of Nordea, the crux of the chapter was then to map out perspectives to account for the lack of women in the top echelons of the organization: historical continuity, managerial work and family (public-private divide), organizational change, and perceived national differences.

Based on our analysis, we suggest that corporate managers be sensitive to gender-related questions in the context of cross-border mergers and acquisitions. The key message here is that the contemporary discourse around management and gender is not something 'natural' or self-evident. Rather, the ideas and meanings are socially constructed. This means that the situation can be changed. Nordea has already taken valuable concrete steps in this direction, correcting pay differentials, locating competent female candidates to managerial positions, and launching practices such as mentoring and 'work-life balance' initiatives to tackle gender segregation and promote equal opportunities in management. Recently, several women were appointed to the board of the Nordea Group.

Our analysis suggests general points that can (and should) be considered in the context of a multinational organization. Attitude change is the basis for equal opportunities. Gendered historical legacies can (and should) be tackled explicitly. Maintaining that 'there are no competent women around' never holds as an excuse in filling organizational positions. For top management, for example, the last option is always to headhunt from outside the focal organization. This is the case even if the merger context entails intensified competition on positions among the existing key actors. Simultaneously, it is important to note that the distribution of women in top management is not a direct reflection of the state of gender equality in the organization as a whole. Balance at the top is, however, a significant (usually positive) signal to stakeholders such as owners, customers, media and political actors. It can also be an encouraging sign for women (and men) within the organization.

Discussions on gender issues are not 'alien' to normal organizational life. Such discussions should not be silenced. Interpretations of competence, for example, are never value free. They are always based on criteria that involve a degree of subjective judgement (cf. Holgersson, 2001). Thus, interpretations of competence are never gender neutral. When these interpretations are made to appear neutral, however, gender segregation in management becomes a self-fulfilling process (Tienari, 2000). It is also highly suspicious to talk about motherhood and potential motherhood as an excuse for hindrances in women's career making.

Further, it should be noted that people's perceptions of gender equality, and the appropriate measures to tackle inequality in a company, may differ somewhat across representatives of different nations or national cultures. This is evident also between the Nordic countries. Synchronizing different conceptions in a multinational organization is a tough managerial challenge. But it cannot be avoided.

REFERENCES

AALTIO-MARJOSOLA, I. (2001). *Naiset, miehet ja johtajuus.* Vantaa: WSOY. (Women, Men and Leadership.)

ABRAHAMSON, L. (2000). *Att återställa ordningen. Könsmonster och förändring i arbetsorganisationer.* Umeå: Boréa. (To Restore Order – Gender Patterns and Change in Work Organisations.)

ACKER, J. (1990). 'Hierarchies, jobs, bodies: a theory of gendered organizations'. *Gender and Society,* 4, 139-158.

ANDERSSON, G. (1997). 'Karriär, kön och familj.' In Nyberg, A. and Sundin, E. (Eds.), *Ledare, makt och kön.* SOU 1997:135. Stockholm: Fritzes. (Career, Gender and Family.)

ANTTONEN, A. (1997). *Feminismi ja sosiaalipolitiikka – miten sukupuolesta tehtiin yhteiskuntateoreettinen ja sosiaalipoliittinen avainkäsite.* Tampere: University of Tampere Press. (Feminism and Social Policy – How Gender Was Made a Core Concept in Social Sciences Theory and Social Policy.)

ASPLUND, G. (1988). *Women Managers. Changing Organizational Cultures.* Chichester: Wiley.

BERGQVIST, C. (Ed.) (1999). *Likestilte demokratier? Kjönn og politikk i Norden.* Oslo: Universitetsforlaget.

BILLIG, M. (1995). *Banal Nationalism.* London: Sage.

BORCHORST, A., CHRISTENSEN, A.-D. and SIIM, B. (2002). 'Diskurser om køn, magt og politik i Skandinavien.' In BORCHORST, A. (Ed.). *Kønsmagt under forandring.* Copenhagen: Hans Reitzel. (Discourses on Gender, Power and Politics in Scandinavia)

CALÁS, M.B. and SMIRCICH, L. (1999). 'Past postmodernism? reflections and tentative directions'. *Academy of Management Review*, 24, 649-671.

CONNELL, R.W. (2001). 'Masculinity politics on a world scale.' In Whitehead, S. M. and BARRETT, F. J. (Eds.). *The Masculinities Reader.* Cambridge: Polity Press.

CZARNIAWSKA-JOERGES, B. (1994). 'Editorial: Modern organizations and Pandora's box'. *Scandinavian Journal of Management*, 10, 95-98.

DeCILLIA, R., REISIGL, M. and WODAK, R. (1999). 'The discursive construction of national identities'. *Discourse and Society*, 10, 149-73.

DUNCAN, S. (1998). 'Theorising gender systems in europe.' In Geisler, B., Maier, F. and Pfau-Effinger, B. *FrauenArbeitsMarkt.* Berlin: Edition Sigma.

ERIKSSON, U. (2000). *Det mangranna sällskapet. Om konstruktion av kön i företag.* Gothenburg: BAS Förlag. (Company to a Man: Constructing Gender in Business.)

FOLDY, E.G. (2002). 'Managing' diversity: Identity and power in organizations. In Aaltio, I. and Mills, A. J. (Eds.). *Gender, Identity and the Culture of Organizations.* London: Routledge.

HEARN, J. (1998). *The Violences of Men: How Men Talk About and How Agencies Respond to Men's Violence to Women.* London: Sage Publications.

HOLGERSSON, C. (2001) 'The social construction of top executives.' In Sjöstrand, S.-E., Sandberg, J. and Tystrup, M. (Eds.). *Invisible Management: The Social Construction of Leadership.* UK: Thomson Learning.

HØJGAARD, L. (2002). 'Tracing differentiation in gendered leadership: an analysis of differences in gender composition in top management in business, politics and the civil service'. *Gender, Work & Organization*, 9, 15-38.

JACOBSON, S.W. and AALTIO-MARJOSOLA, I. (2001). ''Strong' objectivity and the use of Q-methodology in cross-cultural research: Contextualizing the experience of women managers and their scripts of career'. *Journal of Management Inquiry*, 10, 228-48.

JOHNSON, R. and REDMOND, D. (2000). *Diversity Incorporated – Managing People for Success in a Diverse World.* London: Pearson Education.

KANTER, R.M. (1977). *Men and Women of the Corporation.* New York: Basic Books.

KORVAJÄRVI, P. (1998). *Gendering Dynamics in White-Collar Organizations.* University of Tampere Doctoral Dissertation. Acta Universitatis Tamperensis 600.

LAINE-SVEIBY, K. (1987). *Svenskhet som strategi.* Stockholm: Timbro. (Swedishness as Strategy.)

LAINE-SVEIBY, K. (1991). *Suomalaisuus strategiana.* Porvoo: WSOY. (Finnishness as Strategy.)

MELKAS, H. and ANKER, R. (1998). *Gender Equality and Occupational Segregation in Nordic Labour markets.* Geneva: International Labour Office.

MERILÄINEN, S. (2000). 'Discourses of equality and difference in bank managers' talk'. LTA / *The Finnish Journal of Business Economics*, 3, 416-32.

STATISTICS SWEDEN (2000). *Women and Men in Sweden: Facts and Figures.* Örebro, Sweden: SCB.

SUNDIN, E. (2000). 'Women and men as managers in a female dominated sector and company'. LTA / *The Finnish Journal of Business Economics,* 3: 394-415.

SØDERBERG, A-M and HOLDEN, N. (2002). 'Rethinking cross-cultural management in a globalising business world'. *International Journal of Cross-Cultural Management,* 2, 103-21.

TIENARI, J. (2000). 'Gender segregation in the making of a merger'. *Scandinavian Journal of Management*, 16, 111-44.

TIENARI, J., QUACK, S. and THEOBALD, H. (2002). 'Organizational reforms, 'ideal workers' and gender orders: A cross-societal comparison'. *Organization Studies*, 23, 249-79.

VAARA, E. (2000). 'Constructions of cultural differences in postmerger change processes: A sensemaking perspective on Finnish-Swedish cases'. *M@n@gement*, 3, 81-110.

VANHALA, S. (1999). 'Yksityisen sektorin johtajamarkkinat lamasta nousuun.' In Veikkola, E. S. (Ed.). *Onko huipulla tyyntynyt.* Helsinki,

Tilastokeskus / Työmarkkinat 1999:12. (Private Sector Management in the Recovering Managerial Labour Market.)

WAHL, A. (Ed.) (1995). *Men's Perceptions of Women and Management.* Sweden: Ministry of Health and Social Affairs.

ÅSTRÖM, G. (1995). 'Society in a Gender Perspective.' In Wahl, A. (Ed.), *Men's Perceptions of Women and Management.* Sweden: Ministry of Health and Social Affairs.

Chapter 11

TRAVELLERS IN THE LONG HOURS CULTURE

INCREASED PRESSURE ON INDIVIDUALS IN THE NORDIC ORGANIZATION

Janne Tienari & Eero Vaara

INTRODUCTION

As key decision-makers, top managers are involved in restructuring, and creating new kinds of organization. Their work receives public recognition, and they are usually handsomely rewarded for their efforts. Due to their position, top managers face various kinds of expectations from internal and external stakeholders. Active owners and analysts force top managers to work on synergies in merging. Consequently, top managers are often faced with making difficult decisions such as demotions and staff dismissals, which affect the lives of many people. While being change agents, however, top managers themselves are objects of change. This means that while bearing the responsibility for implementing the merger, they are exposed to similar kinds of uncertainty and pressure to change as other organizational members. One reason for this is that their own positions are not secure.

These issues can also be placed in a wider social and societal framework. Contemporary sociologists have pointed to the specific problems created by the globalized market-driven society (see e.g. Bauman, 2000). These analysts have examined the increasing demands put on people to compete, create new ways of thinking, engage in continuous organizational changes, and constantly develop their professional competence. These pressures are often 'invisible' for the involved people, who join the race voluntarily. In a sense, they work and live in a golden cage.

In this chapter, we discuss the demands and pressures put on top managers in the making of Nordea. We ask the question *what types of pressure do managers suffer when going through cross-border mergers?* Based on our interview and documentary material, we elaborate on the antecedents and effects of being socialized into a long hours work culture. We concentrate especially on the extra work created by the merger process, special problems caused by travelling, the ever-changing social environment, and constant uncertainty, which can be seen as specific problems in cross-border mergers and acquisitions. We also discuss measures taken to alleviate the potential problems. Finally, from the perspective of the well-being of individual organizational members, we suggest some general points that need to be considered in merging across borders.

THE GOLDEN CAGE OF CONTEMPORARY BUSINESS ORGANIZATIONS

In most sectors and industries, it has gradually become a natural order of things for individuals in responsible positions to work long hours without extra compensation, also at weekends, when the business situation calls for it. And the business seems to demand this ever more often. Excessive demands for flexibility and availability have become naturalized with the increasingly harshening Zeitgeist. In contemporary corporations, shareholder value seems to dominate over the interests of other stakeholders (see Tainio et al., 2003). This is articulated in rationalistic discourse, which promotes organizational rationalization and efficiency (Vaara and Tienari, 2002). At the level of individuals, a reflection of this is that if one is not willing to sacrifice oneself on the altar of constant availability, there is always the threat that someone else will be ready to step in. It is thereby even harder to say 'no' to more work.

In general, it is evident that such 'greedy' organizations can become seductive for individuals (Hochschild, 1997). This may especially be the case for people in managerial positions as these positions offer several kinds of incentives. At least sporadically, managers are able to exercise control over their own work. They are also relatively independent to make decisions regarding their tasks and ways of working. Their work can even demand a degree of creativity. Managers and experts usually have the opportunity to work with interesting and talented colleagues. They may mingle with powerful people in high positions in organizational hierarchies. Their financial compensation is likely to be satisfactory. In all, it is no wonder managers and experts may be seduced by workaholism. Being there easily becomes a value in itself. Time-space visibility or doing 'face time' (mingling with important people) may become addictive.

On the one hand, it may be argued that this 'long hours culture' is an increasingly universal phenomenon, which is spreading to new contexts. In the West, it is customary to view Japanese work organizations as strongholds of the culture of commitment and loyalty through long working hours and short holidays. However, from a Nordic perspective, companies of Anglo-American origin such as investment banks and management consultancies seem to be characterized by extremely strong normative pressures towards time-space visibility (Meriläinen et al., forthcoming). Multinational companies have become important carriers of the long hours culture. Through imitation and institutionalizing norms, multinationals set the standard for the ways in which this culture is spread in new locations.

In the Anglo-American context, the prevailing model is one of a hierarchical and unbroken career where the ideal worker is flexible. Long working hours is viewed as a symbol of commitment (Lewis, 1997). Consequently, the concept of 'work-life balance' has come to denote company-specific policies and initiatives to take care of the potentially negative consequences for employees working long hours. Often, such policies are initiated under the label 'family-friendly'. As a part of diversity management, initiatives may include job sharing, flexible working, career breaks or reductions in work hours (Johnson and Redmond, 2000). In sum, the long hours culture has given birth to 'work-life balance' policies and initiatives to mend some of its own potentially negative consequences in the short term (Coussey, 2000).

It is important to note that the long hours culture, and the 'work-life balance' policies and initiatives related to it, are gendered. A study conducted in Sweden shows that long hours cultures are particularly nurtured in organizations numerically dominated by men (Wahl and Holgersson, forthcoming). In general, in the long hours culture, women are usually put at a disadvantage as they are still considered to be predominantly responsible for the domestic work in families (see e.g. Meriläinen et al., forthcoming). Thereby, initiatives for 'work-life balance' have in practice become initiatives targeted especially for women. However, women who take up the provisions offered may find themselves marginalized within the organization. This may take the form of less demanding and rewarding work tasks as well as hindrances in making an upward mobile career (Benschop and Doorewaard, 1998).

On the other hand, increasing workload is also a trend rooted in local and societal developments in the Nordic countries. It is the outcome of increased cost cutting and downsizing, which in the Nordic context until recently have been the remnant of the severe economic crises and recession experienced in the early 1990s. It may be argued that the discourse around work has taken problematic turns. This is highlighted, for example, by a number of Finnish academics in a pamphlet titled 'mad work disease' (Riikonen et al., 2002). In their insightful texts, the authors reflect critically on the contemporary work discourse. Their focus is on the backlash – individual stress and burnout as well as tensed social interaction – that the current rationalization craze brings about. The authors' focus is on the public sector, but the ideas are arguably also applicable in corporate settings.

Riikonen et al. (2002) problematize the materializing, technocrat discourse that renders abstract the mundane phenomena in (working) life. Somewhat sarcastically, we would summarize the material consequences of the dominating work discourse: everyone is busy being (or appearing) so busy that they do not have time to do much.

Even more alarmingly, decreased short-term costs provided by extreme work-orientation, rationalization and downsizing may lead to increased long-term costs on societal, company and individual levels.

The problematics of increased work-orientation have recently been the source of public debate in the Nordic countries. In Finland, for example, the balance of different spheres of an individual's life was a recurring topic in the late 1990s and early 2000s (see e.g. Meriläinen et al., forthcoming). Riitta Jallinoja, professor of sociology, studied interviews published in the Finnish media as well as e-mail messages that she had received as response to her own public commentary. Most of the texts were narrated by men in responsible positions at work. Jallinoja (2000) maintains that these texts reflect a shift in public debate in Finland towards a more positive tone regarding family, a development that gained strength in the late 1990s. A recurring theme in the texts studied is the narrator's repentance for dedicating 'all' his/her time to work. The key plot in the texts is a great turnaround, which starts a new stage in the narrator's life. Such texts can be read as heroic stories about individuals sacrificing (at least temporarily) professional careers to 'give time' to family life.

In all, it is evident that a discourse nurturing a long hours culture is gaining ground in contemporary organizational life. Organizations are increasingly 'greedy' about their employees' time. Key individuals may then be seduced to time/space visibility, that is, to work longer hours and do 'face time' at the company premises and customer sites.

MAKING NORDEA: THE TRAVELLERS IN THE LONG HOURS CULTURE

Nordea has been created through a series of domestic and cross-border mergers and acquisitions. It thus provides an illustrative setting for analyzing the pressures and demands that managers in charge of restructuring organizations are facing. Of the many kinds of social and socio-psychological pressure, we focus on the extra work created by the merger process, special problems caused by travelling, the ever-changing social environment, and constant uncertainty.

EXTRA WORK AND THE LONG HOURS CULTURE

For the people involved, post-merger integration builds up on top of ordinary everyday work. It means an added workload. In addition to their 'normal' responsibilities, people have to cope with and manage multiple change projects. It is particularly difficult for those in managerial positions to question this extra work as, by virtue of their positions, they are held accountable for the implications of the structural changes – meaning both financial success and social consequences. It is also the case that both internal and external stakeholders frequently put special pressure on the top decision-makers. For example, stock market analysts are eager to hear both about new merger or acquisition plans and even more so about realized synergies.

In our interviews, the top decision-makers often described the hard work that they had been doing in the context of mergers and acquisitions. This can be seen as a reflection of the contemporary discourse where long hours are an emblem of commitment to the organization. A Finnish top manager described his experience in an illuminative way: *It did mean working night and day because you had to give answers to the organization during the day and take care of the daily* [i.e. 'normal'] *work on the side. What you cannot do during the day, you do in the evening or at night.*

However, the interviewees also described how specific projects had taken their toll. For example, the managers pointed to potential problems in not getting enough rest and sleep. Dr. Kirsti Pakkala, the Chief Occupational Physician and Vice President in the Finnish organization of the Nordea Group, comments on the potential implications of the long hours culture as follows:

When people constantly get too little sleep, this often leads to routinized thinking and a decrease in innovativeness. In the hectic pace, stress is also an ever present risk. It is only when people get tired that they start reflecting on these issues, and try to do something about it on a personal basis.

Further, potential problems in balancing work and family life were discussed by the top managers. As discussed in detail in the chapter 10 on gender, top managers presented family obligations in a specific tone in the cross-border merger context. As a Finnish senior executive puts it: *For the past three weeks ... I've been away for four days* [every week]. *And it doesn't work out if you don't have total freedom, well, from all family responsibilities.* It is clear that managing mergers puts a strain on individuals' private life. *Boundaries between work and spare time are becoming more and more blurred,* remarks Dr. Pakkala. In addition, information technology enables availability 24 hours a day, seven days a week. Managers are disciplined to be constantly available for work-related issues.

Thorleif Krarup, ex-CEO of Nordea, has become a well-known example of the potential problems related to individual work-life balance in the cross-border merger context due to the media coverage around his resignation in August 2002. The main reason given in the public was the pressure put on Mr. Krarup's personal life by the challenges in managing and representing the Nordic organization. *One must take care of the whole person,* Krarup justified his decision to step down in an interview with the Swedish *Dagens Industri.* Although it was speculated by journalists whether pressure on work-life balance was the 'real' reason for Mr. Krarup's resignation, the fact remains that he, like many others, has been facing a tremendous workload due to the need to make the mergers successful.

The case of Thorleif Krarup opens up for the discussion of the issue of balancing work and private life more generally in Nordea. While it may be warranted to view 24-hour availability as a natural part of a modern CEO's work contract, the top echelons of the Nordea organization have all been exposed to similar pressures and demands. Moreover, down the hierarchy, large numbers of employees are facing a similar situation.

THE SPECIAL BURDEN OF TRAVELLING

In cross-border mergers and acquisitions, constant travelling creates a special burden. In making Nordea, the idea of rotating meetings in different countries and the idea of a 'virtual headquarters' have implied a need for constant moving from one place to another. In brief, when Merita and Nordbanken merged in 1997, the top management group alternated between Stockholm and Helsinki. It is illustrative to note that the bank rented flats in both cities to be used and shared by the mobile managers. When MeritaNordbanken and Unidanmark merged in March 2000, it was announced that the new bank would not operate with one formal headquarters. Instead, a virtual headquarters model was decided upon. Top managers would retain their offices in their home country, but travel extensively in the three countries. After the Norwegian CBK joined in October 2000, group executive meetings were to take place once a week either in Copenhagen, Helsinki, Oslo or Stockholm.

This idea of virtual headquarters served to maintain an impression of national balance in the multinational organization. It was perceived as an important signal to employees, customers and other stakeholders. Apart from its potentially positive symbolic effects, however, the virtual headquarters model has proved to be tiresome for those who ran it, that is, the mobile managers. The model meant extensive travelling for the key people. One interviewee mentioned having on average 20-25 flights a month, amounting to 5-6 flights per week. As one of our interviewees sardonically expressed it: *We're not to blame if SAS is showing poor results.*

Nordea managers seem to be agree on the necessity of being mobile: *On average, I'm away abroad for two or three days a week, and the rest is attending meetings back home. But this is my own choice. I have said 'yes' to carrying out this job, so I can't complain.* In such accounts, travelling is seen as an important sign of personal commitment to the emerging Nordic organization. A Norwegian manager reflects: *Usually, it's one day in Stockholm, one day in Copenhagen, and one day in Helsinki ... and then there is Luxembourg in between.*

Many of the top managers have viewed constant travelling as a temporary condition, which is likely to decrease somewhat when the merger enters its stabilization stages:

Due to the travelling alone, during the last year, my normal work time has increased by about 25 percent. And you take that time from your spare time. It means you have weeks with over 80 work hours. That is fine for a period of time, but not on a continuous basis. You just have to take it as an investment in building up the organization you are responsible for. If you did not have the naïve belief that the travelling is going to reduce in the future, you couldn't do it. In this sense, things can only get better.

However, others have grown sceptical as to the possibilities to cut down on the amount of travelling. *I'm running in meetings all day long. At present, it's working out. But sometimes you just want to put up the white flag and say 'I give up!'* For many Swedish and Finnish top managers, the mobile situation has been a reality since the autumn of 1997. One of the managers involved reflects:

You're travelling constantly, for years, and it seems that the project never ends. This is extremely challenging for the people involved. Along with this virtual headquarters thing, it may be that some people are not going to manage it much longer.

In terms of travelling, a specific case concerns those Danes, Finns or Norwegians who have a position in Stockholm, and commute weekly between their home country and Sweden. They say that while being in Stockholm they work extremely long hours, and only have a life outside work when they are back in their home country. Having two work modes may become difficult to handle in the long run – or, on the contrary, it may actually suit some individuals' life situations.

In all, extensive travelling may bring about less efficient work time and deteriorating quality of work, fatigue, as well as more long-term effects on physical fitness. A top manager remarks:

> *Personally, I'm not all too happy about* [travelling]. *I try to do all my travelling as day trips, and then get home to my own bed. I've travelled a lot earlier, too, so I'm a bit tired of it. … It's just a hassle to be delayed at airports and eat airplane food and all that.*

What is making these problems potentially even more severe is that travelling usually takes place during the early morning and late evening hours. When a manager makes a one-day trip abroad, he leaves home around 5.30 a.m. and returns around 9 p.m. or later. This is the general picture outlined in our interviews. 'Round trips' abroad entails flying to one country, spending some time there and flying to a third country before returning home.

THE EVER-CHANGING SOCIAL ENVIRONMENT

A special feature in the building of the cross-border organization is the need to work in different social and cultural environments. This aspect of international restructuring is often portrayed solely in a positive light. Many of the top managers in Nordea expressed working in different social and cultural contexts as *"a positive challenge"*, *"a great learning experience"* and *"a privilege"*.

However, in the conditions of post-merger or post-acquisition turmoil, the need to work in everchanging social environments also puts extra pressure on the people involved. We analyze cultural problematics in detail in other chapters of this book, but it is important to note that constant adjustment to different social and cultural settings is a special challenge for managers involved in cross-border mergers. What seems to have been specifically taxing for the top managers is the fact that they are often forced to quickly take charge of operations in new locations. According to many of our interviewees, this has frequently been much more difficult than expected. This is due to subtle but important differences in the practices, values and norms of the different organizations.

What has added to these cultural challenges is the fact that the managers have rarely had enough time to acquaint themselves with the focal organizations when being forced to change places constantly. One of the managers remarked: *You always have extremely little time. This is what has surprised me the most ... There is no one to do my usual work* [in the different locations]. *This means that I have to be prepared to start organizing, and think in a new way, all the time.*

The Nordea case also shows how social relationships and networks of long standing may become subject to change in post-merger or post-acquisition turmoil. Some networks may in practice be broken. For many top managers, the virtual headquarters model in particular has implied a need to spend a great deal of time away from the home office. Some no longer have a home office. These changes have created a special problem in that these people are not able to participate in small talk, coffee breaks and the like on a constant basis. This kind of informal organizational interaction is something that the managers have apparently missed in terms of being able to maintain friendships, spontaneously discuss difficult issues face-to-face with people and, in general, be able to be informed about how people in their organization feel in the midst of the restructurings.

Respectively, the building of new social relationships and contacts has not been unproblematic when spening little time in particular locations. A Swedish manager pointed to the problems of the increasing size of the cross-border organization:

> *You can take the old Nordbanken [as an example]. There you could call someone and say: 'Hello, I need some help', and then they come and help out. To call Thorleif Krarup, it is like calling Kofi Annan and asking 'can you assist in this process?'. It is just as likely ... So we can say that contacts disappear, and that the whole thing becomes too big.*

What has added to the cultural and social challenges is the use of foreign languages. When Swedish was chosen as the official corporate management language in the MeritaNordbanken merger in 1997, it put extra pressure on the Finnish-speaking Finns. They were forced to work in the Swedish language – and often could not express themselves fully. In some cases, Finns had to cope with feelings of (unjust) professional inadequacy when they were deprived of the ability to communicate in their mother tongue.

When English was set as the new official corporate language in the merger between MeritaNordbanken and Unidanmark in 2000, the situation changed for the Finnish-speaking Finns. For the other nationalities, the switch to English created an additional burden in social interaction. Subsequently, Swedish, Danish and Norwegian managers have at times continued to use Scandinavian (a mixture of Swedish, Danish and Norwegian) especially in more informal interaction. This, again, has been problematic for many Finns. A Finnish top manager pointed to the language use of the CEOs Hans Dalborg and Thorleif Krarup as follows: *"Dalborg ... often wanted to speak Swedish, even in official meetings. Krarup is very careful in that all the meetings are held in English, and that's it."* On the whole, working in a foreign language is a potential source of stress, especially in negotiations requiring persuasion skills.

UNCERTAINTY ABOUT THE FUTURE

Uncertainty about the future is claimed to be the most common source of stress in mergers and acquisitions (see e.g. Cartwright and Cooper, 1990, 1993). This uncertainty is related to future prospects – and often specifically to concerns about one's own future position. It should be emphasized that in organizations such as Nordea, uncertainty is not only related to one-time organizational changes resulting from particular merger or acquisition decisions but is almost an ever-present feature of organizational life. Many of the people involved have incredible 'change histories': the chain of mergers and acquisitions started with domestic arrangements, most notably in the early 1990s, and continued in the form of cross-border manouevres. Uncertainty remains due to pressures to create value, realize synergies, and cut costs. An additional factor that may amplify this uncertainty is the media, which has continuously speculated about new merger and acquisition partners for Nordea.

Top managers are in many ways more informed – and in a better position to control their own future – than other organizational members. This should alleviate the harmful consequences of uncertainty. Yet, in conditions of constant organizational change, especially concerns of their own positions in the organization seem to create special pressure for top managers. A Swedish top manager, for example, described this as follows: *I really think that it is this uncertainty which makes it* [most difficult]. *You don't know if you can stay in the organization. You don't know if you can hold on to your position. You don't know if you can keep your status. That is the biggest problem.*

Apart from being a problem *per se*, uncertainty related to one's own future tends to increase the problems related to the workload in particular ways. It creates a need among managers to show commitment to the organization, for example, through working long hours and producing positive short-term results in their own area of responsibility. This uncertainty also implies a special need to see to their personal interests. As a Finnish top manager puts it: *"We all have brains to think and capacity to open our mouths. Or at least we should have this capacity to open our mouths and express clearly our own views, how we wish things to be."* The message is that you have to speak up for yourself in order to succeed.

Finally, many Nordea managers pointed out how difficult it is to try to constantly make decisions 'fair' for all the parties involved. The multinational element may be especially stressful here. There can be contradictory pressures coming from representatives of their own and other nationalities. A Finnish manager described his difficulties when he was in charge of a Finnish-Swedish unit: *"If I think about those who left* [the Finnish side], *who were disappointed, many of them felt that we should not share all these things with the Swedes. But even more people left because they were disappointed in me, because I did not take a tighter grip of the Swedish organization."* In general, it is clear that making decisions that affect other peoples' lives may turn out a special source of anxiety also for the top decision-makers.

GETTING THE BALANCE RIGHT

Some of the concerns specified and illustrated above have been heard in Nordea. For example, the problems related to a clear-cut virtual headquarters model have led to subsequent changes in practices. From January 2002 most top management and board meetings have been held in Stockholm. The practical reason behind this choice is that Stockholm is geographically the most centrally located of the Nordic capitals. Returning to a more traditional headquarters model enables to reduce the amount of time spent moving from one place to another.

Conducting meetings over telephone or video conference is an alternative practice that has been tried out. This is a two-edged sword. On the one hand, such solutions are about creating and establishing practices that take physical strain off individuals while maintaining the business momentum. On the other, conducting meetings over the telephone or video conference is never a perfect substitute for face-to-face human interaction. The potential technical problems are well known. Even more importantly, managers in Nordea point out that the constant restructurings in the organization mean that people in responsible positions must keep on travelling *"to meet people in order to put the organization in place."*

Further, it is evident that people in specific units in Nordea have worked on the problems related to increased demands and pressures. *Nordea Markets* is a good example. It is part of the Corporate and Institutional Banking business area in Nordea. The Markets unit consists of several business operations: debt capital markets, foreign exchange, money market, fixed income, and derivatives. The unit has approximately 750 employees. It is organized according to business functions, operating as a cross-national organization. This has entailed extensive travelling for a large number of employees. In a financial services company, Nordea Markets is a typical example of a unit whose business is fundamentally international (in contrast to, for example, retail banking). It is no exaggeration to say that the business is run around the clock.

When the Nordea Markets unit was set up, operations such as currency trading were centralized in Copenhagen. As it became the main trading floor, Copenhagen was perceived by many to have become the unit 'headquarters'. However, no members of the management group in Nordea Markets relocated to Copenhagen. As personal meetings were crucial for the functioning of the new organization, constant travelling became part of the weekly agenda of these individuals. Due to feedback from people actively involved in travelling, during the fall of 2002, elaborate steps were taken in Nordea Markets to discuss the issue of life balance or 'balanced lifestyle' (cf. work-life balance above).

A consultancy firm was hired to conduct a preliminary study of the current situation in *Nordea Markets*. Consultants carried out a total of 30 telephone interviews in the unit. In their agenda, 'life balance' and 'gender equality' were seen as closely linked. Both issues were covered in the interviews. This is illuminative of how these issues are commonly – and, it seems, naturally – perceived to somehow go together (see chapter 10 on gender).

The consultancy report singled out strategies to enable balanced lifestyles for the Nordea Markets people. These included (1) improved ability to set personal limits and priorities, (2) flexible working methods, (3) opportunities for part-time work, (4) family agreements, and (5) reduced travel. The report made a distinction between making suggestions for the offer of 'quick fixes' and more long-term actions.

The former includes flexible working (e.g. flexible hours, compressed work week, part-time work), paid time-off, parental leave, exercise benefits, meal service and paid transport when working late, and laundry service. The latter includes the availability of portable computers, childcare referral services as well as programs for personal development and stress management.

In terms of life balance, the consultancy report gives advice to different employee groups at Nordea Markets. The *senior management* is advised to promote the message of the importance of life balance within the unit, establish and maintain a dialogue among managers – and hold them accountable. *Line management* is to act as the primary discussion partner for employees, keeping them informed of the available benefits. Line managers are also to establish a dialogue in the organization through team meetings. The role of *human resources specialists* is to define and establish benefits and guidelines, inform and support line managers and employees, track developments and ensure their adequate reporting (the consultants point out that this process may vary according to differences between national contexts). Finally, *employees* are to take advantage of appropriate benefits, and initiate discussions with managers and HR specialists when necessary. In all, the report claims, each and every individual is responsible for acting as a model for a balanced lifestyle in his or her own capacity.

The findings of the consultancy study were presented and discussed in a seminar with the top 30 managers in Nordea Markets. It was commonly acknowledged that life balance is an important challenge for everyone involved. The head of the Markets unit stressed the importance of life balance in retaining the unit's high performance also in the long term, to avoid the negative consequences of stress and burnout. In the discussion, the responsibility of each manager to pay attention to life balance in his/her own unit was further underlined.

One of the focal topics in discussing life balance was how to profile the Nordea Markets unit in terms of its competitive context. With the nature of its business, the unit operates in an international environment. Discussions at the seminar centered around the question whether the Markets unit should strive for a 'Nordea culture' – or an 'international culture' more in line with the operation of its global competitors. This choice remains to be made. Finally, it was pointed out in the seminar that, in any case, openness about issues related to life balance is crucial, and that more information about the benefits should be made available to employees. It was agreed that the top management in Nordea Markets would return to the issue in the near future.

CONCLUSION

This chapter has taken a critical perspective on dominant economic and organizational values and management practices that put heavy demands and pressures on key individuals in restructuring organizations. We asked the question *what types of pressures do managers suffer when going through cross-border mergers?*, and highlighted potential sources of managerial stress such as extra work, special problems of travelling, the ever-changing social environment, and constant uncertainty. In the cross-border merger context, these are examples of the human and social challenges that managers and other key people face. In our view, by examining these kinds of pressures and their consequences at the level of individual perception and experience, we avoid sustaining a too polished or superficial picture of the nature of managerial work in contemporary corporations.

Our analysis of interviews with top managers in Nordea give rise to general reflections on managerial work in cross-border mergers. On the whole, the specific demands and pressures that managers and other key individuals confront in this context seem to both reflect and reproduce the long hours culture that dominates contemporary working life. This makes it very difficult to break free from the overall norm. Yet, as shown in this chapter, the long hours culture has potentially problematic consequences. At the individual level we can, for example, point to stress and tiredness as well as problems in balancing work and private life. At the organizational level, it seems fair to assume that stressed and tired managers may find it difficult to reach best possible decisions on a continuous basis, to be innovative, and to serve as inspiring examples for others.

What can then be done with these problems in merging multinational organizations? First, there is a need to recognize that these are significant problems. Without overall awareness of the negative consequences of extreme work orientation and the long hours culture, it is unlikely that people will, for example, seek and support individual or collective initiatives to reorganize and reduce working time. The Nordea Markets unit has taken important steps in bringing issues related to life balance into the open. The discussions carry positive symbolic value. The challenge now is to agree on concrete measures to respond to the concerns raised.

Second, there is a clear need to set limits on the extra work created by the restructurings. While it makes sense to work extra hours in the initial stages of a merger, it takes courage from the top managers to subsequently encourage shorter hours at company premises. This is yet likely to secure the long-term commitment of managers and employees. For example, a coordinated plan where intensive projects are followed by longer leaves for individuals can reduce the potential problems resulting from heavy workloads.

Third, policies with regard to travelling need to be reworked after the initial 'getting together' period in cross-border mergers. People should be encouraged to cut down on all unnecessary travelling, and find alternative ways such as telephone and video conferences for social interaction. Fourth, and relatedly, people should also be encouraged to develop more meaningful working conditions in different locations. While cross-cultural interaction should be promoted as such, a constant flood of brief visits abroad also seems to have questionable effects. The transnational business executive may turn out to be everywhere – and nowhere.

Fifth, all members of the organization should 'fight' against uncertainty concerning the future. While it is obviously impossible for top decision-makers to promise that things will not change eventually, at least short and medium term plans should be made clear for the people involved. If this is not done, there is a risk that managers as well as other key people cannot wholeheartedly work for the organization.

Efforts exemplified by Nordea Markets are undoubtedly needed to be able to spread the awareness of the problems caused by excessive demands and pressures on individuals, including managers. However, at the same time, it is important to recognize the practical limits of such projects. Without fundamentally challenging the rationale of extreme work orientation in organizations and in society in general, it is hard to imagine that there will be sustainable change in the dominant long hours culture.

In conclusion, the question of pressure deserves constant attention in merging organizations. Strong statements and personal examples by top managers are needed. We want to emphasize that taking the question of life balance seriously is a positive signal not only to the people within the organization, but also to other stakeholders. And it certainly complies with Nordic ideas and values.

REFERENCES

BAUMAN, Z. (2000). *Liquid modernity*. Cambridge: Polity Press.

BENSCHOP, Y. and DOOREWAARD, H. (1998). 'Covered by equality: The gender subtext of organizations'. *Organization Studies*, 19, 787-805.

CARTWRIGHT, S. and COOPER, C.L. (1993). 'The psychological impact of merger and acquisition on the individual: A study of building society managers'. *Human Relations*, 46, 327-347.

CARTWRIGHT, S. and COOPER, C.L. (1990). 'The impact of mergers and acquisitions on people at work: Existing research and issues'. *British Journal of Management*, 1, 65-76.

COUSSEY, M. (2000). *Getting the right work-life balance*. London: Chartered Institute of Personnel and Development.

HOCHSCHILD, A.R. (1997). *The time bind. When work becomes home and home becomes work*. New York: Metropolitan Books.

JALLINOJA, R. (2000). *Perheen aika*. Helsinki: Otava. (Family Time.)

JOHNSON, R. and REDMOND, D. (2000). *Diversity incorporated – Managing people for success in a diverse world*. London: Pearson Education.

LEWIS, S. (1997). 'Family friendly' employment policies: A route to changing organizational culture or playing about at the margins?' *Gender, Work and Organization*, 4, 13-23.

MERILÄINEN, S., TIENARI, J., THOMAS, R. and DAVIES, A. (forthcoming). 'Management consultant talk: A cross-cultural comparison of normalising discourse and resistance'. *Organization*.

RIIKONEN, E., MAKKONEN, M. and VILKKUMAA, I. (2002). *Hullun työn tauti: lukemisto tulevan työhyvinvointikeskustelun pohjaksi*. Tampere: Vastapaino. (Mad Work Disease.)

TAINIO, R., HUOLMAN, M., PULKKINEN, M., ALI-YRKKÖ, J. and YLÄ-ANTTILA, P. (2003). 'Global investors meet local managers: shareholder value in the Finnish context'. In Djelic, M.-L. and Quack, S. (Eds.). *Globalization and institutions: Redefining the rules of the game.* Cheltenham: Edward Elgar.

VAARA, E. and TIENARI, J. (2002). 'Justification, Legitimization and Naturalization of Mergers and Acquisitions: A Critical Discourse Analysis of Media Texts'. *Organization*, 9, 275-303.

WAHL, A. and HOLGERSSON, C. (forthcoming). 'Male managers' reactions to gender diversity activities in organizations'. In Davidson, M. J. and Fielden, S. L. (Eds.). *Individual diversity and psychology in organizations.* UK: Wiley Handbook Series

THE INTERVIEW GUIDE

This joint interview guide was developed in our research group. It focuses on the following issues and tentative formulations of a series of open questions.

BACKGROUND

How did you get involved in the creation of Nordea?

NEGOTIATIONS BETWEEN MERITA AND NORDBANKEN

How did they start?

Main problems/challenges (e.g. location of headquarters, positions in the board and group management, "equality" concerns)

How did you solve the problems (e.g. specific deals/promises)?

INTEGRATION OF MERITA AND NORDBANKEN

Main problems/challenges when integrating the organizations (e.g. roles and responsibilities in the new organization, motivation/commitment, cultural differences and change)

What did you do to tackle the challenges/solve the problems?

Which issues became politicized/what did you fight about?

How did you deal with expectations and promises (especially "equality")?

Can you give us examples of surprising consequences of specific actions (concerning integration)?

NEGOTIATIONS BETWEEN MERITANORDBANKEN AND UNIDANMARK

How did they start?

Main problems/challenges (e.g. location of headquarters, positions in the board and group management)

How did you solve the problems (e.g. specific deals/promises)?

Did you have to re-open earlier deals/promises?

INTEGRATION OF MERITANORDBANKEN AND UNIDANMARK

Main problems/challenges when integrating the organizations (e.g. roles and responsibilities in the new organization, motivation/commitment, cultural differences and change)

What did you do to tackle the challenges/solve the problems?

What issues became politicized/what did you fight about?

How did you deal with expectations and promises (especially "equality")?

Can you give us examples of surprising consequences of specific actions (concerning integration)?

NEGOTIATIONS BETWEEN MERITANORDBANKEN (PLUS UNIDANMARK) AND KREDIKASSEN

How did they start?

Main problems/challenges (e.g. location of headquarters, positions in the board and group management)

How did you solve the problems (e.g. specific promises)?

Did you have to re-open earlier deals/promises?

INTEGRATION OF MERITANORDBANKEN–UNIDANMARK AND KREDITKASSEN

Main problems/challenges when integrating the organizations (e.g. roles and responsibilities in the new organization, motivation/commitment, cultural differences and change)

What did you do to tackle the challenges/solve the problems?

What issues became politicized/what did you fight about?

How did you deal with expectations and promises (especially "equality")?

Can you give us examples of surprising consequences of specific actions (concerning integration)?

How did it feel to proceed with this "last" integration process when creating Nordea?

CONTINUOUS CHANGE AND PARALLEL INTEGRATION PROCESSES

How far has the integration proceeded?

How far do you want to proceed with integration?

How do you manage parallel integration processes?

How can you cope with continuous/excessive change?

KNOWLEDGE TRANSFER

What actions have you taken to transfer knowledge/capabilities across the organizations?

How have you succeeded in creating new best practices?

CORPORATE CULTURE, NATIONALISM AND NORDISM

What actions have you taken to create a joint corporate culture/identity? (e.g. name, values, focus on "equality" and "fairness")

Can you give use examples of nationalism/international confrontation?

What is meant by "a Nordic bank"?

How do you comment on the campaign on "Nordic ideas"? (show the ad)

GENDER

Has equality between the sexes emerged as an issue in the negotiations or integration decision-making?

How has the cross-border dimension changed views and policies concerning equality?

LEARNING

What are the main differences in the (three) integration processes?

What have you learned as to the management of the integration process?

THE CURRENT SITUATION

What is it like to work with "virtual headquarters" (explain the idea)?

How has your life changed?

What did you do last week?

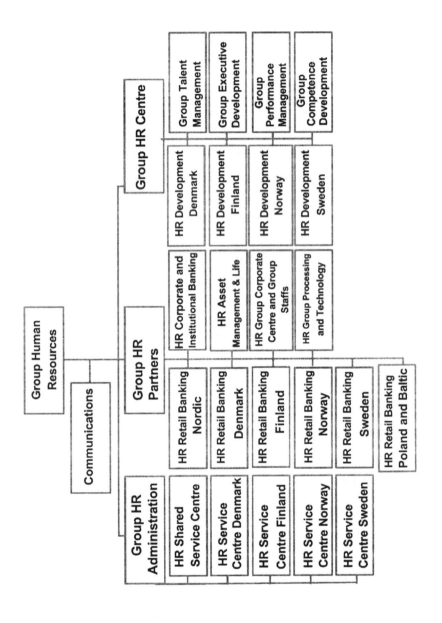

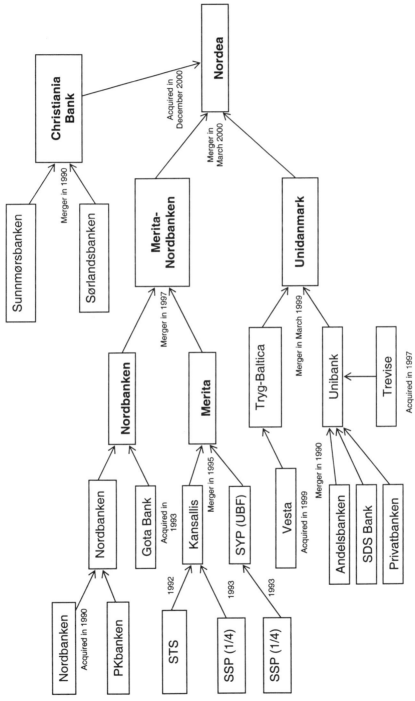